GOLDEN
GUIDES

C000157024

THE COTSWOLDS

William Fricker

BATH
BROADWAY
BURFORD
CHELTENHAM
CHIPPING CAMPDEN
CIRENCESTER
STRATFORD-UPON-AVON

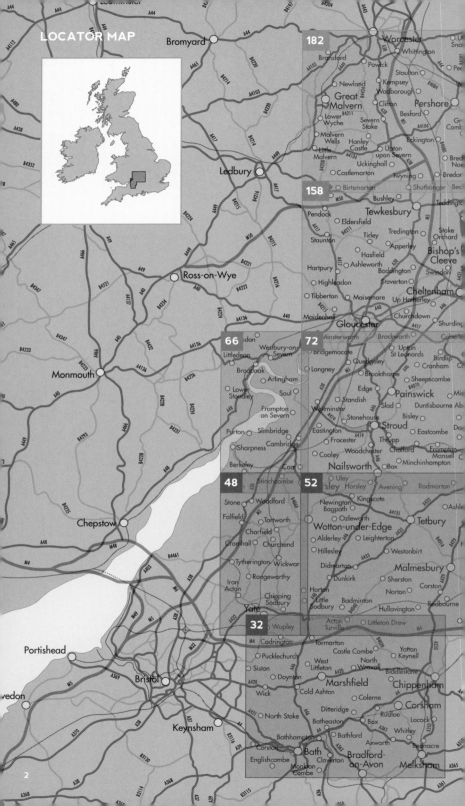

LOCATOR MAP

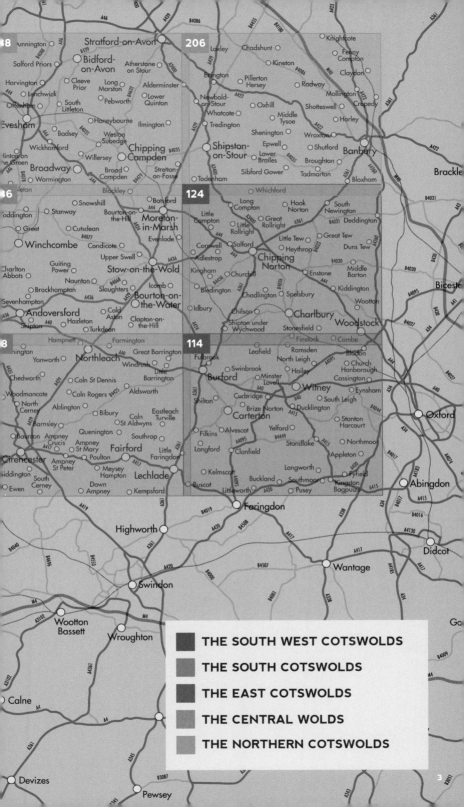

THE SOUTH WEST COTSWOLDS

THE SOUTH COTSWOLDS

THE EAST COTSWOLDS

THE CENTRAL WOLDS

THE NORTHERN COTSWOLDS

To Peter Smith, my Cotswold Agent. Wishing you good health, and many more years on the road. Thank you.

Research & Text: William Fricker
Photography: William Fricker (unless credited with ss)

This, the Second Edition, published by Goldeneye, Broad Street, Penryn, TR10 8JL

Abbreviations in Text

C14	14th Century
Mar-Oct	1 March to 31 October (inc.)
NT	National Trust property
EH	English Heritage property
BH	Bank Holidays
W/Es	Weekends
East	Easter
E/C	Early Closing
TIC	Tourist Information Centre
M	Monday
Tu	Tuesday
W	Wednesday
Th	Thursday
F	Friday
Sa	Saturday
Su	Sunday
ss	Supplied by Subject (reference illustrations)

4 Colin Carruther, Red Rag Gallery, Bath

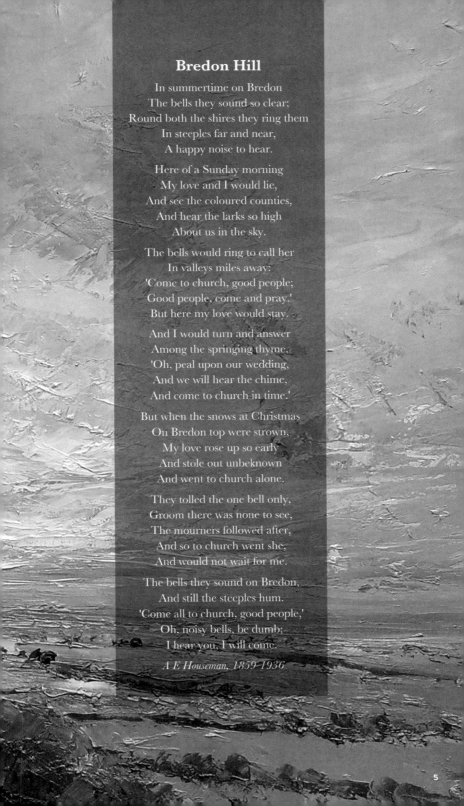

Bredon Hill

In summertime on Bredon
The bells they sound so clear;
Round both the shires they ring them
In steeples far and near,
A happy noise to hear.

Here of a Sunday morning
My love and I would lie,
And see the coloured counties,
And hear the larks so high
About us in the sky.

The bells would ring to call her
In valleys miles away:
'Come to church, good people;
Good people, come and pray.'
But here my love would stay.

And I would turn and answer
Among the springing thyme,
'Oh, peal upon our wedding,
And we will hear the chime,
And come to church in time.'

But when the snows at Christmas
On Bredon top were strown,
My love rose up so early
And stole out unbeknown
And went to church alone.

They tolled the one bell only,
Groom there was none to see,
The mourners followed after,
And so to church went she,
And would not wait for me.

The bells they sound on Bredon,
And still the steeples hum.
'Come all to church, good people,'
Oh, noisy bells, be dumb;
I hear you, I will come.

A E Houseman, 1859-1936

I have a close relationship with all the areas I have produced guidebooks, for. As with siblings, these relationships differ in style and intensity, and develop over time. None of the other regions is quite as close to me as the Cotswolds…my regional twin, if you like.

The Cotswolds were once my base for 30 years. For 20 of those years, I lived and managed Goldeneye in Cheltenham. I walked, drove and cycled around the area; researching, writing and photographing for Goldeneye maps and guides. I played cricket in many of the towns and villages (eventually, ending up at Sheepscombe, on Laurie Lee Field - strange, and ironic, for his prose set me on this journey of adventure, so many years ago), and sampled many a brew in the local hostelries. I eventually married a Cotswold girl, and our wedding took place in Gloucester Cathedral, a privilege rarely granted to those outside the Church. It so happened that her grandfather had been Vicar of Guiting Power for 25-years, and had collapsed, and died, on the High Altar of the Cathedral, while taking a service. A unique event, that gave us entry to the inner sanctum. My mother and father-in-law still live in the Cotswolds, providing me with a base. My original cartographer, David Cox, has lived all his life in West Oxfordshire, and I have the use of many researchers who ply me with new, and up-to-date information. My visits to the area are frequent, and intense. Our Cotswold credentials are significant, and deeply ingrained, and this guidebook represents the sum of our collective years, and all the knowledge, and opinions, that that engenders.

Having produced the Cotswold Map-Guide for many years, it had been a long-standing ambition to extend that publication, and to produce a book on this scale, and my intention, that it be practical, and easy-to-use. A book that is clear to navigate, fun to read and a pleasure to turn the page, and one that will encourage you to delve beyond the surface of the region. There aren't enough pages in this second edition to fit in everything, and so future editions of the book will be refined on a constant, annual basis – in parallel, I hope, with your relationship with the region. For this is more than a simple guidebook - it is meant to be a souvenir, and an object, to treasure.

As well as photography, I have included contemporary and traditional paintings to provide a different perspective. The touring maps offer an immense amount of detail, not necessarily common to guidebooks, and this has saved me a lot of unnecessary, descriptive prose. But, the major difference of this guidebook, compared to many others on the market (who first commission a writer, then gather the images from various picture libraries) is that I have researched, and written it, and taken 80% of the photographs. Repeated visits to chosen sites, at different times of the day, or year, in differing lights and weather, has given me a greater insight into my subject, and has helped create an intense labour of love. Goldeneye's small enthusiastic team work closely together on each guidebook. And they build up an undiluted passion for each region, as well as for the guidebooks, in the series. So, thank you Phil (book designer), Dave (cartographer) and Izy (editor), for sharing this incredible journey.

I realise that for many of you, this may be your first time in the Cotswolds, and so I want you to be made aware of the best the region has to offer. It is home to some remarkable hotels, and some luxurious inns with rooms, and dining pubs, and B&Bs. I believe I have included the finest. Not all, are excessively pricey, but the top hotels are not cheap. They offer an experience that will live with you, forever, and are thus, worthy of a special occasion. It is worth noting that many serve afternoon tea to all comers, so you can experience at least a taste of their luxury. If you prefer to lead the simple life you can always try one of the campsites listed - these are independent sites geared up for those wishing to sleep under (the stars or) canvas.

NEW FOR THIS EDITION:

More variance in budget options – As times are tight and visitors don't always want a five-star meal, or an expensive bed for the night, I have included more options such as Light Bites (cafés, coffee shops, tea rooms, and delis). And, more Inns With Rooms, too.

Navigation & Clarity – For ease of use, the area is split into five regions. At the start of each is an area map followed by the respective guide text and illustrations. Each section is colour-coded and the area maps either overlap, or juxtapose, to allow easy navigation. We have also re-designed the pages with new typography, and many new images, to provide a cleaner, clearer presentation.

I believe the Cotswolds to be a truly magical destination, whether you have a short break, a week, are alone, with friends, or family. Whether, you have a particular interest in the English landscape and village life, literary and music festivals, gardens and historic 'wool' churches, or simple, hedonism. There are no shortages of options available to you. Take a deep breath of country air, shrug off your working persona, and live the life, fantastic.

William Fricker
Cheltenham, May 2016

The Glebe, Bourton-on-the-Water

Slad Valley, Jack Russell Gallery 55

What and where is the region known as the Cotswolds? To those who know it, this may seem like a silly question. However, it is a place that manifests itself in many different ways to different people. Even down to the area they would define as the Cotswolds on a map. To some fashionistas, and magazine editors, the Cotswolds runs comparison to the New York Hamptons and Tuscany. Whilst to others the name is synonymous with wool and hunting, stone walls and majestic churches.

The Cotswolds region is perched on the central section of a ridge of oolitic limestone. The geological structure has thus had a profound and lasting affect on the landscape, and 'look' of the area. The oolitic limestone that forms these hills has the appearance of 1000s of tiny balls, like fish roe and is between 200 and 175 million years old.

This ridge has been tilted on its side, and is run off with streams, and river valleys, that lead off in a south-easterly direction, to feed the Thames basin. On the western edge, the scarp is steep in places with outcrops of rounded hills, notably Cam Long Down, and Bredon Hill, and makes for fine walking country, and pleasing views across to the Malvern Hills and Wales

Linguistically, the Cotswolds derives its name from two Saxon words: 'Cote' - sheep fold, and 'Wold' - bare hill. This references the importance of sheep in the development of the area. And, it is to the Cotswold Lion sheep that one must look to for the origin of wealth and endeavour that brought prosperity to this region

Neolithic Man found refuge on these hills from the swamps of the Severn, and Thames flood plains. The Celtic Dobunni tribe established hill forts where they farmed, bartered their crafts and founded coinage before the Romans arrived. They were not a warlike tribe like their neighbours the Silurians (Welsh), and eased into a compatible relationship with the conquering Romans to build Corinium Dobunnorum (Cirencester) into the second largest Roman settlement in Britain with a populace of 12,000 inhabitants.

The Saxon farmer laid the foundations of prosperity for the medieval wool merchants, and it was these merchants who built the great 'Wool' churches and the great manor houses.

Henry VIII's Dissolution of the Monasteries in the C16 saw the destruction of the Abbeys at Cirencester, Winchcombe, Hailes and Malmesbury. The first, and last battles of the English Civil War, 1641-1651, saw skirmishes at Edgehill, Lansdowne (Bath) and Stow-On-The Wold.

In the more peaceful C18, Bath and Cheltenham epitomised the elegance, hedonism and splendour of the Georgian era.

The landscape is rich in imagery: dry-stone walls divide the vast, sweeping sheep pastures and lazy, winding, trout streams meander through the rich pastureland. And, scattered across this landscape you will come across quaint hamlets undisturbed by coach, sightseer or time itself. All this makes for an idyllic scene rarely bettered in England.

In recent times this region's closeness to London has attracted wealthy residents, and an increase in second homes being bought by out-of-towners. This development brings with it all the associated benefits and disadvantages. Now the region attracts glitzy minor celebrities with their hangers-on in tow, and the seemingly necessary trumpet and fanfare. This has, of course, meant an increase of high-class restaurants and dining pubs which is of benefit to all (if you can afford their prices). And, of course, any money spent in the area ensures that the great historic buildings are being brought back to their original glory, and maintained for future generations – for which I for one, am very grateful.

Broadway Tower

- A Day at Cheltenham Races

- Big Bore Breakfast at The Old Passage Inn, Arlingham

- Christmas Carol Concert (or Evensong), Gloucester Cathedral

- Climb Broadway Tower, to View the 13 Counties

- Enjoy a Theatrical Experience at the Royal Shakespeare Theatre, Stratford

- Follow the "Wool Trail" from the Cotswold Woollen Weavers, to the Cotswold Farm Park, to a "Wool" church

- Follow the "Arts & Crafts Movement Trail" from Kelmscott Manor, to Sapperton Church, to The Wilson - Cheltenham's Art Gallery, to the Arts & Crafts Guild, Chipping Campden

- The Prescott Hill Climb

- Spring Sheep Shearing, the Cotswold Farm Park

- The Rococo Gardens first snowdrops in February

- The Chedworth Roman Villa, followed by a walk and picnic in Chedworth Woods

- Walk a section of the Cotswold Way

- Climb Bredon Hill and listen to the skylark

- Lunch in a Country Pub

- Westonbirt Arboretum, in the Autumn, and Spring

Stanton

The Cotswolds are noted for their wealth of beautiful villages. If you have a short time, and wish to visit just one, or two, this spread will point you in a direction that will not disappoint.

Cotswold villages are often grouped under the same name, for example: Upper and Lower Slaughter, Little and Great Tew, Duntisbourne Leer, Middle Duntisbourne and Dunstisbourne Abbots. And, if so named, it is well worth visiting the collective, for they are never too far apart, and often, connected by footpaths. The reason for your visit may be to explore the church, or perhaps to visit the village pub and, as luck would have it, it is often the case that the two are found opposite, or next door to each other.

1. BIBURY
William Morris described Bibury as one of the prettiest villages in England. It attracts the crowds and is the stop-off point for many coach tours. It is a honey-pot village made up of rose-covered cottages set behind idyllic kitchen gardens.

2. BOURTON-ON-THE-WATER
One of the most popular beauty spots in the Cotswolds, and one that invites mixed opinions. It can be charming on a quiet, frostbitten morning when only the postman is out and about, but is best avoided on a busy bank holiday. Often described as 'The Venice of the Cotswolds' because the River Windrush is spanned with low, graceful bridges.

3. BROADWAY
'The Painted Lady of the Cotswolds' is a term often used to describe this beautiful village. The honey-coloured stone captivates the visitor today, as it did in the C19, when William Morris, and his pre-Raphaelite friends settled here.

4. BURFORD
A fine introduction to the area for there are splendid inns and pretty cottages hidden down the side streets. The churchyard is a quiet spot with some beautifully decorated table tombs.

5. CHIPPING CAMPDEN
If you chose to visit just one Cotswold village. make sure it's this one. There is no better introduction. The harmony of Cotswold stone mirrors the town's prosperity in the Middle Ages as the home of the wealthiest wool merchants.

6. GREAT TEW
A sensationally beautiful village lined with ironstone cottages covered in thatch and stone tiles. Many fell into disrepair, but have now been restored to their former glory.

7. PAINSWICK
Its local description as 'The Queen of the Cotswolds' is fully justified. The houses have a Palladian quality about them. The churchyard is famous for the legendary 99 yew trees.

8. STANTON
A Charming village with houses of honey-coloured stone, and the refurbished Mount Inn is a welcome refuge for those tackling the Cotswold Way, or in need of sustenance.

9. STANWAY
This village is dominated by the outstanding Manor House, and in its grounds stands one of the country's finest tithe barns, and across the road, a thatched cricket pavilion is set on staddle stones.

10. UPPER & LOWER SLAUGHTER
One of the most popular of the twin villages in the Cotswolds, connected by the Eye Stream, and an easy-going footpath. Famous for the Old Mill, and the three prestigious hotels.

Kiftsgate Court Gardens ss

Cerney House Gardens

Rousham Park Gardens ss

Abbotswood Garden, Lower Swell

Alliums and Laburnam, Barnsley House

Sezincote ss

No. 131, Cheltenham

This is a selection to make choosing your B&B, hotel or Inn, an easy and quick process. We suggest you view their website to find one that suits your tastes, expectations and budget.
It is often the unexpected that will surprise you; a luxurious bathroom, an exquisite view, attentive and discreet staff, or a quirky, and fun temperament that will draw you back again, and again. In recent years, the Cotswolds has seen a rebirth in the old-fashioned hostelry - Inns With Rooms. That these establishments are enthusiasts for fine dining is no accident. They would rather draw you to their tables, and be able to offer a comfortable bed to sleep in, and refresh you for another day, so to spend more time at table.

Nowhere in England is the English Country Hotel more in evidence than within the Cotswold triangle. That many now have spas to go with their luxurious lifestyle is no accident, and is a reflection on what the customer expects. But, whatever these businesses offer, when all is said and done, you can not exchange charm, good manners and hospitality, for material things. All entries are described in the following pages.

COUNTRY COTTAGE B&B

Bullocks Horn Cottage, Charlton.
01666 577600 www.bullockshorn.co.uk

Dix's Barn, Duntisbourne Abbots.
01285 821249

Folly Farm Cottage, Back Street, Chipping Campden.
01608 682425 www.follyfarm.co.uk

Grey Cottage, Bath Road, Leonard Stanley.
01453 822515 www.greycottage.ik.com

Harrowfields, Cotheridge Lane, Eckington.
01386 751053 www.harrowfields.co.uk

Pinetum Lodge, Churcham.
01452 750554 www.pinetumlodge.ik.com

Thatch Cottage, Lacock.
01249 730398 www.thatchcottagelacock.com

True Heart, Frampton-on-Severn.
01452 740504 www.thetrueheart.co.uk

White House, Nettleton.
01249 782359 www.thewhitehousebandb.com

COUNTRY HOUSE B&B

Caswell House, Brize Norton.
01993 701064 www.caswellhouse.co.uk

Clapton Manor, Clapton-on-the-Hill.
01451 810202 www.claptonmanor.co.uk

Cotland House, Nr Burford.
01993 822382 www.cotlandhouse.com

Eckington Manor Cookery School, Bredon
01386 751600 www.eckingtonmanor.co.uk

Holmby House, Sibford Ferris.
01295 780104 www.holmbyhouse.com

Home Farm, Little Barrington.
01451 844300 www.homefarmcotswolds.com

Ivydene House, Uckinghall.
01684 592453 www.ivydenehouse.net

Kempsford Manor.
01285 810131 www.kempsfordmanor.com

Lower End House, Manor Road, Eckington.
01386 751600 www.lowerendhouse.co.uk

Lower Farm House, Adlestrop.
01608 658756 www.adlestrop-lowerfarm.com

Luggers Hall, Springfield Lane, Broadway.
01386 852040 www.luggershall.com

Old Manor House, Halford.
01789 740264 www.oldmanor-halford.co.uk

Old Rectory, Cantax Hill, Lacock.
01249 730335 www.oldrectorylacock.co.uk

Old Rectory, Meysey Hampton.
01285 851200 www.meyseyoldrectory.co.uk

Rectory Farmhouse, Lower Swell.
01451 832351

St Anne's B&B, Gloucester Street. Painswick.
01452 812879 www.st-annes-painswick.co.uk

South Newington House, South Newington.
01295 721207 www.southnewingtonhouse.co.uk

Uplands House, Upton.
01295 678663 www.cotswolds-uplands.co.uk

Wren House, Donnington.
01451 831787 www.wrenhouse.net

COUNTRY HOUSE HOTELS

Bibury Court Hotel.
01285 740337 www.biburycourt.co.uk

Buckland Manor Hotel, Nr Broadway.
01386 852626 www.bucklandmanor.co.uk

Foxhill Manor.
01386 852711 www.foxhillmanor.com

Greenway, Shurdington.
01242 862352 www.thegreenway.co.uk

Lords of the Manor, Upper Slaughter.

01451 820243 www.lordsofthemanor.com
Lower Slaughter Manor.
01451 820456 www.lowerslaughter.co.uk
Manor House Hotel, Castle Combe.
01249 782206 www.manorhouse.co.uk
Old Bell Hotel, Abbey Row.
01666 822344 www.oldbellhotel.co.uk
Rectory, Crudwell.
01666 577194 www.therectoryhotel.com
The Painswick.
01452 813688 www.thepainswick.co.uk

FARMHOUSE/BARN B&B
Barn B&B, Pensham.
01386 555270 www.pensham-barn.co.uk
Barn House, High Street, Broadway.
01386 854858
Blackwell Grange.
01608 682357 www.blackwellgrange.co.uk
Bould Farm, Chipping Norton.
01608 658850 www.bouldfarm.co.uk
Bowers Hill Farm, Chipping Campden.
01386 834585 www.bowershillfarm.com
Brawn Farm, Sandhurst.
01452 731010 www.brawnfarmbandb.co.uk
Brooklands Farm, Ewen.
01285 770487
Burhill Farm, Buckland.
01386 858171 www.burhillfarm.co.uk
Cross O' Th' Hill Farm, Clifford Road, Stratford-upon-Avon.
01789 204738 www.cross-o-th-hill-farm.com
Deerhurst B&B.
01684 293358 www.deerhurstbandb.co.uk
Fosse Farm B&B, Castle Combe.
01249 782286. www.fossefarmhouse.com

Lodge Farm B&B, Tetbury.
01666 505339 www.lodgefarm.co.uk
Manor Farm, Weston Subedge.
01386 840390 www.manorfarmbnb.demon.co.uk
Mount Pleasant Farm, Childswickham.
01386 853424 mountpleasantfarmbroadway.co.uk
North Farmcote, Winchcombe.
01242 602304 www.northfarmcote.co.uk
Rectory Farm, Salford.
01608 643209 www.rectoryfarm.info
Rectory Farmhouse, Lower Swell.
01451 832351
Salford Farm House, Salford Priors.
01386 870000 www.salfordfarmhouse.co.uk
Snowshill Hill Estate.
01386 853959 www.snowshill-hill.co.uk
Sudeley Hill Farm, Winchcombe.
01242 602344
Well Farm, Frampton Mansell.
01285 760651 www.well-farm.co.uk
West Farm, West Littleton.
01225 891249 www.westfarmbandb.co.uk
Westley Farm, Chalford.
01285 760262 www.westleyfarm.co.uk
Weston Farm, Buscot Wick.
01367 252222
Whittington Lodge Farm, Whittington.
01242 820603 www.whittingtonlodgefarm.com

GUEST ACCOMMODATION (B&B)
5 Ewlyn Road, Cheltenham.
01242 261243
Georgian House, Castle Combe.
01249 783009
Georgian House, Cheltenham.
01242 515577 www.georgianhouse.net
Hanover House, Cheltenham.
01242 541297 www.hanoverhouse.org
Lacock Pottery, Lacock.
01249 730266 www.lacockbedandbreakfast.com
Moda House, Chipping Sodbury.
01454 312135 www.modahouse.co.uk
No.107 Gloucester Street, Cirencester.
01285 657861
Oxbourne House, Oxhill.
01295 688202 www.oxbournehouse.com

INNS WITH ROOMS
Amberley Inn.
01453 872565 www.theamberley.co.uk
Angel Inn Hotel, Pershore.
01386 552581 www.theangelinnpershore.co.uk
Black Horse, Naunton.
01451 850565
Bull Inn, Charlbury.

Wild Rabbit Bedroom

01608 810689 www.bullinn-charlbury.com

Castle Inn, Bradford-on-Avon.
01225 865657 www.flatcappers.co.uk

Churchill Arms, Paxford.
01386 593159 www.churchillarms.co

Ebrington Arms, Ebrington.
01386 593223 www.theebringtonarms.co.uk

Eight Bells Inn. Church Street.
01386 840371 www.eightbellsinn.co.uk

Falkland Arms, Great Tew.
01608 683653 www.falklandarms.org.uk

Five Alls (The), Filkins.
01367 860875 www.thefiveallsfilkins.co.uk

Fleece, 11 Church Green, Witney.
01993 892270 www.fleecewitney.co.uk

Fleece Inn, Bretforton.
01386 831173 www.thefleeceinn.co.uk

Fox Inn, Lower Oddington.
01451 870555 www.foxinn.net

George Hotel, Shipston-on-Stour.
01608 661453 www.georgehotelshipston.com

Golden Heart, Birdlip.
01242 870261 www.thegoldenheart.co.uk

Highway Inn, 117 High Street, Burford.
01993 823661 www.thehighwayinn.co.uk

Horse & Groom, Bourton-on-the-Hill.
01386 700413 www.horseandgroom.info

Horse & Groom, Upper Oddington.
01451 830584 www.horseandgroom.uk.com

Horse and Groom Inn, The Street, Charlton.
01666 823904 www. horseandgroominn.com

Howard Arms, Ilmington.
01608 682226 www.howardarms.com

Inn For All Seasons, Little Barrington.
01451 844324 www.innforallseasons.co.uk

Kings Arm's, Didmarton.
01454 238245 www.kingsarmsdidmarton.co.uk

Kings Arms, Stow-On-The-Wold.
01451 830364 www.thekingsarmsstow.co.uk

Kings Arms Hotel & Restaurant, Woodstock.
01993 813636 www.kings-hotel-woodstock.co.uk

Kings Head Inn, Bledington.
01608 658365 www.thekingsheadinn.net

Lamb Inn, Burford.
01993 823155 www.cotswold-inns-hotels.co.uk/lamb

Lamb Inn, Shipton-Under-Wychwood.
01993 830465 www.shiptonlamb.com

Lion Inn, Winchcombe.
01242 603300 www.lionwinchcombe.co.uk

Maytime, Asthall.
01993 822068 www.themaytime.com

Plough (The), Kelmscott.
01367 253543 www.theploughinnkelmscott.com

Red Lion, Long Compton.
01608 684221 www.redlion-longcompton.co.uk

Redesdale Arms, Moreton-In-Marsh.
01608 650308 www.redesdalearms.com

Seagrave Arms, Weston Subedge.
01386 840192 www.seagravearms.com

Sign of the Angel, Lacock.
01249 730230 www.signoftheangel.co.uk

Swan Inn, Swinbrook.
01993 823339 www.theswanswinbrook.co.uk

The Chequers at Churchill.
01608 659393 www.thechequerschurchill.com

The Plough at Kingham.
01608 658327 www.thekinghamplough.co.uk

The Swan, Southrop.
01367 850205 www.theswanatsouthrop.co.uk

The White Hart, Stow-On-The-Wold.
01451 830674 www.whitehartstow.com

The Wild Rabbit, Kingham.
01608 658327 www.thewildrabbit.co.uk

Timbrell's Yard, Bradford-On-Avon.
01225 869492 www.timbrellsyard.com

Trout, Tadpole Bridge.
01367 870382 www.trout-inn.co.uk

Wheatsheaf, Northleach.
01451 860244 www.cotswoldswheatsheaf.com

Wheelright Arms, Monkton Combe.
01225 722287 www.wheelwrightsarms.co.uk

White Hart, Winchcombe.
01242 602359 www.wineandsausage.co.uk

Wild Duck at Ewen.
01285 770310 www.thewildduckinn.co.uk

LUXURIOUS B&B

Bradford Old Windmill, 4 Mason's Lane, Bradford-on-Avon.
01225 866842 www.bradfordoldwindmill.co.uk

Cardynham House, Painswick.
01452 814006 www.cardynham.co.uk
Clifton House, Bradford-on-Avon.
01225 309399 www.cliftonhouse-boa.co.uk
Manor Farm House, Ab Lench.
01386 462226
Mill Hay House, Broadway.
01386 852498 www.millhay.co.uk
No.12 Park Street, Cirencester.
01285 640232 www.no12cirencester.co.uk
Old Post House, New Street, Deddington.
01869 338978 www.oldposthouse.co.uk

RUSTIC CAMPING

Apple Tree Park, Eastington.
01452 742362 www.appletreepark.co.uk
Cotswold View Campsite, Charlbury
01608 810314 www.cotswoldview.co.uk
Far Peak Camping, Northleach.
01285 720858 www.farpeakcamping.co.uk
Folly Farm Campsite, Notgrove.
01451 820285 www.cotswoldcamping.net
Long Compton Camping.
01608 684663
Thistledown Farm, Nympsfield.
01453 860420 www.thistledown.org.uk

SELF-CATERING

Frampton Court (The Orangery), Frampton-on-Severn.
01452 740698 www.framptoncourtestate.co.uk
Upper Court, Kemerton.
01386 725351 www.uppercourt.co.uk

SMALL HOTELS

Bay Tree Hotel, Sheep Street, Burford.
01993 822791 www.cotswold-inns-hotels.co.uk/baytree
Burford House, 99 High Street. Burford.
01993 823151 www.burfordhouse.co.uk
Castle Inn Hotel, Castle Combe.
01249 783030 www.castle-inn.info
Close Hotel, Tetbury.
01666 502272 www.theclose-hotel.com
Cottage in The Wood, Holywell Road, Malvern.
01684 588860 www.cottageinthewood.co.uk
Dial House, Bourton-On-The-Water.
01451 822244 www.dialhousehotel.com
Ettington Park Hotel.
01789 450123 www.ettingtonpark.co.uk
Evesham Hotel, Evesham.
01386 765566 www.eveshamhotel.com
Feathers Hotel, Woodstock.
01993 811251 www.woodstockarms.co.uk
Fosse Manor Hotel, Stow-On-The-Wold.

01451 830354 www.fossemanor.co.uk
Grapevine Hotel, Stow-On-The-Wold.
01451 830354 www.fossemanor.co.uk
Hotel du Vin & Bistro, Cheltenham.
01242 370584 www.hotelduvin.com
Kings Arms, Chipping Campden.
01386 840256 www.kingscampden.co.uk
Lower Brook House, Blockley.
01386 700 286 www.lowerbrookhouse.co.uk
New Inn, Coln St Aldwyn.
01285 750651 www.new-inn.co.uk
No. 38 Evesham Road, Cheltenham.
01242 822929 www.no38thepark.com
No. 131 The Promenade, Cheltenham.
01242 8229939 www.no131.com
Noel Arms Hotel, Chipping Campden.
01386 840317 www.noelarmshotel.com
Ormond, Tetbury.
01666 505690 www.theormond.co.uk
Swan Hotel, Bibury.
01285 740695 www.cotswold-inns-hotels.co.uk
The Porch House, Stow-On-The-Wold.
01451 830670 www.porch-house.co.uk
The Inn at Fossebridge.
01285 720721 www.fossebridgeinn.co.uk
The Slaughters Country Inn, Lower Slaughter.
01451 822143 www.theslaughtersinn.co.uk
Three Ways House Hotel, Mickleton.
01386 438429 www.puddingclub.com

SPA & COUNTRY HOUSE HOTELS

Barnsley House, Nr Cirencester.
01285 740000 www.barnsleyhouse.com
Calcot Manor, Tetbury.
01666 890391 www.calcotmanor.co.uk
Combe Grove Hotel & Spa, Nr Bath.
01225 834644 www.combegrove.com
Cotswold House Hotel, Chipping Campden.
01386 840330 www.cotswoldhouse.com
Cowley Manor, Nr Cheltenham.
01242 870900 www.cowleymanor.com
Dormy House Hotel & Spa, Willersey Hill.
01386 852711 www.dormyhouse.co.uk
Lucknam Park, Colerne.
01225 742777 www.lucknampark.co.uk
Lygon Arms, Broadway.
01386 852255 www.barcelo-hotels.co.uk/lygonarms
Soho Farmhouse, Great Tew.
01608 691000 www.sohohouse.com
Whatley Manor, Easton Grey.
01666 822888 www.whatleymanor.com
Woolley Grange, Bradford-on-Avon.
01225 864705 www.woolleygrangehotel.co.uk

38, The Park, Cheltenham ss

The Painswick, Painswick ss

Foxhill Manor, Broadway ss

Wild Rabbit, Kingham ss

Lords of the Manor, Upper Slaughter ss

The Wheatsheaf, Northleach ss

23

The Sign Of The Angel, Lacock

The Chequers, Churchill I ss

Selecting a café, inn or, restaurant with rooms, can make or break, a romantic weekend. It may also determine where you decide to stay. Luckily, you have an amazing choice. The Cotswolds has an over supply of food emporia: from the humble tearoom to the precious dining-pub. These have grown out of the demise of the common pub, and in their place have come young, ambitious chefs to turn what was potentially an attractive building into a restaurant within (what was) a pub. To appease the locals, a couple of bar stools, and a little bar area may remain, (and the skittle alley will be available for two nights a week). The Cotswolds has a fair number of traditional hostelries, and at least three breweries: Donningtons, Hook Norton, and the Uley Brewery. Specialist cider houses have fallen by the wayside.

The English Country House hotel is well represented here, too and they all have prestigious restaurants and (often) a more laid-back brasserie, or bistro, for informal dining. Seek out the Lunch Deals.

Herewith, a representative selection of what follows in the following pages. If the pub/restaurant has rooms, this has been indicated with a B&B, which will help you select a country pub with rooms:-

CAFE/BISTROS/DELIS

Bakery On The Water, Bourton-On-The-Water.

01451 822748 www.bakeryonthewater.co.uk

Broadway deli, 16 High Street, Broadway.

01386 853040

Cacao Bean, Moreton-In-Marsh.

01608 652060 www.cacaobean.co.uk.

Cotswold Lion Cafe, The Old Prison, Northleach.

Hampers Food & Wine Company, Oxford Street, Woodstock.

01993 811535 www.hampersfoodandwine.co.uk

Made By Bob, Corn Hall, Cirencester.

www.foodmadebybob.com

Mrs Bumble of Burford, 31 Lower High Street. Burford.

New Brewery Arts, Brewery Court, Cirencester. B&B.

01285 657181 www.newbreweryarts.org.uk

Old Mill Museum, Lower Slaughter.

01451 820052 www.oldmill-lowerslaughter.com

Quayles, Tetbury.

01666 505151 www.quayles.co.uk

Sweetpeas, Great Tew.

01608 683600 www.sweetpeasofgreattewox7.co.uk

Williams Food Hall & Oyster Bar, Nailsworth.

01453 835507 www.fishandseafood.co.uk

ETHNIC RESTAURANTS

Chef Imperial, High Street, Woodstock.

01993 813593

La Galleria Ristorante Italiano, 2 Market Place, Woodstock.

01993 813381 www.la-galleria.co.uk

La Passione, Chipping Sodbury

01454 326444

Mayflower Chinese Restaurant, 29 Sheep Street, Cirencester.

01285 642777 (also in Cheltenham)

Siam Thai, 1 Horse Street, Chipping Sodbury

01454 850095

FARM SHOPS WITH RESTAURANTS

Daylesford Organic Farmshop.
01608 731700 www.daylesfordorganic.com

The Organic Farm Shop, Burford Road, Cirencester.
01285 640441 www.theorganicfarmshop.co.uk

FOODIE HOSTELRIES/(GASTRO) PUBS

Gumstool Inn, Calcot Manor, Tetbury. B&B.
01666 890391 www.calcotmanor.co.uk

Bell at Sapperton.
01285 760298 www.foodatthebell.co.uk

Churchill Arms, Paxford. B&B.
01386 594000 www.thechurchillarms.com

Five Alls (The), Filkins. B&B.
01367 860875 www.thefiveallsfilkins.co.uk

Horse & Groom, Bourton- on-the-Hill. B&B.
01386 700413 www.horseandgroom.info

Horse & Groom, Charlton.
01666 823904 www.horseandgroominn.com

The Chequers at Churchill.
01608 659393 www. thechequerschurchill.com

The Plough at Kingham. B&B.
01608 658327 www.thekinghamplough.co.uk

Kings Head Inn, Bledington. B&B.
01608 658365 www.thekingsheadinn.net

Lion Inn, 33 North Street, Winchcombe. B&B.
01242 603300 www.lionwinchcombe.co.uk

Maytime, Asthall. B&B.
01993 822068 www.themaytime.com

Plough (The), Kelmscott. B&B.
01367 253543 www.theploughinnkelmscott.com

The Swan, Southrop. B&B.
01367 850205 www.theswanatsouthrop.co.uk

Sign of the Angel, Church Street, Lacock. B&B.
01249 730230 www.signoftheangel.co.uk

Swan Inn, Swinbrook. B&B.
01993 823339 www.theswanswinbrook.co.uk

Village Pub, Barnsley. B&B.
01285 740421 www.thevillagepub.co.uk

The Swan, Southrop. B&B.
01367 850205 www.theswanatsouthrop.co.uk

The Wheatsheaf, Northleach. B&B.
01451 860244 www.cotswoldswheatsheaf.com

The Wild Rabbit, Kingham. B&B.
01608 658327 www.thewildrabbit.co.uk

LUNCH IN FORMAL SURROUNDINGS

Barnsley House (& garden visit), Nr Cirencester.
01285 740000 www.barnsleyhouse.com

Bath Priory Hotel, Weston Road Bath
01225 331922. www.thebathpriory.co.uk

Bibury Court Hotel.
01285 740337 www.biburycourt.co.uk

Buckland Manor, Nr Broadway.
01386 852626 www.bucklandmanor.co.uk

Calcot Manor, Nr Tetbury.
01666 890391 www.calcotmanor.co.uk

Close Hotel, Long Street, Tetbury.
01666 502272 www.theclose-hotel.com

Cotswold House Hotel, The Square, Chipping Campden.
01386 840330 www.cotswoldhouse.com

Lords of the Manor, Upper Slaughter.
01451 820243 www.lordsofthemanor.com

Lower Slaughter Manor.
01451 820456 www.lowerslaughter.co.uk

Lucknam Park, Colerne.
01225 742777 www.lucknampark.co.uk

The Painswick, Kemps Lane. Painswick.
01452 813688 www.thepainswick.co.uk

The Royal Crescent Hotel, 16 Royal Crescent, Bath.
01225 823333 www.royalcrescent.co.uk

RESTAURANT WITH ROOMS

Angel, 14 Witney Street, Burford.
01993 822714 www.theangelatburford.co.uk

Old Passage Inn, Arlingham.
01452 740547 www.theoldpassage.com

Russell's, Broadway
01386 853555 www.russellsofbroadway.co.uk

The Rectory, Crudwell.
01666 577194 www.therectoryhotel.com

Three Ways House Hotel, Mickleton.
01386 438429 www.puddingclub.com

Timbrell's Yard, 49 St Margaret's Street, Bradford-On-Avon.
01225 869492 www.timbrellsyard.com

Wesley House, Winchcombe.
01242 602366 www.wesleyhouse.co.uk

Wild Garlic, 3 Cossack Square, Nailsworth.
01453 832615 www.wild-garlic.co.uk

TOWN RESTAURANTS

Champignon Sauvage, 24-26 Suffolk Road, Cheltenham.
01242 573449 www.lechampignonsauvage.co.uk

5 North Street, Winchcombe.
01242 604566

No. 131 The Promenade, Cheltenham.
01242 8229939 www.no131.com

The Circus Restaurant, 34 Brock Street, Bath.
01225 466020 www.thecircuscafeandrestaurant. co.uk

The Suffolk Kitchen, Cheltenham.
01242 237057 www.thesuffolkkitchen.co.uk

Woods, 9-13 Alfred Street, Bath
01225 314812 www.woodsrestaurant.com

Five Alls, Filkins ss   *Swan Hotel, Bibury* ss   *Seven Tuns, Chedworth* ss

TRADITIONAL PUBS (NOT ALL SERVE FOOD – BUT, MOST DO)

Bakers Arms, Broad Campden.
01386 840515

Bathurst Arms, North Cerney.
01285 831281 www.bathurstarms.com

Bear at Bisley.
01452 770265 www.bisleybear.co.uk

Beehive, 1-3 Montpelier Villas, Cheltenham.
01242 579443

Butcher's Arms, Sheepscombe.
01452 812113 www.butchers-arms.co.uk

Ebrington Arms, Ebrington. B&B.
01386 593223 www.theebringtonarms.co.uk

Falkland Arms, Great Tew. B&B.
01608 683653 www.falklandarms.org.uk

Fleece Inn, Bretforton.
01386 831173 www.thefleeceinn.co.uk

Fox Inn, Lower Oddington.
01451 870555 www.foxinn.net

George Inn, 4 West Street, Lacock.
01249 730263 www.georgeinnlacock.co.uk

Golden Heart, Birdlip. B&B.
01242 870261 www.thegoldenheart.co.uk

Kings Head Inn, Wootton.
01993 811340 www.kings-head.co.uk

Lamb Inn, Sheep St. Burford. B&B.
01993 823155 cotswold-inns-hotels.co.uk/lamb

Lamb Inn, Shipton-Under-Wychwood.
01993 830465 www.lambinn.co.uk

Old Spot Inn, Hill Road, Dursley.
01453 542870 www.oldspotinn.co.uk

Plough Inn, Ford.
01386 584215 www.theploughinnatford.co.uk

Ram Inn, Station Road, South Woodchester.
01453 873 329

Morris Clown, High Street, Bampton.
01993 850217

Ram Inn, South Woodchester.
01453 873 329

Royal Oak, Ramsden.
01993 868213

Seven Tuns, Chedworth.
01285 720242

The Trout, Tadpole Bridge. B&B.
01367 870382 www.trout-inn.co.uk

Tunnel House Inn, Tarlton Road, Nr. Cirencester.
01285 770280 www.tunnelhouse.com

Volunteer, Chipping Campden.
01386 840688

Weigh Bridge Inn, Longfords, Nailsworth.
01453 832520 www.2in1Pub.co.uk

Woodstock Arms, Market Street.
01993 811251 www.woodstockarms.co.uk

Woolpack Inn, Slad.
01452 813429

Yew Tree Inn, Conderton.
01386 725364

Wild Rabbit, Kingham ss

George Inn, Lacock

The Bar, The Painswick ss

THE GOLDEN FLEECE OF THE COTSWOLD SHEEP

Sheep have grazed on the Cotswold hills for more than 2,000 years - and the most famous breed was The Cotswold, whose lustrous, curly fleece was famous throughout Europe.

Here is the story of that sheep - known as The Lion of the Cotswolds...

Today, there is not much more than a ton or two of Cotswold fleece-wool available each year. It is long-stapled (more than 6 inches), reasonably lustrous and of mid 40's quality (For comparison Merino is mid 60's plus, Lincoln about mid 30's). Until recently, Cotswold wool was for many years lumped in with other English lustre-wools - and used mainly for carpets and industrial cloths.

During the early 1980's Cotswold Woollen Weavers recognised its potential and revived its use. In particular, the natural lustre and the clarity with which it accepts dye made the wool ideal for loose-twist worsted spinning, and weaving into soft-furnishing cloths - a range of dramatic block-weave throws and rugs.

Cotswold Woollen Weavers' activities have coincided with a renewed interest in the Cotswold breed, and is thus a good time for a re-appraisal of the breed. For too long, the historic pedigree of Cotswold wool has been ignored as irrelevant.

But it was not always so. The Cotswolds are marked with the history of the Cotswold sheep and its fleece. But, it is a puzzling, clouded history. For, although the great Wool Churches stand four-square in many a Cotswold village, as solid testimony to the power and wealth of the medieval merchants who endowed them, not much can be said with certainty about the wool which the Cotswold sheep provided. There is certainly a lot of superstition: even a bogus derivation of the very word Cotswold (sheep cot on the wold, or open hillside) has been widely used to puff the influence of wool in the area.

Certainly wool has long been an important English commodity, and the Cotswolds an important source for it. 500 years ago wise men agreed that half the wealth of England rides on the back of the sheep - wool exports paid for Richard the Lionheart's ransom to the Saracens.

The Lord Chancellor sits in The House of Lords to this day on a sack stuffed with wool to show the preeminent position which the wool industry has played in this country's affairs. The medieval weavers of C12 Flanders happily sang:

The best wool in Europe is Cotswold, and the best wool in England is Cotswold.

But what sort of wool was it that they prized so highly?

The Medieval Cotswolds

There is evidence that the Romans brought sheep with them as they battled northwards, and perhaps they introduced them to the Cotswold hills around the important Roman settlement of Corinium, (Cirencester). They would have valued these sheep for their milk and for their fleece: shivering Southern European mercenary soldiers needed warm winter coats. There is further evidence, based mostly on scanty skeletal remains, that these Roman imports were the ancestors of the great flocks of Medieval Cotswolds - and indeed of all the English longwool breeds.

The temptation is to look at a Cotswold sheep today, to sink one's hand in its thick lustrous long-wool fleece, and think fondly of an unbroken pedigree stretching back 2,000 years to those early Roman farmers. The problem is that for most of the intervening years virtually nothing is known for sure.

Shepherds reasonably enough have rarely thought it sensible to spend their time writing down descriptions of their flocks: the first book in English entirely about sheep was not published until 1749 (Ellis- The Shepherd's Sure Guide), and the first comprehensive resumé of English wool not until 1809 (Luccock - An Essay on Wool). But by then, the early C19, the heyday of the Cotswold sheep was over. And of course, woollen cloth gets worn out, and is attacked by moth and mould: there is very little extant medieval woollen cloth available for analysis.

During the Early Medieval centuries England was a relatively underpopulated country, with plenty of rolling hill-pasture to sustain vast land-hungry flocks of sheep kept for their fleece. Perhaps 500,000 sheep roamed the Cotswolds, and most of their wool was exported to Flanders and Lombardy; more densely populated countries which could not spare land for wool growing. Thousands upon thousands of packhorses laden with wool-bales wound their way down from the High Cotswold hills to The Thames. They crossed the river at Radcot and proceeded southwards to Southampton, or saw their loads shipped on barges to London. The continental weavers paid royally for the wool, the Cotswold merchants grew rich and built their churches, and the English crown paid its way with the taxes levied on the trade.

But was this Golden Fleece (the Cotswold sheep was long known as The Lion of the Cotswolds) the long, heavy, lashy wool that the modern Cotswold bears, or something shorter, softer and more like the Ryeland wool from Herefordshire which was equally important to the medieval weavers?

There are memorial brasses in Northleach church which show what look like newly shorn Cotswolds just like those which crop the grass today, and some commentators suggest the Cotswold was always a big, longwoolled breed (Youatt, for instance, quotes that sage Gervase Markham to this effect). But others suggest that the wool was once much softer: Michael Drayton, writing at the end of the C16 suggests that Cotswold wool was very fine: it comes very near that of Spain, for from it a thread may be drawn as fine as silk.

This Spanish comparison is important, because one conundrum revolves around the export - widely noted by contemporary commentators - of Cotswold sheep to Spain, particularly by Edward IV but up to 1425 when the export was banned as part of the increasingly draconian network of laws to safeguard the interests of the burgeoning English wool-weaving industry. Spain was the home of the fine-woolled merino sheep, and it is inconceivable that English, and specifically Cotswold sheep, could have been so fine as to be worth cross-breeding with merinos. The most likely explanation is that Cotswolds were different from merinos: long-woolled enough to provide fleece to make alternative cloths.

Clattering Loom-shuttles

Until the late C19, and advanced mechanical innovation, it was not possible to spin worsted yarn from short fibre. The wool from which worsted yarn was spun had to be combed by hand to eliminate short hair (noils) and to align every fibre parallel to the direction of the yarn. Then tight, flat yarn could be spun and tough, sleek cloth could be woven: quite different from the spongy, less sophisticated cloths which could be woven from yarn woollen spun from shorter merino and down-breed fleece. Perhaps medieval Cotswold sheep were shorter and softer fleeced than they are today, but their wool was still lustrous and strong enough to be ideal for worsted spinning. If nothing else, Cotswold fleece could provide Spanish soldiers with tough, resilient serge uniforms, and nobles with flowing, draping cloaks to wear over their shirts of soft, fluffy merino.

During the C16 and C17s, the rising clatter of loom-shuttles in the valleys around Stroud presaged England's transition from raw-fleece exporter to major woollen cloth manufacturer. So complete was this change that the crown eventually forbade the export of fleece altogether, and it remained illegal until 1824. Although, gradually, vast amounts of wool began to be imported from the wide, open spaces of Australia and South Africa (ideal for extensive sheeprearing) but it was the pre-eminence of English combing wools (including Cotswold) which helped establish England's superiority as a woollen textile manufacturer.

To some extent this issue of the nature of Cotswold wool is one of semantics: as William Marshall wrote, after he rode the Cotswold hills at the end of the C18, the Cotswold is a breed which has been prevalent on these hills, [since] time immemorial: it has been improved, but has not changed. (During the Improving Years of the C18, the Cotswold certainly increased in size as shepherds learnt new husbandry techniques.) Or as Ezra Carman wrote disarmingly in 1892, as he strove to sum up the evidence of three hundred years of literature about Cotswold fleece: It is difficult to reconcile these opinions, nor indeed is it necessary; the Cotswolds beyond the memory of our day have long been a longwoolled race and valuable... for their wool.

So, superstitions and all, in this volatile world perhaps it is acceptable, even necessary that there are these noble, mythic links with the past. If this be so, then The Golden Fleece, which might have provided uniforms for the Roman legions, paid for the Crusades, clothed C18 Europe with West of England Broadcloth and today makes splendid block-weave rugs, is certainly an ideal candidate.

Richard Martin
Cotswold Woollen Weavers, Filkins

Pulteney Bridge, Bath

For Architecture, Cultural Festivals, Luxurious Hedonism, Shopping Sprees, Walking the Cotswold Way...

Bath is arguably the most beautiful town in England. It is second to London in the number of visitors it attracts and is thus a fine place to eat, drink and be merry, and to shop and attend cultural events. The surrounding villages are accordingly affluent and well-heeled (and expensive) places to live. Bath is expensive but you can find more reasonably priced accommodation outside the town limits and many of these are listed in this book.

There are pretty and attractive villages aplenty outside Bath. The most popular being Castle Combe and Lacock. Both grew out of the wool industry, and both have been so well maintained that they amount to showcase villages. Sadly, you won't witness a herd of cattle being walked through at dawn and dusk, only perhaps the drayman upsetting the balance of this new life.

Cross the M4 and you encounter two towns of comparative interest: Malmesbury and Tetbury. Malmesbury was the home of Athelstan, the first King of All England. And, Tetbury is the home of Prince Charles, next in line for the throne of England, and its protectorates. But, if these two men and their burghs don't hold your interest, and you still have a spring in your step after tramping the streets of Bath. Look to the Cotswold Way, a long distance footpath that leads north to Chipping Campden. It follows the edge of the escarpment, passes through many pretty villages and gorgeous woodland and will reward you with fine views and hours of solitary reflection. And, if trees take your fancy you must visit Westonbirt Arboretum, an arboreal paradise, second to none.

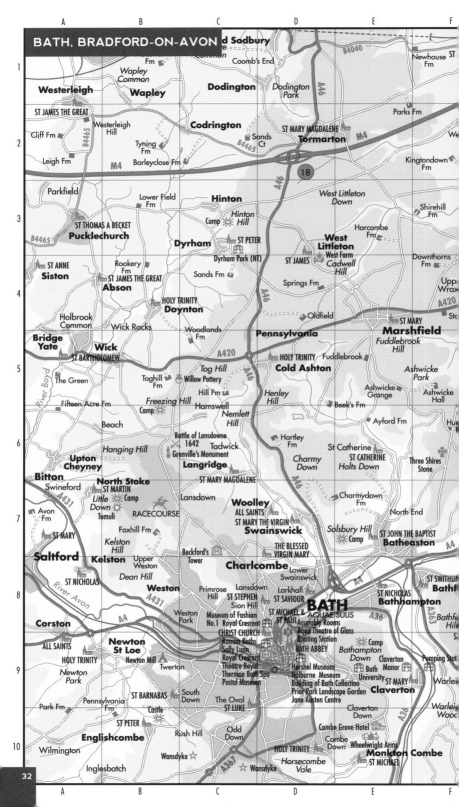

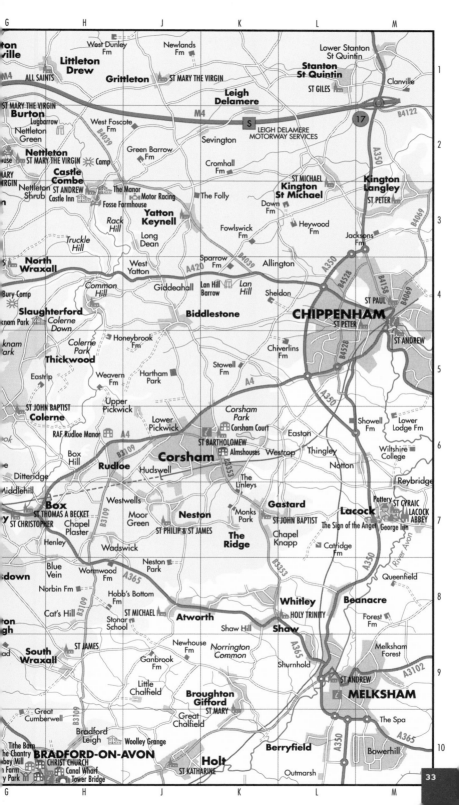

Golden Light, The Circus, Bath.

Golden Morning, The Circus, Bath.

BATH

Is Bath the most beautiful city in England? Many believe so, for, it is second only to London, in the number of visitors it attracts. It will captivate you today, as it has done so down the centuries, from the Romans to Jane Austen, to Robert Southey and the Romantic Poets, to the Rugby aficionados jostling to get into the Recreation Ground.

There is surely only one way to see Bath (apart from the top of an open double-decker bus, or from a hot-air balloon) and, that is to walk. So, prepare yourself, first with a good night's sleep, and second, with a comfortable pair of shoes, and a clear map. The day will be long and exhausting. Your eyes will be worn out with an overload of images, and your feet in need of a soothing bath. However, the next day you will be raring to go and see more of this visual feast and to revisit your favourite crescent. You have become a Bathophile. The Bath springs or hot waters were discovered by the mythical King Bladud (or Blaiddyd) in 863 BC, King of the Britons, and father of King Lear. The Celts venerated the site but it was the Romans in about 60-70 AD who developed the hot springs and built a wall around the 23 acre site naming it Aquae Sulis. The site held warm to hot to very cold baths, sweating rooms, massage areas and fitness rooms. It prospered for 400 years until the Romans withdrew from Britain in 410 AD. In 973 the Abbey was chosen as the setting for the coronation of King Edgar, and in 1157 it received the seat of a Bishopric. The city saw much prosperity in the Middle Ages due to the sale of Cotswold wool. The building of today's Abbey started in the C15. But, the heyday of Bath began over a 40- year period when three men of immense vision transformed the city from a populace of 3,000 into the Georgian city of 30,000 citizens. The three men, Beau Nash (Master of Ceremonies, manners and fashion), John Wood, (Architect), and Ralph Allen, (benefactor, financier and quarry owner who supplied

Cafe Culture, Bath Abbey, Bath.

the building materials). Today, Bath is an educational centre and host to many festivals: Cricket, Fashion, Literature, Music, to name, but a few. It is a bustling shopping centre with more than your average number of independent retailers. For those seeking refreshment there appears to be a café, or bar, on every corner, and it boasts some of the West Country's finest restaurants. Listed and described below, are the most notable attractions to visit. For those arriving by car there are three Park & Rides, from the M4 there is the Race Course at Lansdown on the northern side of the City. In the City, 13 car parks, one is beneath the Podium Shopping Centre. Beware of bus lanes. More details below. E8)
www.visitbath.co.uk

SPECIAL PLACES OF INTEREST...

Assembly Rooms (NT), Bennett Street. Designed in 1769 by John Wood the Younger. These public rooms epitomise the elegance of fashion conscious life in Georgian society. These magnificent rooms were let out for parties and functions in the C18, as they are, today. Café. Open daily 10.30-4. (D9) 01225 4771734
www.nationaltrust.org.uk

Bath Abbey. The Church of St Peter and St Paul has seen three churches occupy this site: an Anglo-Saxon church in 757, and a Norman Cathedral in 1090, but, later in 1137 much was destroyed by fire. Today's building was founded in 1499, to replace the ruin damaged

Punting on the Avon, Bath

by fire. However, it had again to be rebuilt in 1611 following Henry VIII's Dissolution of the Monasteries. In simple architectural terms, it can be described as Perpendicular Gothic, and cruciform, in plan. The fan vaulting of the Nave is very fine and was designed by Robert and William Vertue, designers of Henry VII's chapel in Westminster Abbey. It was never finished until Gilbert Scott completed the original designs in the 1860s. Note, the Stairway to Heaven on the West Front: two ladders of carved angels are climbing towards Christ. Tower Tours. Open daily. (D9) 01225 422462 www.bathabbey.org

Bath Aqua Theatre of Glass, 105-107 Walcot Street. Demonstrations of glass blowing (from 10.30am) with a history of glass, stained glass, and museum. Gift shop. Open daily 9.30-5. (D9) 01225 428146 www.bathaquaglass.com

Bath Boating Station, Forrester Road. Try your hand at 'Wind in the Willows' on the River Avon. You can hire skiffs (rowing boats), punts and canoes (Canadian and kayaks) and navigate between Bathampton Weir and Pulteney Bridge. Boatman Restaurant. Self-catering units. Open daily 10-6. (D9) 01225 312900 www.bathboating.co.uk

Bath Contemporary, 35 Gay Street. A classically beautiful, light and airy, art space, with Atrium given to showing established and emerging artists who are considered to be original, intelligent and inquisitive. 01225 461230 www.bathcontemporary.com

Bath Rugby Club, Recreation Ground. Loyalty to this club hath no bounds. The West Country's premier rugby club has won glory in all competitions, from the Heineken Cup to the Premier Division. Who can forget the sight of Jeremy Guscott, Stuart Barnes and Ben Clarke in full flow? (D9) 01225 325200 www.bathrugby.com

Beckford's Tower, Lansdown Road. Designed by Henry Goodridge in 1825 for the eccentric collector William Beckford, (1760-1844) to house his library of rare books, prints and paintings. For panoramic views over Bath, you must climb the spiral staircase of the 120ft neo-classical Tower. Open East to 31 Oct W/Es & BH Ms 10.30-5. (C7) 01225 460705 www.bath-preservation-trust.org.uk

Building of Bath Collection, The Paragon. A fascinating study of how Bath was transformed, from a provincial town into the world-renowned Georgian city, thought of, (at the time) as the finest city in

Western Europe, and how classical design influenced the architects, builders and visionaries. Open mid-Apr to 30 Oct, W/Es & BHs 10.30-5. (D9) 01225 460705 www.bath-preservation-trust.org.uk

David Simon Contemporary, 4 Bartlett Street. Paintings, sculpture and ceramics specialist since 2,000. Bath in all its glory, from Rugby to its minutae. 01225 460189 www.davidsimoncontemporary.com

Fashion Museum, Assembly Rooms. A major collection started by Doris Langley Moore; collector, costume designer and author. From the C18, to the present day: with accessories, corsets, 'Dress of the Year', archives and research facilities. Open daily from 10.30-5. (D9) 01225 477789 www.fashionmuseum.co.uk

Gallery Nine, 9b Margarets Buildings. The very best of jewellery, shell ceramics, sculptures in wood and engravings. Open M-Sa 10-5.30. 01225 319197 www.gallerynine.co.uk

Georgian Garden, Royal Victoria Park. A place to sit, and meditate, after pounding the streets amidst a simple, formal garden of variegated leaves and double-flowers. Open daily. (D9)

Herschel Museum of Astronomy, 19 New King Street. A celebration of the many achievements of William and Caroline Herschel, distinguished astronomers and talented musicians whose research broached new knowledge of the solar system. In 1781 William discovered Uranus. Open daily except W Feb to mid-Dec, M-F 1-5, Sa, Su & BHs 11-5. (D9) 01225 446865 www.herschelmuseum.org.uk

Holburne Museum of Art, Great Pulteney Street. A collection of fine, and decorative art, founded by Sir William Holburne in the C19. The paintings include landscapes by Guardi and Turner, portraits by Stubs, Zoffany and Gainsborough. Cafe. Open daily 10-5. (D9) 01225 388569 www.holburne.org.uk

Jane Austen Centre, 40 Gay Street. Jane lived in Bath from 1801-1806 and the experience had a profound effect on her writing. There are costume displays from TV's Persuasion and there are guided tours of Jane's Bath. Bookshop. Tearoom. Open daily. (D9) 01225 443000 www.janeausten.co.uk

Komedia, Westgate Street. An arts venue with daytime cafe and evening bar. Comedy Club, music from jazz to pop, and post-punk. Film. 0845 293 8480www.komedia.co.uk/bath

Little Theatre Cinema, St Michael's Place. Part of the Picturehouse chain of cinemas showing a mix of mainstream and art house films. Built in 1935, the cinema has retained the charm of the 30s, whilst being refurbished, with up-to-date technology and comfort. (D9) 0871 902 5735 www.picturehouses.com

Museum of Bath at Work, Julian Road. Set in an C18 Real Tennis Court, the museum traces the development of Bath from the C17, to the present day, by illustrating engineering, printing, tourism and car making. Open daily Apr-Oct 10.30-5. (D9) 01225 318348 www.bath-at-work.org.uk

Museum of East Asian Art, 12 Bennett Street. Founded by Brian McElney whose collection of fine ceramics, jades and bronzes from China, Japan, Korea and South East Asia date from 5,000 BC to the present day. Open Tu-Sa 10-5,Su 12-5. (D9) 01225 464640 www.meaa.org.uk

No 1 Royal Crescent. Built between 1767 and 1774 by John Wood the Younger, to be the fines house in Bath. It was considered to be the very embodiment of C18 urban architecture, and was used to accommodate wealthy visitors and royalty. It portrays a vivid picture of Georgian Bath and you, too, can bathe in the brilliance of C18 life, by experiencing the Entrance Hall, Dining Room, Study, Drawing Room, Bedroom and Kitchen. Open Tu-Su 10.30-5.30, M 12-5.30. (D9) 01225 428126 www.no1royalcrescent.org.uk

Postal Museum, 27 Northgate Street. History of the postal system from ancient Egypt to today, and the men who developed Bath's system: Ralph Allen, John Palmer and Thomas Moore Musgrave. Wonderful display of the British postbox. Open M-Sa 11-5 (4.30 in winter). (D9) 01225 460333 www.bathpostalmuseum.org

Prior Park Landscape Garden (NT). The brainchild of C18 entrepreneur Ralph Allen. Within an enchanting and wild wood, lies a Palladian bridge. The views of Bath from here are spectacular. Parking only for the disabled. Access is via a steep path

from the railway station that passes by Widcombe's shops. Open daily except Tu, mid-Feb to 30 Oct and winter W/ Es, 11-5.30 (dusk in winter). (D9) 01225 833422 www.nationaltrust.org.uk

Pulteney Bridge. Built by Robert Adam in 1773, for the entrepreneur Francis Pulteney, who planned to connect Bath with his new town, Bathwick. The plans were shelved, and this was sadly, Adam's only building in Bath. It was based on the Ponte Vecchio (Florence) and the Ponte di Rialto (Venice). (D9)

Roman Baths, Abbey Church Yard. The centre of this great city, and the centrifugal force of nature that created Bath. This is where the story began in 863 BC when King Bladud discovered the hot springs, whose rich mineral waters were to have magical healing powers. The Romans built a great temple around the spring, and dedicated it to the goddess, Sulis Minerva. What is extraordinary to fathom, is that the hot water erupts at 46 degrees centigrade, at a rate of 240,000 gallons (1,170,000 litres) per day. Where does it all go after this, you may well ask? The main features are: the Sacred Spring, the Roman Temple, the Roman Bath House and the Georgian Pump Room, a neo-classical salon where the hot spa water is available for consumption, along with morning coffee, lunch and afternoon teas. Open daily from 9.30 to dusk. (D9) 01225 477785 www.romanbaths.co.uk

The Drawing Room, No1 Royal Crescent ss

Royal Crescent

Sally Lunn's Refreshment House & Museum, 4 North Parade Passage. The oldest house in Bath, and home of the original Bath bun. It houses a museum, as well as, providing coffee, lunch and cream teas. Open daily. (D9) 01225 461634 www.sallylunns.co.uk

The Circus. Originally named King's Circus, the vision and brilliance of John Wood the Elder, was built between 1754 and 1768. Sadly, he never saw his plans reach fruition. It was left to his son to complete the project. It was John Wood's intention to create a classical Palladian architectural landscape, inspired by Rome's Colosseum. The Circus is made up of 33 terraced houses. Thomas Gainsborough lived in No.17 from 1765-1774. In 1942 several were destroyed during the blitz. (D9)

The Royal Crescent. Built by John Wood the Younger between 1767 and 1774, and all houses were occupied by 1778. Today, the 30 original homes are split into flats, houses and an hotel, and many are privately owned. A society was founded in 1973 to protect the Crescent for future generations. Interestingly, it took the society 18 years to persuade the council to ban tourist buses and coaches from entering the crescent. (D9) www.royalcrescent.co.uk

Theatre Royal. A lively theatre with a busy Young People's Theatre, and locally sponsored events.   It is one of the country's oldest theatres, first built by George Trim

in 1705 with many guises, thereafter. The present building was renovated in 1982 and opened with "A Midsummer Night's Dream" starring Paul Scofield, Marsha Hunt and Jack Shepherd. The Vaults Restaurant. (D9) 01225 448844 www.theatreroyal.org.uk

Thermae Bath Spa. Combine the rich mineral waters of Bath with contemporary design, and the full range of spa treatments, and you have this haven of relaxation and hedonism. You can enjoy two-hour, four-hour or full day sessions, intermingled with the aromatic steam rooms and various massages on offer. Children under 16 are not permitted. Open daily from 9am. (D9) 01225 331234 www.thermaebathspa.com

Victoria Art Gallery, Bridge Street. Free admission provides a full programme of contemporary art, decorative art and British paintings by Sickert, Whistler, Zoffany and Gainsborough. Don't miss the hilarious caricatures depicting C18 Bath life. Open Tu-Sa 10-5, Su 1.30-5. (D9) 01225 477233 www.victoriagal.org.uk

Westbury Fine Art, 16 Alfred Street. Considered by its Peers to be the leading Fine Art gallery outside London. Consultants in Old Master paintings and sculpture, advising on acquisitions and offering advice on art investment and consultancy. Paintings and tapestries from the Renaissnce, to the Baroque, to C17 sculptures. Open

M-Sa 10.30-6. 01225 330022 www.westburyfineart.co.uk

WHERE TO EAT & DRINK...

Browns, Orange Grove. Browns does not offer an intimate dining experience, (100 seats) but the menu and ambience will be familiar to many who have a Browns in their locale, for sometimes, there is comfort in familiarity, especially when it tastes so good! Menu based on classic recognisable dishes. The building was once a police station and a Magistrates Court and retains the entrance doors suitable for horse-drawn Police vehicles! Open from 9 am. 01225 461199 www.browns-restaurants.co.uk

Casanis, 4 Saville Row. A popular French bistro-restaurant that has carved out a little corner of France in the south-west of England, oozing Gallic charm and style. The unfussy interior complements the authentically French menu (which includes regional specialities). 'A place where locals feel at home and visitors feel special.' 01225 780055 www.casanis.co.uk

Demuths Vegetarian Restaurant, 2 North Parade Passage. Long-established restaurant catering for vegetarians,and vegans as well as all who love a tasty feast. Unpretentious, and uncomplicated vegetarian food. Open for breakfast, lunch and dinner. Special childrens' menu. Organic wine list. They also run a cookery school. 01225 446059

Firehouse Rotisserie, 2 John Street. The owners of the Firehouse have transferred a little bit of the American Southwest to a listed Georgian building that was formerly a wool shop. From the rustic restored interior and furnishings, to the open kitchen and friendly service, and finally to the menu influenced by Californian, Mexican, Pacific Rim and Creole cuisine. Open for lunch and dinner.01225 482070 www.firehouserotisserie.co.uk

Hudson Steakhouse Bar & Grill, 14 London Street. A mix of steakhouse, and lively cocktail bar, all set in an old Edwardian pub. This apparent clash of genres results in a relaxed and surprisingly glamorous restaurant. Steaks come from grass-fed herds of Angus and Limousin Staffordshire cows slow-matured, for 28 days. Also fusion, seafood and classic dishes. 01225 332323 www.hudsonsteakhouse.co.uk

King William, 36 Thomas Street. This tastefully designed pub serves award-winning food along with a drinks menu that includes four tasty real ales from local micro-breweries - all kept cool in their very own Georgian wine cellar! . 01225 428096 www.kingwilliampub.com

Olive Tree, Queensberry Hotel, Russel Street. A sophisticated restaurant with modern art lining the walls, set in the basement of a luxury boutique hotel. Classy, high quality and modern British cuisine served with understated skill in a relaxed environment. Rarely does the quality of a hotel restaurant match the quality of the hotel itself. In this case, both get high marks. 01225 447928 www.thequeensberry.co.uk

Woods, 9-13 Alfred Street. Woods is owned, and run by an Anglo-French couple, and their children, and the Gallic in this paring shines through in the design of the place, from the wicker chairs outside the front of the restaurant, to the paraphernalia on the walls inside. Menus offer a range of gourmet European dishes. 01225 314812

COFFEE/LIGHT BITES... On every street corner, and within every square and arcade you will be tempted to enter an eatery; from a specialist coffee shop, to an organic deli, to a full-scale restaurant. The choice is far and wide. Around the Abbey and Roman Baths, tourists flock. The locals tend to patronise the eateries north of Milsom Street, or off it, and in the squares, e.g. Kingsmead, and within the narrow lanes of Margaret Buildings and Bartlett Street. Chains, like **Jamie's** and **Carluccios** are not included. You will pass them by, as you meander through the streets. I prefer to list the independent enthusiasts. Below, is a our selection. First head to the Royal Crescent. If No 16 (hotel) doesn't take your fancy, pass by No 1 (historic building) and on your L is the walkway, Margaret's Buildings. Up on on the R, **The Foodie Bugle Shop** at No 7. An eclectic mix of farmhouse kitchen, street cafe and hardware shop. The food is fresh, from sandwiches to soups, to hot chocolates. Silvana's produce will prepare you for your day in Bath, and maybe, provide some inspiration. 07762 330519 www.thefoodiebugleshop. com. Moving on to The (Kings) Circus, on your L, **The Circus Restaurant**, 34 Brock Street for a more formal coffee or lunch, or dining experience. Lunch may include fresh fish from Newlyn, or a Rib Eye steak, aged for 28 days. 01225 466020 www. thecircuscafeandrestaurant. co.uk Leave The Circus heading south, down Gay Street, and turn L onto George Street. This is where your choice of eateries multiplies. Across the road is a popular sandwich bar, and on you L, The Porter, where

you can sit, al fresco, and watch the world tumble by. Cross the road into Milsom Street, and look half-way down, for Milsom Place on your L. Pass by Jamie's, and upstairs is **Colonna & Hunter**. This is where you can refresh yourself with a delicious craft beer, on tap or bottled. Or, sit at a table and visit your laptop, or iPad, all acceptable behaviour in this internet cafe. Coffee and savouries for sale, too. 07821 975033 www.colonnaandhunter. co.uk

Refreshed? Now for some shopping, exercise or culture vulturing. After which you may as well head for Kingsmead Square, to the **Society Café**, in the corner. Popular with students, and locals, and off the beaten track. Parties and cakes, loose leaf teas, and artisan hot chocolates, and al fresco seating. www. society-cafe.com. If you are in need of a gift to take home, or some baked sustenance, head north towards the Theatre Royal, on your L, and into Barton Street where you will come to **The Thoughtful Bread Company**, at No 19. An award-winning artisan bakery where you can sit, and digest a coffee, croissant, and or, their delicious sour dough. 01225 471747 www.thethoughtful breadcompany.com

Now, finally, if coffee is the real thing with you, and If you happen to be in the Queens Square area you must, just must visit **Colonna & Small's**, 6 Chapel Row. Enthusiasm, and an obsession for the coffee bean, begins and ends, here. Its an award-winning business. They import the beans direct from the producers, and will talk up coffee, all day. Be warned. www. colonnaandsmalls.co.uk Bon Chance!

The Royal Crescent Hotel ss

WHERE TO STAY...

4 Brock Street. You can't get much better in terms of location, and the B&B accommodation is pretty special, too. Set between the Royal Crescent, The Circus and Victoria Park, this Georgian house has been decorated with great care and period style. The rooms are full of books, antique furniture and paintings. For those wanting privacy or for families, the top floor with one double and one twin bedroom can provide a little space. (D9) 01225 338374
www.brocksguesthouse.co.uk

14 Raby Place, Bathwick Hill. Small B&B set in a Regency house filled with modern art and stunning pictures and objects scattered throughout. (D9) 01225 465120

77 Great Pulteney Street. Situated, as it is, right in the centre of trendy Bath, this B&B seems reasonably priced. The comfortable and airy rooms makes you feel like you are staying with friends. (D9) 01225 466659
www.77pulteneyst.co.uk

Bath Paradise, 86-88 Holloway. Small, privately owned hotel located in a pretty Georgian house and garden. Raised above the town, the views are excellent. Accommodation is a mix of traditional elegance and modern comfort. (D9) 01225 317723
www.paradise-house.co.uk

Bath Priory Hotel, Weston Road. The Priory epitomises luxury and efficiency. Comfortable rooms with delightful garden views from the windows. Michael Caines is Head Chef here at the Michelin-starred Priory restaurant and at their sister hotel, Gidleigh Park, in Devon, Caines brings his uniquely classic, yet innovative style to dining. (D9) 01225 331922.
www.thebathpriory.co.uk

Bathwick Gardens, 95 Sydney Place. A Regency townhouse B&B, the façade adorned with wrought iron balustrades. The interior is tastefully decorated with period touches. A self-catering 4-bed coach house situated at the

bottom of the garden, is also available. (D9) 01225 469435
www.bathwickgardens.co.uk

Dorian House, 1 Upper Oldfield Park. Think of the Dorian (Grey) that walks, and not the image trapped on canvas when you think of Dorian House. For every inch of this B&B is gorgeous, and full of period charm. From the bedrooms upstairs, to the drawing room, and gardens downstairs. (D9) 01225 426336
www.dorianhouse.co.uk

Dukes Hotel, Great Pulteney Street. In the heart of Bath sits this Grade I Palladian townhouse. Faithfully restored to high Georgian standards with a layer of contemporary comforts. Dukes has a pleasing ambience. Bedrooms and Suites are dressed in period furnishings and fabrics. Cavendish Restaurant & Bar. (D9) 01225 787960
www.dukesbath.co.uk

Milsoms Hotel, 24 Milsom Street. Belongs to the Loch Fyne Restaurant group, and

represent 'restaurants with rooms' in the truest sense. Built around a Loch Fyne restaurant, this small stylish hotel has dispensed with a concierge and room service, and in their stead is a modern, pared- back elegance in concord with a Grade II listed building, set in the centre of this historic city. Relaxing and elegant simplicity. 01225 750128
www.milsomshotel.co.uk

Newton Mill Holiday Park and Campsite, Newton Road. Caravanning and camping site open all year. Idyllic setting in a sheltered valley bordered by trees and a meandering stream. Convenience store and licensed bar/restaurant. (B9) 01225 333909
www.newtonmillpark.co.uk

The Residence, Western Road. This boutique townhouse is truly unusual in a number of ways. It offers a range of bedrooms and suites that have been tastefully designed in a variety of shades of Georgian. Each room is pleasingly different - for a touch of glamour, stay in the Queen's room with its floor to ceiling windows overlooking Royal Victoria Park, or try the King's room or the Loft if romance is on the agenda. Billed as a comfortable home from home, the Residence has a library, breakfast room, bar and private dining room. You have the use of a small, well-

equipped professional kitchen for the duration of your stay or you can use the hotel's rent-a-chef service if you simply can't be bothered. Last surprise - a decent sized garden complete with summerhouse in the middle of the city! 01225 750180
www.theresidencebath.com

The Royal Crescent Hotel, 16 Royal Crescent. The Royal Crescent occupies two listed buildings which were built by John Wood the Younger and have remained fairly unchanged since the C18. This makes a perfect setting for what is an extravagantly luxurious hotel full of period details. Step into the Royal and you enter a more sumptuous world - one of overstated luxury. Rooms are filled with period details and paintings from C18 masters. Behind the hotel lies a surprise - the beautiful and secluded gardens, perfect for afternoon tea, and overlooked by the "Dower House" restaurant and bar. The former coach houses are now the Bath House Spa. 01225 823333
www.royalcrescent.co.uk

Tasburgh House, Warminster Road. The hotel is set on the outskirts of Bath in seven acres of gardens and meadow park running down to the Kennet and Avon canal making you feel like you're in the countryside whilst remaining close to the city centre. Rooms are tastefully decorated and the

service is friendly and efficient. Breakfast in the conservatory followed by drinks on the garden terrace or a quick game on the croquet lawn. 01225 425096
www.tasburghhouse.co.uk

SPECIAL PLACES TO VISIT OUTSIDE BATH....

Claverton Church of St Mary. Norman church renovated in 1858. Ralph Allen, who financed the building of Georgian Bath, is buried here. Peel of bells. (E9)

Claverton Manor. An important Museum of Americana that displays furniture and decorative arts, and fosters anglo-american friendship. Fascinating collection of American furniture, decorative arts, silver, and textiles, taking you on a journey through American history. Important resource for students. Café and garden open from 10.30. Gift shop. Open mid-Mar to 30 Oct Tu-Su & BHs 12-5 & late Nov to mid-Dec. (E9) 01225 460503
www.americanmuseum.org

Claverton Pumping Station. This attractive Grade II listed building is built of Bath stone, and is a feature on the Kennet and Avon Canal. From 1813-1952, it pumped gallons of water, per hour, from the river Avon into the canal 47 feet above. (F9) 01225 483001
www.claverton.org

Claverton Manor ss

Dyrham Park

Dyrham Park (NT). C17 William and Mary mansion house set in a deer park with elegant formal gardens. The house belonged to the family of Sir William Blathwayt's wife, Mary Wynter. Blathwayt was Secretary of War to William III (1671-1720). Sir William started to remodel the dilapidated Tudor mansion on site in 1692-1699. Victorian domestic quarters, Splendid collection of Dutch paintings. Film location for 'Remains of the Day' (1993). Open 5 Mar to 30 Oct daily 10-5. Park open all year. (C3) 0117 9372501 www.nationaltrust.org.uk

Willow Pottery, Toghill House Farm. Ceramics by Kim Donaldson. (C5) 01225 891919 www.willowpottery.com

Grenville Monument (EH), Lansdowne Hill. This was built in 1720, in honour of Sir Bevil Grenville, who led his Cornish Pikemen in the Battle of Lansdowne in 1643, during the English Civil War. Erected on the spot where he lay mortally wounded. He was taken to the Rectory at nearby Cold Ashton, where he died on the 5th July. He was buried on the 26th July at Kilkhampton, North Cornwall. (B6)

WHERE TO STAY OUTSIDE BATH...

Combe Grove Hotel & Spa, Brassknocker Hill. An C18 manor house set in 70 acres of woodland. Fitness Club, Spa treatments and the pastoral location will enliven your sensory glands to indulge in some much-needed rest and wholesome foods. (E10) 01225 834644 www.combegrove.com

Lucknam Park, Colerne. Drive six miles from Bath, and you enter another era. This Palladian manor house built in 1720 was a family home until 1987 from whence it was transformed into a Country House Hotel restored to the elegance, and style, of the Georgian period. Set in 500 acres of listed parkland and gardens the hotel offers luxurious comfort in its 41-bedrooms including 13 suites. Fine dining in the Park Restaurant. More humble dining in the Brasserie. Spa, Equestrian Centre. 01225 742777 www.lucknampark.co.uk

Whatley Manor, Easton Grey. Set in a 12-acre traditional English country garden, Whatley Manor is a beautifully restored Cotswold manor house, made to feel more like a private home than a hotel. Bedrooms and suites are filled with contemporary, and antique furnishings to feed the senses. For those mixing business with pleasure, there is a boardroom and business centre including a 40-seat cinema. Spa. 01666 822888 www.whatleymanor.com

Wheelwrights Arms Hotel, Monkton Combe. A C18 carpenter's home and workshop converted into a public house in 1871. The workshop has been transformed into charming, light and airy B&B accommodation. (E10) 01225 722287 www.wheelwrightsarms.co.uk

Grenville Monument

Tithe Barn, Bradford-on-Avon

BRADFORD-ON-AVON

Situated in the Vale of Pewsey, and on an adjoining hillside, Bradford on Avon is the last Cotswold town in west Wiltshire, close to the borders of Somerset. The town centre is full of narrow streets lined with shops, as well as, impressive Roman and Norman architecture. It is dissected by the River Avon, and the Kennet and Avon Canal, which provide a glimpse into the mill-related past of the town. The surrounding hillside is scattered with weaver's cottage of all shapes, and sizes, built from Cotswold stone. A climb through the narrow passageways, between the houses, and up to St Mary's Tor, provides an excellent vantage point to view the town in its entirety, and beyond it, the shimmering Marlborough Downs, the Mendip Hills and Westbury White Horse. It is no wonder that due to its proximity to Bath, and the beauty of the domestic architecture, it has become a less pricey place to live. (H10)

SPECIAL PLACES OF INTEREST...

Abbey Mill. Built in the mid-1800s, Abbey Mill has been used as a cloth mill, a rubber factory, offices, and has recently been transformed into 53-flats for age exclusive housing. Best viewed from across the river. (H10)

Barton Farm Country Park. A 36-acre park bounded by the River Avon on one side, and the Kennet and Avon Canal, on the other. The park offers something for everyone; from walking, rowing, and fishing, to relaxing with a picnic by the river. Sections of the park are managed specifically to encourage a wide range of wildlife. At the entrance to the park, the C14 farmhouse, granary and tithe barn of the original Barton Grange farm. Open all year, free of charge. (H10)

Canal Wharf & Lock. There are two wharfs on the Kennet and Avon Canal, both of which were busy commercial wharfs from 1810 to 1930. Lock Inn Cottage Café at the lower wharf. The larger wharf is the upper wharf by the lock. (H10)

Holy Trinity Church. The church is originally Norman and was extensively modified in the early 1300s, and throughout the following century. (H10) 01225 864444

Pack Horse Bridge. It spans the River Avon and was built in C14 to allow produce to be carried across the river by packhorses for storage in the tithe barn at Barton Grange farm. (H10)

Saxon Church. Near to Trinity Church is the Saxon church of St Laurence. This C7 building is all that remains of a monastery which once existed in the area. Throughout the C17 and C18 the Saxon church had various secular uses as, among other things, an ossuary, cottages and a free school for boys. Now protected by a trust. (H10)

The Chantry. Visible from the churchyard this striking building was once the home of a successful local clothier. (H10)

The Shambles. A crooked lane running between Silver Street and Market Street with a variety of shops. The name derives from the Anglo-Saxon word 'scamel,' meaning a bench on which goods were laid out for sale. (H10)

Tithe Barn. Formerly part of the estate of Shaftesbury Abbey, the C14 barn was used to collect 'tithes' or income in the form of produce, and livestock, for the Abbey. The barn is 51 metres (168ft) long and has a spectacular timber-cruck roof which is one of the largest stone roofs in Europe. Open all year 10.30am-4pm. Free. (H10) 01225 868644

Town Bridge. The Town Bridge crosses the 'broad ford' on the Avon which is likely to be the origin of the name Bradford on Avon. Originally built by the Normans, the bridge was very narrow and without parapets so a second bridge was built alongside to widen it - you can see the join if you look under the bridge. You can also still see two ribbed and pointed arches of the original

Town Bridge, Bradford-on-Avon

Norman construction on the eastern side. The tiny C17 building on the bridge was originally a chapel (see the early Christian symbol on the weather vane). Later it became a small prison or 'Blind House' where local drunks and troublemakers were left overnight to cool off. (H10)

Wiltshire Music Centre, Ashley Road. Hosts in excess of 90 concerts a year; classical, folk and jazz, many world-class artists in a 300-seat auditorium. Family shows and storytelling venues. 01225 860110 www.wiltshiremusic.org.uk

LIGHT BITES...

Bridge Tea Rooms, 24a Bridge Street. Housed in a charmingly wonky former blacksmith's cottage dating from 1675, the tea room specialises in traditional afternoon tea and cakes served by waitresses in Victorian costume. Also, open for evening meals. (H10) 01225 865537 www.thebridgetearooms.co.uk

Fat Fowl Restaurant, Silver Street. The Fat Fowl, right in the centre of town is a bustling licensed café with an outdoor terrace during the day and a busy restaurant in the evening. Open daily for breakfast, lunch and dinner. (H10) 01225 863111 www.fatfowl.com

WHERE TO STAY...

Bradford Old Windmill, 4 Mason's Lane. A stay at the Old Windmill will leave you with plenty to talk about for some time. The quirky and historic windmill, set high above Bradford, is stuffed with character, from the Grimm's fairy tale building itself – once viewed as the haunt of ghosts and witches - to the romantically themed bedrooms, especially those, set up in the circular rafters, and finally, your hosts, who are full of welcome, and weird stories. (H10) 01225 866842 www.bradfordoldwindmill.co.uk

Castle Inn, Mount Pleasant. Revived from dilapidation and a failing reputation, this listed Georgian building is now a thriving freehouse pub with boutique bedrooms, stunning views and a large and sunny garden and terrace. (G10) 01225 865 657 www.flatcappers.co.uk

Clifton House, Bath Road. A small family-owned hotel providing stylish B&B accommodation. Originally a coaching inn dating from the C17 with a Victorian façade, Clifton House has a charming and comfortable interior. Guests are encouraged to spend lazy Sunday's lounging in their 4-poster bed, the drawing room or garden with the Sunday papers. (G10) 01225 309 399 www.cliftonhouse-boa.co.uk

Timbrell's Yard, 49 St Margaret's Street. Great food and atmosphere, luxurious bedrooms with quirky pieces of decor, and all within a handsome riverside building overlooking the Avon. (G10) 01225 869492 www.timbrellsyard.com

Woolley Grange, Woolley Green. The original Luxury Family Hotel is set in a beautiful Jacobean Manor House standing in 14 acres of grounds on the outskirts of Bradford. All the comfort and sophistication parents might crave with all the activities and adventure a kid could want. (H10) 01225 864705 www.woolleygrangehotel.co.uk

Church of St Laurence

CASTLE COMBE

One of the prettiest, and most visited villages in the south Cotswolds lies sheltered in a hidden valley surrounded by steep, wooded hills. In former times, a flourishing medieval wool centre, as evidenced by the weavers and clothiers cottages that descend from the Market Cross to By Brook, and the three-arch bridge. Its great claim to fame followed its appearance in the 1966 film of 'Doctor Doolittle' starring Rex Harrison. The village remains a popular location for TV commercials, and period dramas, because of its rows of quaint cottages undisturbed by time, or any life. More recently, used in the film 'War Horse'. You rarely see children or families (who can't afford to live here), and the post office has closed, as have most, or all, of the shops, too. There is parking at the top, and bottom end of the village. (H3)
www.castle-combe.com

SPECIAL PLACES OF INTEREST...

Colham Farm Trail. The circular trail starts opposite the Dower House in Castle Combe and takes you through ancient woodland in Parsonage Wood and down into the By Brook valley where the meadow is a Site of Special Scientific Interest. Resident species include the green winged meadow orchid. (H3)

Dower House. The finest house in the village built in the C17. Note the beautiful shell-hooded doorway. (H3)

Motor Racing Circuit. Regular car and motorcycle race days take place at this circuit through the summer. One of the longest established tracks in the UK. Track Days for motorcyclists. (J3) 01249 782417
www.castlecombecircuit.co.uk

St Andrew's Church. Originally C13, the nave was added in the C14 and the tower completed in the C16. In the 1850's much of the church had to be rebuilt. Note the beautiful fan vaulting reminiscent of Bath Abbey. Also, the medieval faceless clock, one of the most ancient working clocks in the country. (H3)

Village Museum. Run by locals, this tiny museum provides a fascinating insight into the history of the village, and its surrounding countryside. Many artefacts, including archaeological finds, old photographs and maps. Open East to Oct Su and BHs 2-5, or by prior arrangement. (H3) 01249 782250

WHERE TO EAT & DRINK...

White Hart, Market Place. C14 pub at the heart of the village with a sunny conservatory and patio gardens to the rear. (H3) 01249 782295

WHERE TO STAY IN CASTLE COMBE...

Castle Inn Hotel. This is a pretty honey-coloured building set in the market place. Many features of the original C12 construction remain thanks to considerate restoration. The eleven bedrooms are individual in character. You can choose

fine dining in the restaurant or more simple bar food in the bar itself. (H3) 01249 783030
www.castle-inn.info

Manor House Hotel. A manicured hotel within an C18 build, more at home in Surrey rather than a dingly dell in Wiltshire. Popular with corporate events, and Americans seeking the "English Style." All surrounded by 365 acres of gardens, woodland and, an 18-hole golf course. (H3) 01249 782206
www.manorhouse.co.uk

OUTSIDE CASTLE COMBE...

Fosse Farm B&B. Set conveniently close to the north-west corner of the village's circular walk. Caron's home is furnished in English vintage and French Brocante. Your hostess is a resource of local knowledge and warm hospitality. Dogs and children welcomed. Self catering, too. (H3) 01249 782286.
www.fossefarmhouse.com

White House B&B, Nettleton. Set in open countryside two miles outside Castle Combe. Accommodation is in an annexe to a thatched cottage containing bedroom and shower room. There are plenty of places to sit and relax in the orchard and garden. (G2) 01249 782359
www.thewhitehousebandb.com

West Farm B&B, West Littleton. The family-run working farm is a substantial climber-covered red-roofed building. Ensuite bedrooms are bright and airy. (D3) 01225 891249
www.westfarmbandb.co.uk

The Bridge, Castle Combe

Almshouses, Corsham

CORSHAM

Attractive town of Cotswolds stone and lime-washed houses dominated by the Methuen-Campbell's home, Corsham Court. Make sure you have time to admire the exterior of the noted Alshouses. Recently used as a backdrop for the current Poldark TV series. (J6)

SPECIAL PLACES OF INTEREST...

Corsham Court. Home of the Methuen-Campbells since the C15 - the current inhabitants are 8th generation. The building dates back to 978 when it was a summer palace for the Kings of Wessex. Major alterations were undertaken in the C16 and C18s, with the house being converted to an E-plan in 1582. In C19, however, major dry rot problems were found which set back the family's finances. The gardens were laid out by Capability Brown. The current mansion has a superb collection of paintings by Joshua Reynolds, Van Dyke and Phillipo Lippi among others, as well as Chippendale furniture. Open summer, late Mar to 30 Sept daily except M & F 2-5.30, winter 1 Oct to late Mar W/Es 2-4.30 (closed Dec). (K6) 01249 712214 www.corsham-court.co.uk

RAF Rudloe Manor (now know as JSU Corsham). This was a Royal Air Force station above an MOD underground tunnel complex which, during WWII, was the Central Ammunitions Depot for the UK and the world's largest underground factory. A Beaverbrook aircraft engine factory was also created here as a fallback should the factories in Bristol be damaged by bombing - but it was never used. The labyrinth of caverns supplied 2,250,000 square feet (209,000 m2) of space, divided into many smaller chambers and including 14 miles of conveyor belts. There was cause for much rumour and conspiracy theories during its time, and until very recently, most of Corsham's inhabitants were unaware of the tunnel complex, some parts of which are still classified. Nowadays, a wine merchant rents out some areas for wine storage, and amateur cavers often explore (and gaffitti) the tunnels. (H6)

LACOCK

This is a show village owned and protected by the National Trust. You could be forgiven for thinking you were on a film set. Not surprisingly, it is a favourite for location scouts. Pride and Prejudice, Cranford and Wolfman are just some of the TV/Film projects produced here. The houses are lime-washed and half- timbered, and many date from the C13. There are some old inns and tearooms, and gift shops awaiting your custom. (M7)

SPECIAL PLACES OF INTEREST ...

Lacock Abbey (NT). Founded in 1232 by Lady Ela, the Countess of Salisbury as a nunnery for the Augustinian order. The abbey prospered from the wool trade in the Middle Ages but its religious foundation came to a sad end following the Dissolution of the Monasteries. It was converted into a country house around 1540 and eventually passed into the Talbot family. In the C19, William Fox-Talbot lived here, and began experimenting with photography. In 1835 he invented the negative-positive process. His achievements can be seen in the museum. The gardens are a great attraction especially the Victorian woodland and Fox-Talbot's botanic garden. Abbey & Museum open daily mid-Mar to 1 Nov from 11 am (Abbey closed Tu & W, Museum open winter W/Es). (M7) 01249 730459 www.nationaltrust.org.uk

Lacock Pottery, 1 The Tanyard. Coloured glazes cover the stoneware pieces. The B&B is set in the old workhouse. A most impressive building overlooking the church. (M7) 01249 730266 www.lacockbedandbreakfast.com

WHERE TO EAT & DRINK...

George Inn, 4 West Street. The George Inn dates back to 1361. Its interior is so evocative of 'Ye Olde Worlde' that you would be forgiven for imagining that the man at the bar is Cromwell, and that the dogwheel by the huge open fireplace is still being turned by a specially bred dog known as a turnspit. 01249 730263 www.georgeinnlacock.co.uk

Lacock Abbey

WHERE TO STAY....

Old Rectory, Cantax Hill.
Built in 1866, this Victorian Gothic house has an impressive entrance hall with original Victorian tiles and stained glass windows. The bedrooms are elegant with large windows and guests have use of the drawing room, dining room and garden including orchard and croquet lawn. 01249 730335
www.oldrectorylacock.co.uk

Sign of the Angel, Church Street. C15 coaching inn full of character; wood fires, flagstone floors and top nosh combine to make this a magnetic destination. Upstairs, a cosy wood-panelled lounge. Crooked corridors and low doorways lead into the snug bedrooms which are furnished with dark, carved, period furniture. One has an enormous carved bed that once belonged to Isambard Kingdom Brunel. Bedrooms, also, in the Garden Cottage. 01249 730230
www.signoftheangel.co.uk

Thatch Cottage, Folly Lane.
Why not stay in your own cute C16 thatch cottage? Enjoy the privacy of your own living room and front door without the inconvenience of having to fix breakfast– the main house kitchen is adjacent.
01249 730398
www.thatchcottagelacock.com

Corsham Court

Tortworth Chestnut

CHIPPING SODBURY

An ancient medieval town that has escaped the hectic intrusions of tourism, and with its close neighbour Yate (which provides the commerce) has become a quality place to live and work. The wide main street formerly held sheep fairs and market fairs. For Light Bites; coffee and cakes, the smart Hamptons Deli, for a taste of the Mediterranean, La Passione is popular, but the most highly recommended eatery is Siam Thai at the bottom of the High Street on 01454 850095. Forgive their English, just enjoy their food if you can find them. They spell their address 1 Horse Street on their menu and 1 Hose Street on their business card! (D9)

WHERE TO STAY...

The Moda House, 1 High Street. Enjoy B&B with an international flavour if you can pull yourself away from the photo-covered walls, you will settle easily into the comforts of this idiosyncratic C18 home. 10 comfy bedrooms. Relaxed sitting room and snugs, ideal for families. Wifi. (D9) 01454 312135_ www.modahouse.co.uk

SPECIAL PLACES OF INTEREST IN CHIPPING SODBURY...

Jack Russell Gallery, 41 High Street. Jack was Gloucestershire's and England's wicketkeeper, and (saviour) batsmen, for many years in the late 1980s and 90s. He started painting cricket scenes in the West Indies, in 1990, and has since built an international reputation. His paintings cover diverse subjects; cricket, landscape, the Legal profession, portraits and wildlife. Originals and prints for sale. Open M-Sa 9.30-1. (D9) 01454 329583 www.jackrussell. co.uk

OUTSIDE CHIPPING SODBURY...

Brackenbury Ditches. An unexcavated Iron Age earthwork in an impregnable position on the Cotswold Way. The ramparts and entrance are vaguely visible from the south side. Good viewpoint. (E3)

Kingswood Abbey Gatehouse. Almost sole remnant of Abbey built in the C16 for the Cistercian Order. Of interest, the richly decorated mullioned window. Open daily to view. (E4)

Tortworth Chestnut. An enormous sweet chestnut tree. Age is unknown, but reckoned to be about 1,000 years old. The tree sits in St Leonard's churchyard and continues to gather legends. Follow the signs to the Farm shop, and continue down the lane for a further 200 yards. (C4)

Tyndale Monument. Built by the people of Berkeley in 1866 to honour the memory of their famous son, and martyr, William Tyndale, 1490-1536. Tyndale translated the Old and New Testaments which was considered, at the time, a heretical offence, and he was summarily executed for his transgressions. His work became the foundation of the King James Version of the Bible. The monument rises to 111 feet and has an inner spiral staircase which ascends to a stupendous viewpoint. Open as advertised. (E2)

Cricket-On-College-Field, Jack Russell Gallery ss

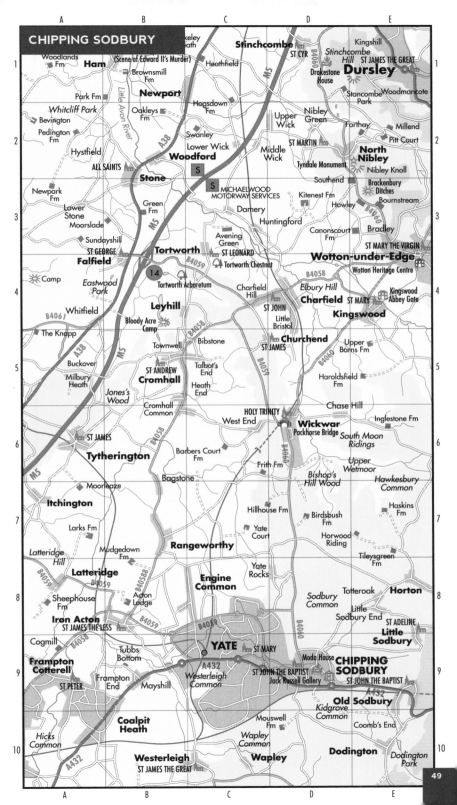

Arlington Row, Bibury

Overgrown, Whittington

Cottage Garden, Guiting Power

Gothic Door, Windrush

Cottage Garden, Windrush

Entering Lower Slaughter

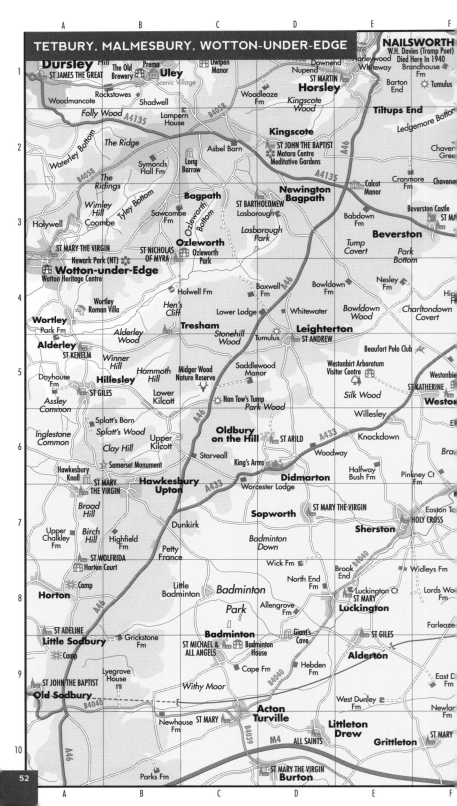

NAILSWORTH
W.H. Davies (Tramp Poet)
Died Here In 1940

Dursley Hill
ST JAMES THE GREAT
The Old Brewery
Prema
Uley
Scenic Village
Owlpen Manor
Downend
Nupend
Harleywood Whiteway
Brandhouse Fm

Woodmancote
Rockstowes
Shadwell
Woodleaze Fm
ST MARTIN
Horsley
Kingscote Wood
Barton End
Tumulus

Folly Wood A4135
Lampern House
Tiltups End
Ledgemore Botton

The Ridge
Asbel Barn
Kingscote
ST JOHN THE BAPTIST
Matara Centre
Meditative Gardens
Chaver
Gree

Waterley Bottom
Symonds Hall Fm
Long Barrow
A4135
Calcot Manor
Cranmore Fm
Chavena

The Ridings
Bagpath
Sawcombe Fm
ST BARTHOLOMEW
Lasborough
Newington Bagpath
Babdown Fm
Beverston Castle
ST MA

Wimley Hill
Coombe
Tyley Bottom
Ozleworth Bottom
Lasborough Park
Tump Covert
Beverston

Holywell
ST MARY THE VIRGIN
Newark Park (NT)
ST NICHOLAS OF MYRA
Ozleworth
Ozleworth Park
Park Bottom

Wotton-under-Edge
Wotton Heritage Centre
Holwell Fm
Boxwell Fm
A46
Bowldown Fm
Nesley Fm
Hig

Wortley Roman Villa
Hen's Cliff
Lower Lodge
Whitewater
Bowldown Wood
Charltondown Covert

Wortley
Park Fm
Alderley Wood
Tresham
Stonehill Wood
Tumulus
Leighterton
ST ANDREW
Beaufort Polo Club

Alderley
ST KENELM
Winner Hill
Midger Wood Nature Reserve
Saddlewood Manor
Westonbirt Arboretum Visitor Centre
Westonbi
ST KATHERINE

Dayhouse Fm
Hillesley
ST GILES
Hammoth Hill
Nan Tow's Tump
Silk Wood
Weston

Assley Common
Lower Kilcott
Park Wood
Willesley

Inglestone Common
Splatt's Barn
Splatt's Wood
Upper Kilcott
Oldbury on the Hill
ST ARILD
A433
Knockdown
Bra

Clay Hill
Starveall
Woodway

Hawkesbury Knoll
Somerset Monument
ST MARY THE VIRGIN
Hawkesbury Upton
A433
King's Arms
Worcester Lodge
Didmarton
Halfway Bush Fm
Pinkney Ct Fm

Broad Hill
Dunkirk
Sopworth
ST MARY THE VIRGIN
Easton To
HOLY CROSS

Upper Chalkley Fm
Birch Hill
Highfield Fm
Badminton Down
Sherston

ST WOLFRIDA
Horton Court
Petty France
Wick Fm
Brook End
B4040
Widleys Fm

Camp
Little Badminton
Badminton
North End Fm
Luckington Ct
ST MARY
Lords Wo Fm

Horton
Park
Allengrove Fm
Luckington
Farleaze

ST ADELINE
Grickstone Fm
Giant's Cave
ST GILES

Little Sodbury
Camp
Badminton
ST MICHAEL & ALL ANGELS
Badminton House
Hebden Fm
Alderton
East D Fm

Lyegrove House
Cape Fm
B4040

ST JOHN THE BAPTIST
Withy Moor
West Dunley Fm
Newlar Fm

Old Sodbury
B4040
Newhouse Fm
ST MARY
Acton Turville
Littleton Drew
ST MARY

A46
Parks Fm
M4
B4039
ALL SAINTS
Grittleton

ST MARY THE VIRGIN
Burton

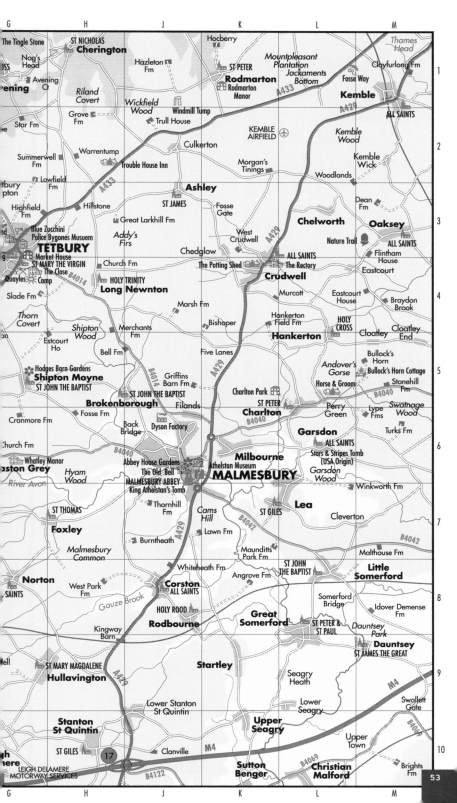

Market House, Tetbury

TETBURY

A market town with a fine church, St. Mary's. The town's recent claim to fame has been due to its proximity to Highgrove, Prince Charles' home at Doughton. The opening of his Highgrove shop on the High Street has brought an influx of new visitors to the town, with coach outings bringing the traffic to a standstill. How this helps the rest of the town's merchants, one can only surmise?

Today, it is the Cotswold's major centre for antiques. It has, also, had much welcome investment in the shape of new shops, galleries, and places to eat and drink. Nearby is Gatcombe Park, the home of Anne, The Princess Royal. The Woolsack Races on May Bank Holiday are fun to watch, and do cause great merriment to the bystanders, but not the participants who are forced to carry the heavy woolsack. (G3)

SPECIAL PLACES OF INTEREST...

Beverston Church of St Mary. Saxon sculptures. Norman additions. Three pointed arches on south arcade are of interest. Screen with some C15 work. (F3)

Beverston Castle. A substantial ruin incorporated into a C17 house. King Harold stayed here in 1051. It was besieged by King Stephen in 1145. The Berkeleys lorded over it, and added a gatehouse. The gardens have an impressive collection of orchids, and are open for the National Garden Scheme. (F3)

Chavenage. A haunted Elizabethan manor house that has remained virtually unchanged for 400 years. A replica of a bygone age. It contains two complete tapestry rooms, furniture and relics of the Civil War. Guided tours by the family. Specialises in weddings and corporate events. Location for much of the current Poldark TV series. Open East Su & M, also May to Sept Th & Su 2-5. (F3)
01666 502329
www.chavenage.com

Parish Church of St Mary the Virgin. The Early Gothic revivalism gives the interior a sparse ambience. There are some box pews of interest. The whole is surrounded by an enclosed cloister housing some ancient tombs of knights and local dignitaries. It is best viewed from afar, across the fields on the south side of town. (G3)

Market House. A substantial building of c.1655 supported by thick Tuscan pillars. It dominates the Market Place of this affluent little town, and is often the venue for Saturday markets. (G3)

Matara Centre Meditative Gardens, Kingscote Park. Labyrinths, ponds, sculptures, Shinto woodlands, meadows and a Meditative Walled

Garden. A place of calm and healing. Specialises in weddings with accommodation on hand. Open May to Sept M-Th 9-5. (D2) 01453 861050 www.matara.co.uk

Nan Tow's Tump. A Long barrow. 9ft high and 100ft in diameter crowned with trees. Believed to contain skeleton of Nan Tow, a local Witch buried upright. (C5)

Westonbirt Arboretum. If you believe trees to be the most beautiful things in creation, then a visit to this arboreal wonderland must be at the top of your agenda. Here, in this paradise garden, you will find 600 acres of magnificent trees and shrubs from around the world. With no less than 15,500 individual specimens of 3,000 different tree types, and a good 17 miles of footpaths ahead, you will need comfy footwear. Needless to say, it is quite a sight in Spring and Autumn, and popular too. Oak Hall Visitor Centre, giftshop and courtyard cafe. Plant centre. Open daily 9-dusk. (E5) 0300 067 4890 www.forestry.gov.uk/westonbirt

Westonbirt School. Girls independent school. Grade 1 listed house. Former home

Ross Poldark, Chavenage ss

Chavenage ss

Green Acer Bush, Westonbirt Arboretum

of Robert Stayner Holford (1808-1892), the founder of Westonbirt Arboretum. Formal Italian gardens noted for exotic trees, shrubs and rustic walks. Gardens open, as locally advertised. (F5) 01666 880333 www.westonbirt.org.uk

Spa-Indoor Pool, Calcot Manor 55

Brecciarolis 63, Badminton ss

WHERE TO STAY, EAT & DRINK...

Calcot Manor. This is a leisure complex combining an English country house hotel furnished in contemporary, up-to-the-minute designs, that flow with ease into the C14 Cistercian barns, and all ideally suited for a family, business or leisurely stay. Adjacent, you have Calcot Spa for health, beauty and relaxation, for pampering the Self. And if, after all this hedonism, you need some simple refreshment, a glass of ale, or some nourishment, then next door, to the Gumstool Inn. Location is ideal for exploring the southern Cotswolds, and Bath. (E3) 01666 890391 www.calcotmanor.co.uk

Close Hotel, Long Street. This traditional Cotswold hotel built a fine reputation but has since been overtaken by the more contemporary and luxurious. However, lunch is exceptional value and a comfortable chair awaits you whilst you digest and look forward to your afternoon cuppa. (G3) 01666 502272 www.theclose-hotel.com

The Ormond, 23 Long Street. This former coaching inn has been completely revamped into a modern small hotel furnished with colour and panache. Restaurant, bar, lounge and courtyard for al fresco refreshments. (G3) 01666 505690 www.theormond.co.uk

The Kings Arm's, Didmarton. C17 coaching inn on the edge of the Badminton Estate. Specialises in dishes of seasonal game and English lamb. B&B. (D6) 01454 238245 www.kingsarmsdidmarton.co.uk

SPECIAL PLACES OF INTEREST...

Badminton. Known throughout the world as the venue for the Badminton Horse Trials, and the home of the Dukes of Beaufort. The buildings are of a soft Cotswold stone or with lime washed exterior. (C9)

Badminton House. The home of the Dukes of Beaufort, and venue for the annual Badminton Horse Trials. The Estate was bought by the Worcesters in 1682. It was the 3rd Duke who was responsible for the house as we see it today. First, he invited James Gibbs to set about remodelling the East and West wings, then William Kent finished the North Front in the Palladian style. Fox hunting has been a great passion of the Beauforts. Their early forebears hunted all the way to London and back. Publishing was another passion. From 1885 to 1902 they devised The Badminton Library of Sports & Pastimes - an aristocratic leather bound series of books that was more like a combination of Punch, and your High Street cricket, or football magazine, albeit, a little more high brow. And, of course, the game of Badminton was reintroduced here in 1873 following its Indian origins. The House is closed to the public. The closest you'll get is to visit during the Three Day Horse Trials (www.badminton-horse. co.uk). (C9) www.badmintonestate.co.uk

Green Trunk, Westonbirt Arboretum

Malmesbury Abbey & Churchyard

MALMESBURY

Claims to be the oldest borough in England (although Barnstaple, in North Devon may dispute this) - established in 880 AD. Military strategists have described its hilltop location as the best naturally defended inland position of all ancient settlements. No wonder then that King Athelstan, the first King of all England, chose it as his home. Set on the edge of the Cotswold escarpment, it is a cheaper place to stay than the more central towns. Its spirit though lies with the Wiltshire landscape. Dyson, the innovative design company of vacuum cleaners, is the major employer and has brought some much needed zest, style and money to this isolated town. However, James Dyson was not the first inventor to work in the town. You must go back to the free-spirited monk, Eilmer, in the C11, who designed and built his own hang glider (see Malmesbury Abbey for details). (J6)

SPECIAL PLACES OF INTEREST...

Abbey House Gardens. The home of the Naked Gardeners, so be prepared for a surprise! View their website for Clothes Optional Days. There are bulbs galore, especially the 70,000 tulips in Spring and a massive range of 2,200 different roses, herbaceous borders, specimen trees and shrubs. Open daily 21 Mar to end Oct 11-5.30. (J6) 01666 822212 www.abbeyhousegardens.co.uk

Athelstan Museum, Cross Hayes. Wonderful collection of Roman and Saxon coins, as well as bicycles, fire engines, Tom Girtin drawings and local bygones. Open daily 10.30-4.30. (J6) 01666 829258 www.athelstanmuseum.org.uk

Charlton Park. Palatial mansion built in 1607. Home to the Earls of Suffolk since the C16. There are 4,500 acres of arable and woodland with trout fishing and game shooting on hand. It is also the venue for WOMAD, the World of Music, Arts & Dance festival, with its own park and camp facility. (L5) 01666 822146 www.charltonpark.com

Dyson Factory, Tetbury Hill. The headquarters of the firm established by James Dyson: a temple of innovation and engineering design, and world leader in the manufacture of vacuum cleaners, and hand dryers. Dyson is the market leader in the USA. The first vacuum cleaner took 5 years, and 5,127 prototypes, to develop. (J6) www.dyson.co.uk

Malmesbury Abbey Church of St Peter & St Paul. Founded as a Benedictine Monastery in 676 AD   by the saintly and scholarly Brother Aldhelm. King Athelstan was buried here in 941 AD. By the C11 the monastery held the second largest library in Europe and was a place of learning and pilgrimage. The Abbey was built and completed by 1180. The tall spire rose to 431 feet (131m) and was to be seen for miles around. However, in 1500 it collapsed destroying the Nave and the   Transept. A few years later, in 1550, the West Tower

Entrance to Malmesbury Abbey

Dyson Factory, Malmesbury ss

also collapsed. What you see today is less than half of the original structure. Yet, it still remains a formidable church, and a sight to behold. It was also a place of great inspiration, for in 1010, the monk Eilmer of Malmesbury became the first man to fly by jumping off the roof of the Tower, and fly his hang glider 200 yards before crashing and breaking both his legs - Leonardo da Vinci was to design a similar machine 350 years later! Open daily East-Oct 10-5, Nov-East 10-4. (J6) 01666 826666
www.malmesburyabbey.com

Market Cross. Built in 1490 to shelter the poor and despondent from the rain. (J6)

The Old Bell Hotel, Abbey Row. England's oldest purpose built hotel dating back to 1220. A fine place to stay if you seek comfort coupled with historic charm. Dine in the formal Edwardian Restaurant, or the less formal Hanks Room. (J6) 01666 822344
www.oldbellhotel.co.uk

WHERE TO STAY, EAT AND DRINK...

Bullocks Horn Cottage, Charlton. Log fires in winter and in summer dine outside in the cool shade of the arbour or by candlelight in the conservatory. 01666 577600
www.bullockshorn.co.uk

The Horse and Groom Inn, The Street, Charlton. All the charm of a true country inn in a beautiful setting. Great food and stylish bedrooms and even an outside bar for those warm summer nights! (L5) 01666 823904
www.horseandgroomcharlton.com

The Rectory, Crudwell. This is a really lovely C16 house that has been transformed into a small, comfortable country house hotel with 12-bedrooms. Three acres with Victorian walled garden, croquet lawn and heated, outdoor swimming pool. Beauty and Health therapies on hand. Noted, however, for its cuisine. (K4) 01666 577194
www.therectoryhotel.com

The Rectory, Crudwell ss

Ozleworth Church

the town's oldest building, but, it is to St Mary the Virgin that all historians will be drawn. (A4)

SPECIAL PLACES OF INTEREST...

Newark Park, Ozleworth (NT). Former Tudor hunting lodge with an eclectic art collection. Countryside walks. Plant sales. Open Mar to May W & Th,(& W/Es June to 1 Nov) 11-4. (B4) 01793 817666 www.nationaltrust.org.uk

Ozleworth Park. C18 house with rose garden and spacious lawns. Next door, Church of St Nicholas with its C12 hexagonal tower, rare weathercock and C13 font. (B3)

St Mary the Virgin, Wotton-under-Edge. The first church on this site was probably destroyed by King John's mercenaries in the C11. The present structure was consecrated in 1283. Its Perpendicular tower, one of the county's finest has corner buttresses crowned with crocketed pinnacles. The marble tomb and the C15 brasses of Thomas, Lord Berkeley and his wife are outstanding. Note the C16 stained glass. Edward Barnsley in the

WOTTON-UNDER-EDGE

As the name suggests, Wotton hangs on the southern edge of the Cotswold escarpment. In its long history, the Berkeley family have dominated the town with varying success. King John's mercenaries devastated the Berkeley's property in the C11. Later, the simmering dispute between the de Lisles and the Berkeleys was sorted out in the latter's favour at the Battle at Nibley Green in 1470. The Berkeleys were generous patrons; Katherine Lady Berkeley established one of the country's first grammar schools here in 1384. Weaving and cloth making grew from cottage industries in the C13. Wotton is a quiet market town with some splendid C17 and C18 buildings. Isaac Pitman, 1813-97, who invented shorthand lived on Orchard Street. The Ram Inn is probably

Ozleworth Walk

Gimson tradition (Arts & Crafts Movement) designed the new altar and reredos on the north wall. The organ originally came from St. Martin in the Fields and had been a gift from George 1. George Handel played on it. Yet, despite all of this the church still lacks the beauty of Burford, or Chipping Campden, and cannot be described as one of the notable "Wool" churches. (A3)

The Bottoms: Waterley Bottom, Tyley Bottom and

Ozleworth Bottom. Deep combes (valleys) of rare, and solitary beauty, rich in wild flowers and bird life. And, all can be viewed from countless footpaths. Strange to believe, but in the C17 and C18 Waterley operated 15 fulling mills (to cleanse and thicken cloth) within a radius of 5-miles. (B3)

Wortley Roman Villa. Believed to be in existence from the C1 to C4. It was accidentally discovered in 1981

when an archaeological dig by the University of Keele unveiled Roman and Saxon coins, painted wall plaster, pottery and a damaged hypocaust. Much is now on display in Stroud Museum. (A4)

Wotton Heritage Centre, The Chipping. Run by the local Historical Society. Museum and research room. Open Tu-F 10-1 & 2-5 (2-4 in winter), Sa 10-1. (A4)
01453 521541
www.wottonheritage.com

The Maytime, Asthall

Dachsund, Five Alls, Filkins 55

The Sign of the Angel, Lacock 55

Horse & Groom, Bourton on the Hill 55

Falkland Arms, Great Tew

Skittle Alley, Seven Tuns, Chedworth

The Chequers, Churchill ss

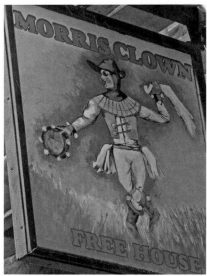

Wild Poppies, Little Barrington

For art and bohemia, 'Wool' churches, river valleys, roman remains, gastro-pubs, hunting and polo, industrial archaeology, gardens, idyllic villages, rolling hills and woodland...

You are now in the heart of the Cotswold experience. From the deep-sided valleys surrounding Stroud to the gentler slopes of the southern Wolds drained by the rivers Churn, Coln and Windrush. Out of these valleys have sprung hamlets with matching stone...made up of the manor house beside the church surrounded by cottages covered in roses and clematis.

The property developer has been busy in this Cotswold landscape. Rarely do you spy an old barn or hayloft that has not been converted into a domestic dwelling. Never has the picture-postcard village looked so perfect.

The Roman influence is notable in the fast-flowing A-roads that pass by Cirencester: Fosse Way, Ermin Way and Akeman Street where you can imagine the auxiliary cavalry units charging up and down these thoroughfares . A visit to the Corinium Museum will connect you to Hadrian and Caesar and you will learn that the conquering Romans built Corinium Dobunnorum (Cirencester) into the second largest Roman settlement in Britain with a populace of 12,000 inhabitants.

A few miles east of Cirencester lies the medieval town of Fairford, home to perhaps the finest stained glass in the Cotswolds. An example of which is displayed on the opposite page.

In the Stroud area there is much to interest the industrial archaeologist. Tours are organised to the woollen mills where you can see for yourself the looms in action.

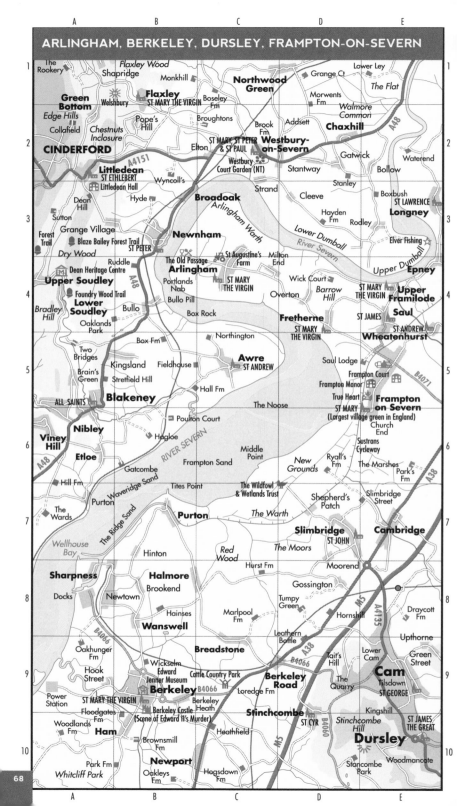

The Rookery
Flaxley Wood
Shapridge
Monkhill
Lower Ley
Grange Ct
The Flat

Green Bottom
Flaxley
ST MARY THE VIRGIN
Welshbury
Boseley Fm
Northwood Green
Morwents Fm
Walmore Common

Edge Hills
Collafield
Pope's Hill
Broughtons
Addsett
Chaxhill

Chestnuts Inclosure
Elton
Brook Fm
Westbury-on-Severn
ST MARY, ST PETER & ST PAUL
Stantway
Gatwick
Waterend

CINDERFORD
Littledean
ST ETHLEBERT
Littledean Hall
Wyncoll's
Westbury Court Garden (NT)
Strand
Cleeve
Hayden Fm
Rodley
Bollow
Boxbush
ST LAWRENCE
Longney

Dean Hill
Hyde
Broadoak
Arlingham Worth
Lower Dumball
River Severn

Sutton
Grange Village
Newnham
ST PETER
Elver Fishing

Forest Trail
Blaze Bailey Forest Trail
Upper Dumball
Epney

Dry Wood
Ruddle
The Old Passage
St Augustine's Farm
Milton End
Wick Court
ST MARY THE VIRGIN
Upper Framilode

Dean Heritage Centre
Arlingham
Portlands Nab
ST MARY THE VIRGIN
Overton
Barrow Hill
ST JAMES
Saul

Upper Soudley
Foundry Wood Trail
Lower Soudley
Bullo
Bullo Pill
Box Rock
Fretherne
ST MARY THE VIRGIN
ST ANDREW
Wheatenhurst

Bradley Hill
Oaklands Park
Box Fm
Northington
Saul Lodge

Two Bridges
Kingsland
Fieldhouse
Awre
ST ANDREW
Frampton Court
Frampton Manor

Brain's Green
Stretfield Hill
Hall Fm
The Noose
True Heart
Frampton on Severn
ST MARY
(Largest village green in England)

ALL SAINTS
Blakeney
Poulton Court
Church End

Viney Hill
Nibley
Hagloe
RIVER SEVERN
Middle Point
New Grounds
Ryall's Fm
Sustrans Cycleway
The Marshes
Park's Fm

Etloe
Gatcombe
Frampton Sand
The Wildfowl & Wetlands Trust
Shepherd's Patch
Slimbridge Street

Hill Fm
Waveridge Sand
Tites Point
Purton
The Warth
Cambridge

The Wards
Purton
Slimbridge
ST JOHN

Wellhouse Bay
The Ridge Sand
Hinton
Red Wood
The Moors
Moorend

Sharpness
Halmore
Brookend
Hurst Fm
Gossington

Docks
Newtown
Hainses
Marlpool Fm
Tumpy Green
Hornshill
Draycott Fm

Wanswell
Breadstone
Leathern Bottle
Upthorne

Oakhunger Fm
Wickselm
Edward Jenner Museum
Cattle Country Park
Berkeley Road
Tait's Hill
Lower Cam
Green Street

Hook Street
Berkeley
Loredge Fm
The Quarry
Cam
Tilsdown
ST GEORGE

Power Station
ST MARY THE VIRGIN
Floodgates Fm
Berkeley Castle
(Scene of Edward II's Murder)
Berkeley Heath
Stinchcombe
ST CYR
Kingshill
ST JAMES THE GREAT

Woodlands Fm
Ham
Brownsmill Fm
Heathfield
Stinchcombe Hill
Dursley

Park Fm
Whitcliff Park
Newport
Oakleys Fm
Hogsdown Fm
Stancombe Park
Woodmancote

ARLINGHAM PENINSULA

This is one of Gloucestershire's hidden gems that lies tucked away between a sweeping bend in   the River Severn's southern course. Centuries of floods and silt have made this peninsula into rich agricultural land. You can enjoy all of this by following one, or all, of the four circular walks that   start from a map board beside the Red Lion Inn on Arlingham's High Street. All walks have kissing gates and bridges, and can be muddy. So take your pick of either, the Hare Walk, Gloucester   Cattle Walk, Salmon Walk, and or, the Skylark Walk, before or after, luncheon. All walks take about 2.5 hours, and are between 4.5 to 5 miles in length. (C3

SPECIAL PLACES TO VISIT...

The Old Passage. This 'restaurant with rooms' has a magical and spellbinding quality, the restaurant is a light and airy space given to fine views across the Severn, only bettered by the view from the bedrooms above. This continues to be a sea-foodies delight: prawns, devilled whitebait, freshly shucked oyster, Pembrokeshire lobster, roast halibut, et al. Meat, too. Accommodation.

Special Severn Bore breakfasts. Closed Ms. (B3) 01452 740547 www.theoldpassage.com

St Augustine's Farm. Working farm where you can stroke and feed the animals, and buy free range eggs. Open Mar to Early-Sept W-Sa from 11 & school hols. (C3) 01452 740720 www.staugustinesfarm.co.uk

BERKELEY

An attractive small town with wide streets that lies at the centre of the Vale of Berkeley. It has been   in the midst of English history for over 1,000 years, all vividly displayed in its three outstanding attractions: Berkeley Castle, the Edward Jenner Museum and St Mary's Church. For some refreshment, there is the Berkeley Arms Hotel with coffee lounge, bars and a restaurant. (B9) 01453 811177 www.hotelinberkeley.co.uk

SPECIAL PLACES TO VISIT...

Berkeley Castle. Home of the Berkeley family for the last 850 years. It remains a splendidly preserved Norman fortress with an enclosing curtain wall. Scene of Edward II's murder in 1327. Lovely terraced gardens. Superb

Butterfly House. Open East to Oct Su & BH Ms, Su-Th June to Aug, 11-5.30. (B9) 01453 810303 www.berkeley-castle.com

Cattle Country Park. Unusual breeds of cattle, and a full panoply of kids activities; play area, pets corner, climbing net, assault courses, and more. Open daily from East/Apr-Oct W/Es and BHs 10-5. (C9) 01453 810510 www.cattlecountry.co.uk

Edward Jenner Museum. A Queen Anne House with traditional and modern displays that celebrate the life of Edward Jenner, the surgeon who discovered a vaccine for smallpox. Open Apr to end Oct, Tu-Sa & BH Ms 12.30-5.30, Su 1-5.30, & daily June to Aug, Oct Su 1-5.30. (B9) 01453 810631 www.jennermuseum.com

Parish Church of St Mary's. One of Gloucestershire's most historic and interesting churches with a mass of features: Ring of ten bells, Norman doorway, C12 font, C13 chancel, C13-15 murals, C15 rood screen, C16 brass, Berkeley family tombs from the C15, and life-size effigies in alabaster, Jenner family vault and separate Gothic tower built in 1753. (B9) www.stmarys-berkeley.co.uk

Berkeley Castle

Berkeley Tombs, Church of St Mary's, Berkeley

DURSLEY

This ancient market town, nestling in a wooded valley, on the very edge of the Cotswold escarpment, modestly hides its innovative, and industrial past. The Market House is a magnificent building that was funded by the Estcourt family of Shipton Moyne in 1738. It has a hipped tile roof and white-washed stone columns. There are some splendid Georgian town houses on the northern fringes of the town. Industry and enterprise are synonymous with Dursley's heritage: from the manufacture of C15 woollen cloth to the mighty C19 diesel, paraffin and petrol engines built by the engineering firm of R A Lister who also employed the failed inventor and genius, Mikael Pedersen. Pedersen invented the centrifugal cream separator (cream and whey from milk) and the Dursley Pedersen Bicycle, a machine of classic design and rare beauty. Architectural innovation carries on with the new Library in May Lane and the splendid new school on the Berkeley Road. Let's hope Dursley is another Cotswold town (like its neighbours, Nailsworth and Tetbury) that is on the up.

For some much-needed refreshment try "the pub of a thousand local's" - **The Old Spot Inn on Hill Road**. The pub of the late, much missed, Old Ric (Sainty). One of CAMRA's favourites and if you are drawn to fine watering holes, then rest your heels here, awhile. (E10) 01453 542870 www.oldspotinn.co.uk

Stinchcombe Common. Superb viewpoint over the Vale of Berkeley and River Severn. Walks. Golf courses. (D10)

FRAMPTON-ON-SEVERN

An enchanting, straggling village with one of the largest village greens in England. Cricket is played here in summer on Saturday afternoons - so beware of men dressed in shimmering white garb chasing projectiles. It is a haven of wild flowers, bird life and insects due to the absence of ploughing, spraying or cultivation for the past 250 years. Two inns side The Green: The Bell and The Three Horseshoes. (E5) www.framptononsevern.com

Elver Fishing. The elver is a baby eel which arrives here in Spring after a two-year journey from the Sargasso Sea. They are fished with nets at Epney on the Severn and considered to be a culinary delicacy (if par-boiled and fried in bacon fat), and

are reputed to be aphrodisiac, in effect. The elvers mature in isolated ponds then return across the Atlantic to spawn. In days of old, Easter Monday would herald an elver eating contest and the winner would then be allowed to rest in a quiet bedchamber with their beloved, sic. (E5)

SPECIAL PLACES TO VISIT...

Frampton Court. A Grade I Vanbrugh House, garden and family home. Fine panelling, original furniture and porcelain,1732. Superb Gothic C18 garden building, The Orangery for self-catering accommodation (sleeps 8). Fine landscaping with park, lake and ornamental canal. Home of the 'The Frampton Flora' a famous wild flower painting. C16 Wool Barn for hire. Country fair in September. (E5) 01452 740698 www.framptoncourtestate.co.uk

Frampton Manor. Grade I timber-framed medieval Manor House with walled garden and barn. C12 Birthplace of 'Fair Rosamund' Clifford, mistress to Henry II. House and garden open by written appointment, for groups of 10, or more. (E5) Tours: 01452 740268.

WHERE TO STAY...

The True Heart, The Street. A sweet little cottage with all the right credentials. It's eco-friendly, fair trade, organic, stylish and comfortable. Within walking distance of the two inns, and a maze of footpaths. (E5) 01452 740504 www.thetrueheart.co.uk

Dursley Library

Frampton Manor Garden ss

Orangery, Frampton Court ss

Tapestry & 4-Poster Room, Frampton Court ss

SPECIAL PLACES TO VISIT...

Wildfowl & Wetlands Trust, Slimbridge. Founded by the late Sir Peter Scott in 1946, and home to the world's largest collection of flamingos, swans, geese and ducks - with over 35,000 wildfowl in winter. In historic terms, it is most probably the birthplace of modern conservation. Restaurant. Shop. Picnic areas. Free wheelchairs for the disabled. Open daily Apr to Oct 9.30-5.30, Nov-Mar 9.30-5. (C7) 01453 891900
www.wwt.org.uk

AND, ACROSS THE RIVER...

Littledean Hall. One of the oldest houses in Britain dating from C11. Archaeological site of Roman Temple. Lovely ancient trees and bluebells in Spring. Open for pre-arranged guided tours. (A3)
www.littledeanhall.co.uk

Westbury Court Garden (NT). C17 Dutch water garden laid out between 1696 and 1705. Designed with canals, yew hedge and vegetable plots. Open East to Oct W-Su & BH Ms 10-5 & daily July & Aug 10-5. (C2) 01452 760461
www.nationaltrust.org.uk

Flamingos, Wildfowl & Wetlands Trust, Slimbridge

Littledean Hall

Toadstool, Thistledown Farm

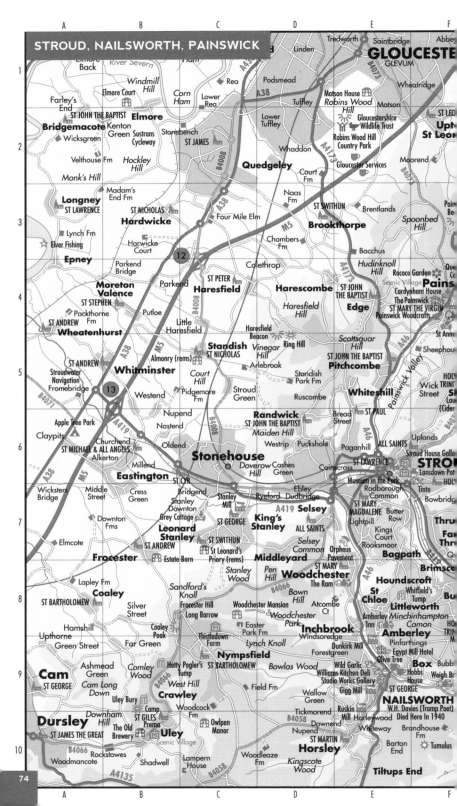

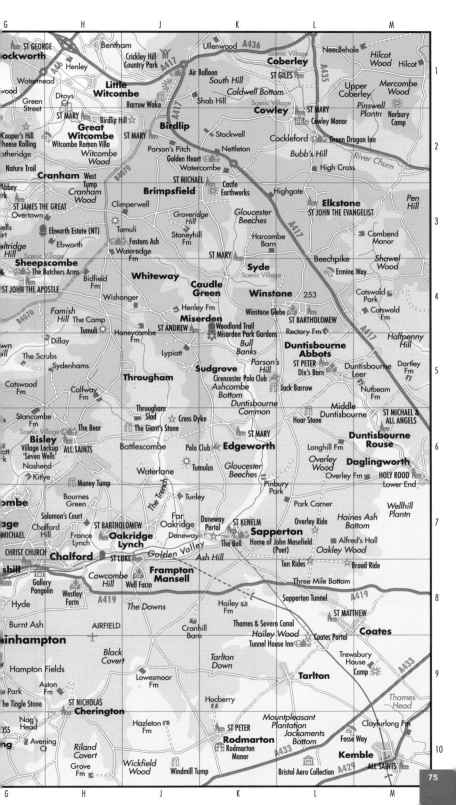

Dusk on Saltridge Wood, Sheepscombe

STROUD

This is not a pretty, pretty, almost too perfect, Cotswold town. No. Stroud was as close to the grime of the industrial revolution as any other town in the Gloucestershire Cotswolds. It has few architectural gems. However, its attraction lies in its energy and artistic ambitions (or pretensions). There has been a liberal, bohemian attitude at play here since the group of Tolstoyan Anarchists settled at Whiteways in 1898. There is a lively community of writers and artists living in the surrounding valleys. Many will have read Laurie Lee's "Cider With Rosie" about his early life in the Slad Valley but artists Michael Cardew, Lyn Chadwick and Norman Jewson settled here, too. And Damien Hirst has a business making up his prints and artworks in nearby Chalford. So, supposedly the claim that it is the Arts and Crafts centre of the Cotswolds is justified. A busy café culture pervades, too. The weaving industry all began in a couple of cottages up the hill in Bisley, This moved into the town where 150 mills were soon in action using the water-powered valleys. But, as the C19 progressed much of this cloth making moved north to the West Riding of Yorkshire. The surrounding valleys provide wonderful walks through combes and woodland that are so very different from the Central Wolds. Look out for the Subscription Rooms built around 1833. Fringe Festival - 2nd week of September.

Arts Festival - October. (F6) www.stroudfringe.co.uk

Mueseum in the Park ss

LIGHT BITES...

Head for the bookshop at the top of the High Street. From this point, cross the street into Witheys Yard, to **Mills Cafe** where they serve all-day breakfasts, toasted tea cakes and homemade cakes. For lunch; soups and Specials, spinach and lasagne, all with al fresco seating. Or, cross to Church Street, to **The Retreat,** a wine bar which opens at noon until 11pm. The chef, Stuart, has a loyal following who are regularly fed bubble and squeak, wild boar chilli and hot chicken sarnies, their all-time favourites. You'll be greeted with a warm welcome, and the beers go down a treat, too. 01453 750208 www.retreatstroud.com. If you seek an all-day breakfast of Eggs Benedict, and the like, turn R out of the bookshop into Union Street to **JRool Bistro**, open Tu-F from 10, and Sa from 9. The menu changes fortnightly. Its all meat and fresh veg, and fresh fish. 01453 767123 www.jrool.co.uk

SPECIAL PLACES TO VISIT...

Stroud Valley Cycle Trail. A flattish route ideal for family cycling takes you along the Nailsworth valley, a former railway track. Start from the Kings Stanley car park, cross the A46, to Dudbridge Roundabout and follow the trail to Egypt Mill. (D7)

Gallery Pangolin, Chalford. Specialises in modern and contemporary bronze sculptures that have been caste in their foundry, and also sculptures' drawings. Open M-F 10-6, Sa 10-1. (H8) 01453 889765 www.gallery-pangolin.com

Lansdown Pottery. A small group of potters work here developing their own different styles. It is, also, a centre for learning and art shows with the Studio, Glaze room, Kiln Room and extensive Library. Open M-F 10-5. (E6) 01453 753051 www.lansdownpottery.co.uk

Museum In The Park, Stratford Park. Innovative and colourful displays and changing exhibitions ranging from Dinosaurs to the Uley Roman Temple to the world's first lawnmower and contemporary sculpture. A Must-See for all Cotswold enthusiasts Open Apr to Sept Tu-F 10-5, W/Es & BHs 11-5. Oct to Mar Tu-F 10-4, W/Es 11-4. (E6) 01453 763394 www.museuminthepark.org.uk

Stroud House Gallery, Station Rd. A presentation of contemporary art in 5-spacious rooms. Around 10 annual exhibitions. Open W-Sa 10.30-5. (E6) 01453 750575 www.stroudhousegallery.co.uk

Woodchester Roman Villa. This huge villa was excavated by Lysons in 1993 and revealed 64 rooms including the Orpheus Pavement. Today, there is little to see. The pavement lies buried and plans to uncover it lie dormant. (E7)

FARMERS' MARKET

This is held every Saturday from 9am to 2pm. There are over 85 stalls, much of which are organic, and they change weekly, so there are regulars and guests to keep it fresh, like the produce. It is considered one of the best in the country, and must not be missed if you are in the area, come Saturday. There are buskers and entertainers to keep the kids happy, and the local ale flows from the bars. Parking is the only handicap. Be prepared to walk.

01453 758060 www.madeinstroud.org

Stroud Farmers' Market ss

Wild Garlic, Nailsworth ss

MINCHINHAMPTON

A large village noted for the Market House, Holy Trinity and rows of weavers' cottages. The Parish Church of the Holy Trinity has an unusual Coronet Tower and some richly ornate monuments. A living and working village, off the tourist route, and better for it. The wide, open spaces have room for three golf courses. So pack your clubs. (F9)

Market House. Impressive building built in 1698 with stone columns and row of wooden pillars. (F8)

Minchinhampton Common (NT). A wide, open space, popular with dog walkers, riding horses, golfers, and the ancient Saxons final resting place - see the Long Barrows and Earthworks. (F8)

Painswick Rococo Garden

NAILSWORTH

In the last few years this little town has come alive! Transformed into a thriving, bustling shopping centre with bakery, restaurants, tearooms, arts and craft shops. An eclectic mix of Cotswold domestic and industrial architecture is to be seen dotted about the hillside overlooking a wooded valley. Its position is convenient as a centre for visiting Bath, and the southern Cotswolds. (E9)

SPECIAL PLACES TO VISIT...

Dunkirk Mill Centre. A mill with machinery driven by the largest working water wheel in Gloucestershire. Displays on the finishing processes of fulling, teasel raising and cross cutting. Access is via the Cycle Track by Egypt Mill. Open Apr to Sept on odd W/Es 2-4. (E9) 01453 766273 www.stroud-textile.org.uk

Gigg Mill, Old Bristol Road. Historic mill with weaving shed containing ancient and modern looms. Open as Dunkirk Mill, above. (E9)

Ruskin Mill. A thriving arts, craft and education centre set in a restored 1820s woollen mill. (E9) 01453 837500 www.rmet.org

Studio Works Gallery, 26 Fountain St. Work by Paul Bradley; Early Studio Pottery, Clive Bowen and others. Open daily. (E9) 01453 833733

LIGHT BITES...

From the X-roads, head East. Beside the stream on your L is **Hobbs House, 4 George Street.** Busy bakery and deli serving coffee, cakes, panninis and sandwiches. You can eat upstairs, or outside overlooking the stream. (E9) 01454 832629 www.hobbshousebakery.co.uk

Around the corner, opposite the Morrisons entrance is the **Olive Tree, 28 George Street.** Just the place to sit and wile away lazy days in the sunshine, or perhaps, to write the next Harry Potter. Breakfasts, coffee, lunch and suppers. Daily Specials can be Fish Pie, Ratatouille Crumble or Rump Steak. Open M-Sa from 8.30am. (E9) 01453 834802 www.theolivetree-nailsworth.com. Returning to the X-roads to Fountain Street (the Bath Road) is **William's Food Hall & Oyster Bar, 3 Fountain Street.** In need of a lunch time sandwich, or seafood (delivery Thursdays) to take home and bake. This deli has been spoiling the locals for so long they have probably forgotten how lucky they are to have it. Restaurant opens for breakfast and coffee. Open daily. (E9) 01453 832240 www.williamsfoodhall.co.uk. Continue up this street where there are all manor of interesting independent shops and galleries, to **No.28 Cafe.** It has the best coffee in town, and opens for breakfast at 8.30-5. Its artisan and rustic, and serves homemade cakes. Artworks line the walls. For the famous 2 in 1 pie, and a pint of ale, you must drive eastwards out of Nailsworth towards Avening to the **Weigh Bridge Inn, Longfords.** Home of the famous 2 in 1 pie. Half of the bowl contains the filling of your choice: steak and mushroom, chicken, ham and leek, pork, bacon and celery...the other half is brimming with home made cauliflower cheese. Freehouse with log fires and cosy corners to sample fine ales. (E9) 01453 832520 www.2inpub.co.uk And now, for something substantial:

Wild Garlic, 3 Cossack Square. Cosy ambience, fresh organic produce, making friends, modern British food cooked by the former head chef of nearby Calcot Manor. What more could you wish for? Perhaps, a bright and colourful bedroom to rest, and digest your food. (E9) 01453 832615 www.wild-garlic.co.uk

Sculptured Yew Trees, Painswick

PAINSWICK

Its local description as 'The Queen of the Cotswolds' is fully justified. The houses and cottages are built from a grey, almost white, limestone, in marked contrast to Broadway and Chipping Campden, and some of the buildings have an almost Palladian, statuesque quality about them.

Look out for the Court House and **The Painswick** (hotel). Wander down the pretty side streets, but above all, you must, and it's tricky to ignore, visit the churchyard famous for the legendary 99 yew trees. The 100th yew tree has been planted, time and again, but has never survived. Painswick is one of the gems of the southern Cotswolds, and is a worthy base from which to explore this region. It is also connected to a network of footpaths including the Cotswold Way, so you can arrive by car, or taxi, and then just walk for the rest of your stay. (F4)

SPECIAL PLACES TO VISIT...

Painswick Beacon. Fine viewpoint. Footpaths. Parking. (F3)

Painswick Woodcrafts, 3 New St. Dennis French specialises in British woodware,

hand-turned on the lathe - table lamps, bowls, vases. Open W-Sa & BH Ms from 9.30. (F4) 01452 814195 www.painswickwoodcrafts.co.uk

Parish Church of St Mary. It is the soaring spire that will first captivate you, then as you enter, it will be the line of yew trees and then, as you wander around the churchyard, the tombs or monuments carved with their intricate figures. But, do look up and admire the gold clock. The spire has been struck by lightning on many occasions, in 1763 and 1883. The 100th yew tree always fades away. So much, for hope. (F4)

Prinknash Abbey Park. Benedictine Monastery with C14 and C15 origins set amidst an idyllic, rolling landscape. Abbey church opens 8-5. Monastery garden with possible

Tudor origins. Café and grounds open daily. (G2) 01452 812455 www.prinknashabbey.org.uk

Prinknash Bird Park. Collection of over 50 wildfowl, waterfowl and tame deer. New Visitor Centre and café. Open daily from 10. (F2) 01452 812727 www.thebirdpark.com

Rococo Garden. A beautiful C18 Rococo garden set in 6 acres, dating from a period of flamboyant and romantic garden design, nestles in a hidden Cotswold valley. Be sure you visit in February for the display of magical snowdrops. Open daily mid-Jan to end Oct, 11-5. Restaurant and Gift Shop. (F4) 01452 813204 www.rococogarden.co.uk

The Painswick, Painswick ss

Fields from The Woolpack, Slad

View of Lower Slad

Upper Slad Valley

Slad Valley

Duntisbourne Abbots Churchyard

WHERE TO STAY...

Cardynham House, Tibbiwell Street. A luxurious B&B set within an enchanting C15-16 former wool merchant's home. Each room is individually decorated from 'Old Tuscany' to 'Cottage Rose' but if you seek a real treat try the 'Pool Room.' Bistro. (F4) 01452 814006 www.cardynham.co.uk

The Painswick, Kemps Lane. This Palladian-style Cotswold rectory has been transformed, again, but this time (thankfully) back into a comfortable country house hotel with contemporary furnishings, feastings of lovely food and various hedonistic treatments. (F4) 01452 813688 www.thepainswick.co.uk

St Anne's B&B, Gloucester Street. A listed, C18 former wool merchant's house with a relaxed family atmosphere. Within easy walking distance of pubs and restaurants. (F4) 01452 812879 www.st-annes-painswick.co.uk

VILLAGES OF INTEREST...

Bisley. Home of the novelist, Jilly Cooper, and the sculptor, the late Lynn Chadwick. Noted for the Well Dressing on Ascension Day and its rows of beautiful stone cottages. Two pubs. Village stores. (H6)

Duntisbournes. A group of hamlets dotted along a beautiful wooded valley. Duntisbourne Abbot stands at the head of the valley. The Dunt Brook flows through each hamlet. The road to Duntisbourne Leer lies beneath a stream. Middle Duntisbourne and Duntisbourne Rouse are two farming hamlets, the latter famous for its idyllic Saxon Church. (L5)

Sapperton. In a splendid position overlooking woodland and the Golden Valley.

Home of the William Morris protégés, Ernest Gimson and, Sydney and Ernest Barnsley of the Cotswold Arts and Crafts Movement, creators of beautiful furniture who also built their own cottages in the village. Their fame rose after completing restorative work at nearby Pinsbury Park which became during World War II, home to the Poet Laureate, John Masefield. Ernest Gimson died young at 59 and is buried in the churchyard. The area is rich in industrial heritage, woodland and circular walks. The dining pub, The Bell, is on hand to refresh you. (K7)

Sheepscombe. A straggling village surrounded by beautiful woodland, rolling pastures and green hills. The view down the valley looking towards Painswick church is a beauty. It is the ancestral home of Laurie Lee whose parents moved to Slad. He maintained a connection with the village by purchasing a field for the cricket club, so named "Laurie Lee Field." A network of footpaths leads through woodland to Painswick, Cranham and Slad. (G4)

Slad. One of the Stroud villages where cloth was spun in the little cottages before it all moved to South Riding, Yorkshire. Hundreds flock here to walk in the shadow of Laurie Lee's "Cider With Rosie" and to sample the brew still available in the Woolpack Inn. If you have recently read the book, which captures an England long forgotten, you will recognise the woods and valleys, so described. You may wish to make your way to Bulls Cross, the hanging place, and now the start- off point for a circular walk. Laurie Lee lies buried in the churchyard, opposite the Woolpack. (F5)

Uley. A long, attractive village with some fine Georgian houses, and famous as a centre of the cloth industry in the C17 and C18s. In 1608 three Uley clothiers represented 29 local weavers of broadcloth, and also, the 13 weavers from Owlpen. The site of a Roman settlement, too. (B10)

SPECIAL PLACES OF INTEREST...

Cotswold Canals. The Stroudwater Navigation was opened in 1779 linking Stroud to the River Severn, to serve the cloth industry of the Stroud Valleys. The Thames and Severn Canal was built to link the Stroudwater to the River Thames via the Sapperton Tunnel. The towpath is open and the best places to see the restored canal are at Eastington, near Stonehouse and at both portals of the Sapperton Tunnel, and west of the Spine Road in the Cotswold Water Park. The restoration work is on-going and is actively creating freshwater habitats where wildflowers abound, notably 'Lilies of the Valley.' (L8) 01453 752568 www.cotswoldcanals.com

Elmore Court. Home of the de Guise family, Baronets of Gloucestershire, who have lived here since 1274. The current generation have miraculously, transformed and saved, this crumbling pile into a special venue for weddings and events. (B1) 01452 720293 www.elmorecourt.com

Frocester Court's Medieval Estate Barn. This is an enormous barn, built between 1284 and 1306. It remains the second largest in England, and is one of the best preserved with a massive oak roof,   and is used every day by the farmer who owns it. For conducted tours (of 5 or more) phone 01453 823250. (B7)

Jet Age Museum, Brockworth Enterprise School. Collection of Gloucester built aircraft with artefacts representing the county's contribution to aviation. Open W/Es & BHs 10-4. (H1) 01452 260078 www.jetagemuseum.org

Misarden Park Gardens. The home of the Wills family, of tobacco fame has shrubs, a traditional rose garden, perennial borders, extensive yew topiary, magnolia Goulangeana and spring bulbs amidst a picturesque woodland setting. Rill and Summerhouse. The Elizabethan mansion has mullion windows and was extended by Waterhouses in the C19 and by Lutyens who added a new wing between 1920-21. The gardens are open Apr to Sept Tu, W & Th, 10-4.30. Miserden Nursery open daily except M, from mid-March. (K5) 01285 821303 www.misardenpark.co.uk

Owlpen Manor. An iconic group of picturesque Cotswold buildings: Manor House, Tithe Barn, Church, Mill and Court House. Water Garden and terrace. The Tudor manor dates from 1450-1616, but the whole estate has 900 years of history to tell. Holiday cottages for hire. Events. (C10) 01453 860261 www.owlpen.com

Prema, Uley. Independent rural arts centre shows new work by emerging artists in their converted Bethesda chapel. Open daily. (B10) 01453 860703 www. prema.org.uk

Rodmarton Manor, Cirencester. This is a unique building built by Ernest Barnsley and his Cotswold group of craftsmen for the Biddulph family from 1909 to 1929. It displays Cotswold "Arts and Crafts" furniture, metalwork and wall hangings. The 8-acre garden is a series of outdoor rooms and is a marvel throughout the year. Refreshments. Open Feb, then May to Sept W, Sa & BHs 2-5. (K10) 01285 841442 www.rodmarton-manor.co.uk

St Mary's Mill, Chalford. An 1820 mill housing a large water wheel and a powerful Tangye steam engine. Open for 'Open Days' on 01453 887186/766273 (H8) www.stroud-textile.org.uk

The Old Brewery, Uley. The mill owner, Samuel Price built this brewery in 1833 to assuage his workers thirst. It was restored in 1984 and has since won many awards for their Old Spot, Pigs Ear and Uley Bitter. It is not open to prying visitors, only the trade. You can sample their wares in the Old Crown Inn at the top of the village, or in various hostelies around the Cotswolds. (B10)

Thistledown Farm, Nympsfield. Promotes the awareness of agricultural and environmental practices by tackling ecological issues head on in a fun way with courses and events. Wild camping and wildlife trails. Farm shop and Fieldfare Café. Organic campsite. Open daily 10-5.30. (C8) 01453 860420 www.thistledown.org.uk

Whiteway Colony. Founded in 1898 by a group of Tolstoyan Anarchists made up of liberal minded teachers and clerks from Croydon who found land they could buy for £7 an acre and who built small, wooden houses. They grew their own vegetables, buried their own dead and invited musicians and intellectuals to visit them. The men wore shorts and beards, the women, smocks. They housed a number of Republican refugees from the Spanish Civil War which later had a profound effect on Laurie Lee's education and travels. Today, many of their descendants still live here from whom you can buy fresh honey and vegetables. (J4)

Woodchester Mansion. Be prepared for a good 1-mile walk from the car park down to this   unfinished masterpiece of Victorian stone masonry set in a secret Cotswold valley. The restoration project is on-going and ambitious. Bat Exhibition. Open Tu-Su & BH Ms, late Mar to end Oct 11-5. (C8) 01453 861541 www.woodchestermansion.org.uk

Owlpen Manor, Uley

View from Coaley Peak, The Cotswold Way

CHURCHES TO VISIT...

Coates. Norman. Perpendicular tower. Brasses. Best viewed from across the fields. (L8) **Coberley**. C15 Gargoyles. Enter through farm gates. (L1)

Daglingworth. Saxon carvings. (M6)

Duntisbourne Rouse. Small Saxon. Saddleback Tower. Norman additions. Lovely situation. (M6)

Edgeworth. Early Saxon with some Norman additions: nave, chancel and south door. A restored C13 porch and C14 stained glass. Look for the cross in the churchyard with medieval base and mutilated head. (K6)

Elkstone. Famous Norman Cotswold church known for its Tympanum and claimed to be the highest in the Cotswolds. (L3)

Miserden. Late Saxon in origin, with a Norman font and windows. Some C16 tombs in churchyard. Sadly much was destroyed by the amateur architect, the Reverend W H Lowder, in 1886. Note the War Memorial by Lutyens, and the beech, and yew trees. (J4)

Sapperton. Noted for its monuments, oak panelling supplied from the Manor House and woodcarvings, its hundreds of crocuses in Spring, and not forgetting, its superb position overlooking the Golden Valley. (K7)

Selsey. Spectacular position set high on the Cotswold escarpment. Stained glass by pre- Raphaelites, Edward Burne-Jones and William Morris. (D7)

Uley. In a spectacular position overlooking the valley. Noted for the Norman font, fine roof and stained glass. (B10)

SPECIAL PLACES OF NATURAL INTEREST...

Cam Long Down. A humpbacked ridge of oolitic limestone that once seen, is never forgotten. From the top, it's a good viewpoint crossed by the Cotswold Way, surrounded by beech woods and bracken. (A9)

Chalford Valley Nature Trail. Passes beside the River Frome and the Thames & Severn Canal. Parking near Round House by the Industrial Estate. (H8)

Coaley Peak. On the edge of the Cotswold escarpment, affording fine views. Picnic area. Ice cream van. (B8)

Cooper's Hill. 137 acres of common land in which to roam wild, crossed by nature trails. Start from the car park at Fiddler's Elbow. The scene of the Cheese-Rolling ceremony on Whit Monday at 6pm - a large cheese (originally representing the Sun in a Pagan ceremony) is chased down the hill. Only for the fittest, and craziest at heart, for limbs have known to be fractured here on many occasions. Scene of an Iron Age fort. (G2)

Cranham Woods. Bluebells and white garlic bloom in Spring and a web of footpaths are spread throughout this tangled woodland. Best approached from Birdlip in early summer when the foliage is green and new. (H3)

Ebworth Estate (NT). Woodland walks through beech woods rich in wildlife managed by English Nature. No parking facilities. (H3) 01452 814213

Frocester Hill. A superb viewpoint rising to 778 feet provides superb views over the Severn Estuary, Welsh Hills and Forest of Dean. (C8)

Gloucestershire Wildlife Trust, Robinswood Hill Country Park. Visitor Centre, exhibition and giftshop. Open daily 9-5, W/Es 11-4.30. (E2) 01452 383333 gloucestershirewildlifetrust.co.uk

Golden Valley. Runs from Sapperton to Chalford, and is especially fine with the arrival of the Autumnal colours of beech, ash and oak. (G8)

Haresfield Beacon & Standish Wood (NT). High open grassland at 700 feet that was a natural fort held by Iron Age and Roman settlements. Delightful when the bluebells and primroses bloom in the Spring. (D4)

Rodborough Common (NT). 800 acres of open space provides great walks and views across the Stroud Valleys. (E7)

ANCIENT MONUMENTS TO VISIT...

Barrow Wake. Deep scarp edge. Favourite viewpoint. Roman pottery found at the bottom of scarp. Car park. (J1)

Ermin Way. Roman road linking Cirencester with Gloucester and Kingsholm; two encampments on the edge of Roman civilisation that was built and manned by troops. This undulating road still leaves a marked pattern across the landscape. (L4)

Hetty Pegler's Tump Uley Tumulus. Neolithic Long Barrow 120ft x 22ft, 4 chambers, 38 skeletons found in C19. Torch and Wellington boots needed. (B9)

Uley Bury Iron Age Hill Fort. This is the Cotswolds most famous Iron Age site. The deep ramparts provide superb views across the Severn Vale, Welsh Hills, Dursley and Owlpen Woods. It's an enclosed area of about 32 acres and is used for arable crops. Of more interest, it has an easy circular walk possible for large wheeled buggies and pushchairs. (B9)

HOSTELRIES WORTHY OF A SPECIAL VISIT...

Bear at Bisley. Bisley's oldest pub is traditional, and friendly, and the bar is well stocked with a range of traditional ales. (H6) 01452 770265
www.bisleybear.co.uk

Bell at Sapperton. Popular dining pub given to natural stonewalls, polished flagstone floors, and the winter log fires provide a comfortable ambience. Local beers. Al fresco in summer. (K7) 01285 760298
www.foodatthebell.co.uk

Butcher's Arms, Sheepscombe. The Butchers Arms has an unlikely national claim to fame - the much photographed carved sign of a butcher sipping a pint of beer with a pig tied to his leg. 'Pie and a Pint' meal deal. (G4) 01452 812113
www.butchers-arms.co.uk

Five Mile House, Gloucester Road, Duntisbourne Abbots. Billed as 'a traditional pub serving food, not a restaurant.' Children and dogs welcome. (M4) 01285 821432 www.fivemilehouse.co.uk

Golden Heart, Birdlip. Centuries-old coaching inn serving a range of local ales, and food, from sandwiches to good pub-grub. Garden with pastoral views. (K2) 01242 870261
www.thegoldenheart.co.uk

Ram Inn, Station Road, South Woodchester. Large outside sitting area. (E8) 01453 883163

Tunnel House Inn, Tarlton Road, Nr. Cirencester. Rural pub in idyllic location beside the Thames and Severn Canal. Childrens play area. Dogs welcome. Camping. (L9) 01285 770280
www.tunnelhouse.com

Woolpack Inn, Slad. Traditional Cotswold pub with exceptional food, simply cooked, and home to a cup of Rosie's cider, and the spirit of Laurie Lee. The Landlady has the voice of an angel, and can she sing! Newspapers, a pastoral view, Beer Fest, cricketers...bliss. (F5) 01452 813429
www.thewoolpackslad.com

WHERE TO STAY...

Amberley Inn. This old favourite overlooks the five Stroud valleys. The kitchen provides meals using local Cotswold ingredients. Pretty rooms. B&B. (E8) 01453 872565
www.theamberley.co.uk

Apple Tree Park, Eastington. New camping and caravan site with 100 pitches in 6-acres, a mile from the A38. (B6) 01452 742362
www.appletreepark.co.uk

Cowley Manor. A chic, and stylish (unstuffy) country hotel, set in 55 acres with four lakes and a Victorian cascade. Techno-gadgets galore. Child-friendly (including play stations). Spa with all the pampering (and more) that you may well need in this crazy world. Friendly staff, a plus. (L2) 01242 870900
www.cowleymanor.com

Dix's Barn, Duntisbourne Abbots. This converted barn overlooks the Area of Outstanding Natural Beauty. Fishing and riding nearby. 01285 821249

Grey Cottage, Bath Road, Leonard Stanley. Comfortable C19 cottage with lots of personal details. Dinners by arrangement. No dogs. No Children U-10. (C7) 01453 822515
www.grey-cottage.co.uk

Well Farm, Frampton Mansell. Charming building set in 20 acres of fields and garden in a peaceful location with stunning views. (J8) 01285 760651
www.well-farm.co.uk

Westley Farm, Chalford. 80-acre hill farm of ancient woodlands, flower-rich hay meadows, and steep banks of limestone grassland with traditional stone (self-catering) cottages spread over the hillside. For the more adventurous try one of the two Turkoman style yurt tents situated in 'the diddlydumps.' 01285 760262 www.westleyfarm.co.uk

Cowley Manor SS

Andoversford Point to Point

Grey Twin, Cirencester Park

Beaufort, Polo Club, Westonbirt

The horse, Equus ferus caballus, has evolved over 45 to 55 million years. They began to be domesticated about 4,000 BC and by 2,000 BC their use had spread across much of Europe, Central Asia and the Middle East. The only wild horse still in existence is the Przewalski, of Mongolian origin and now a protected species.

To many who live in the Cotswolds the horse is synonymous with their lifestyle. Whether it be hunting with hounds, training hunters for racing, point-to-pointing, playing polo, running a livery stable or just owning a horse for the simple pleasure of exercise, and because you adore these beautiful creatures. You can't travel very far in the Cotswolds without coming across a horse being ridden down a country lane or seeing ponies chasing each other around a field. The Cotswold countryside is criss-crossed with hundreds of miles of bridleways. For starters, you could try the Sabrina Way, a 44-mile (70km) route from Forthampton to Great Barrington. For details of more routes log on to: www.ride-uk.org.uk. For those wishing to join this merry band there are many riding stables just itching to teach you.

The Cotswold calendar is choc-a-bloc with events: from Cheltenham's National Hunt festival in March, to the Badminton Horse Trials in May, to the Gatcombe Park festival in August. In between are point-to-points, pony club meets and hunts. A few useful websites below to appease your appetite:

RIDING STABLES:

Bourton Vale Equestrian Centre, Bourton-On-The-Water. 01451 821101
www.bourtonvaleequestrian.co.uk

Camp Riding Centre, Miserden. 01285 821219
www.ridingschoolgloucestershire.co.uk

Glebe Farm, Wood Stanway. 01386 584404
www.woodstanway.co.uk

The Vines, Stanton. 01386 584250
www.cotswoldsriding.co.uk

UK Chasers Cross Country Course, Notgrove. 07776 077271
www.notgrove.com

TRAINERS' STABLES:

Adlestrop Stables, Moreton-in-Marsh. 01608 5810

Down Farm, Slad.

Jackdaws Castle, Temple Guiting. 01386 584209

Grange Hill Farm, Naunton. 01451 85027

Wyck Hill Farm, Stow-on-the-Wold.

CLUBS:

Beaufort Polo Club, Down Farm, Westonbirt 01666 881510
www.beaufortpoloclub.co.uk

Cirencester Park Polo Club, Cirencester 01285 653225 www.cirencesterpolo.co.uk

Edgeworth Polo Club, Fieldbarn, Stroud 01285 821695 www.edgeworthpoloclub.co.uk

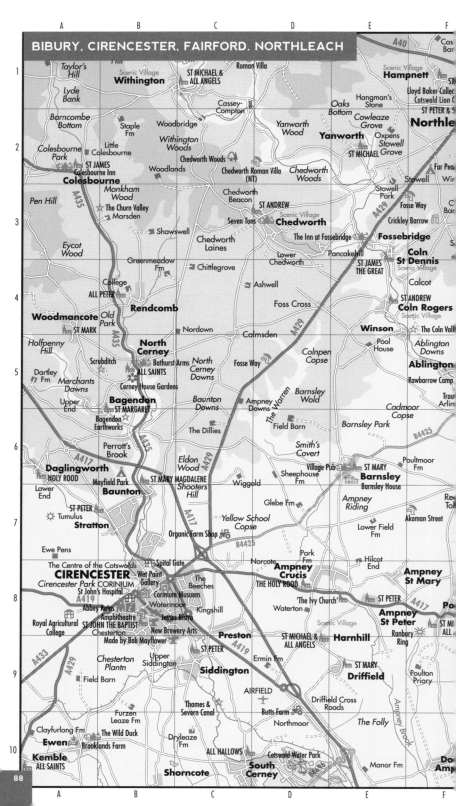

A40

Cas
Bar

Row 1
Taylor's Hill
Withington
ST MICHAEL & ALL ANGELS
Roman Villa
Scenic Village
Scenic Village
Hampnett
Lloyd Baker Collec
Cotswold Lion C
Lyde Bank

Row 2
Barncombe Bottom
Staple Fm
Woodbridge
Cassey-Compton
Oaks Bottom
Hangman's Stone
Cowleaze Grove
ST PETER & S
Northle
Colesbourne Park
Little Colesbourne
Withington Woods
Yanworth Wood
Yanworth
Oxpens Stowell Grove
ST JAMES
Colesbourne Inn
Woodlands
Chedworth Woods
Chedworth Roman Villa (NT)
Chedworth Woods
ST MICHAEL
Stowell Park
Far Pea
Win
Colesbourne
Stowell

Row 3
Pen Hill
Monkham Wood
The Churn Valley
Marsden
Chedworth Beacon
ST ANDREW
Seven Tuns
Scenic Village
Chedworth
The Inn at Fossebridge
Fosse Way
Crickley Barrow
Fossebridge
Coln St Dennis
Eycot Wood
Shawswell
Chedworth Laines
Lower Chedworth
Pancakehill
ST JAMES THE GREAT
Scenic Village
Calcot
Greenmeadow Fm
Chittlegrove
Ashwell
Foss Cross
ST ANDREW
Coln Rogers
Scenic Village

Row 4
College
ALL PETER
Rendcomb
Old Park
Nordown
Calmsden
Winson
The Coln Vall
Woodmancote
ST MARK
Pool House
Ablington Downs
Ablington

Row 5
Halfpenny Hill
North Cerney
North Cerney Downs
Fosse Way
Colnpen Copse
Rawbarrow Camp
Dartley Fm
Scrubditch
Bathurst Arms
ALL SAINTS
Cerney House Gardens
Barnsley Wold
Cadmoor Copse
Trou
Arlin
Merchants Downs
Upper End
Bagendon
ST MARGARET
Bagendon Earthworks
Baunton Downs
Ampney Downs
The Warren
Field Barn
Barnsley Park
B4425

Row 6
Perrott's Brook
Eldon Wood
The Dillies
Smith's Covert
Village Pub
ST MARY
Barnsley
Poultmoor Fm
Daglingworth
HOLY ROOD
Mayfield Park
ST MARY MAGDALENE
Shooters Hill
Wiggold
Sheephouse Fm
Barnsley House
Lower End
Baunton
Glebe Fm
Ampney Riding
Re
Tol

Row 7
ST PETER
Tumulus
Stratton
Yellow School Copse
Organic Farm Shop
B4425
Park Fm
Norcote
Hilcot End
Akeman Street
Lower Field Fm
Ampney St Mary
Ewe Pens
The Centre of the Cotswolds
Spital Gate

Row 8
CIRENCESTER
Wet Paint Gallery
The Beeches
Ampney Crucis
THE HOLY ROOD
Ampney St Mary
Cirencester Park CORINIUM
St John's Hospital
Corinium Musuem
Watermoor
Kingshill
'The Ivy Church'
Waterton
ST PETER
A417
Po
Abbey Ruins
Amphitheatre
Jesses Bistro
Scenic Village
Ampney St Peter
ST MI
ALL
Royal Agricultural College
ST JOHN THE BAPTIST
Chesterton
New Brewery Arts
Made by Bob Mayflower
Preston
ST MICHAEL & ALL ANGELS
Harnhill
Ranbury Ring

Row 9
Chesterton Plantn
Upper Siddington
ST PETER
Ermin Fm
ST MARY
Driffield
Field Barn
Siddington
AIRFIELD
Poulton Priory
Driffield Cross Roads

Row 10
Clayfurlong Fm
Furzen Leaze Fm
The Wild Duck
Dryleaze Fm
Thames & Severn Canal
Butts Farm
Northmoor
The Folly
Ampney Brook
Do
Amp
Ewen
Brooklands Farm
ALL HALLOWS
Cotswold Water Park
Manor Fm
Kemble
ALL SAINTS
Shorncote
South Cerney

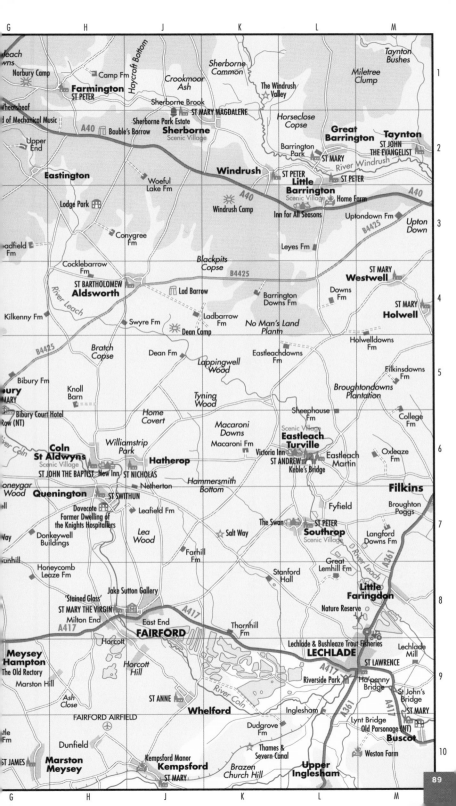

Map labels

G / H / J / K / L / M (top and bottom column markers)

1 / 2 / 3 / 4 / 5 / 6 / 7 / 8 / 9 / 10 (row markers)

Taynton Bushes

Norbury Camp

Camp Fm

Hoycroft Bottom

Crookmoor Ash

Sherborne Common

Miletree Clump

leach wns

Farmington ST PETER

Wheatsheaf

Sherborne Brook

ST MARY MAGDALENE

The Windrush Valley

d of Mechanical Music

A40

Bauble's Barrow

Sherborne Park Estate

Sherborne Scenic Village

Horseclose Copse

Great Barrington ST JOHN THE EVANGELIST

Taynton

Upper End

Barrington Park

ST MARY

River Windrush

Eastington

Woeful Lake Fm

Windrush

ST PETER

Little Barrington Scenic Village

ST PETER

A40

Lodge Park

A40

Windrush Camp

Inn for All Seasons

Home Farm

Uptondown Fm

B4425

Upton Down

adfield Fm

Conygree Fm

Leyes Fm

Blackpits Copse

B4425

ST MARY **Westwell**

Cocklebarrow Fm

Lad Barrow

Barrington Downs Fm

Downs Fm

ST BARTHOLOMEW **Aldsworth**

River Leach

ST MARY **Holwell**

Kilkenny Fm

Swyre Fm

Ladbarrow Fm

Dean Camp

No Man's Land Plantn

Holwelldowns Fm

B4425

Bratch Copse

Dean Fm

Lappingwell Wood

Eastleachdowns Fm

Filkinsdowns Fm

Bibury Fm

Knoll Barn

Tyning Wood

Broughtondowns Plantation

College Fm

ury MARY

Home Covert

Sheephouse Fm

Bibury Court Hotel

Row (NT)

Coln St Aldwyns Scenic Village

Williamstrip Park

Macaroni Downs

Scenic Village **Eastleach Turville**

Oxleaze Fm

r Coln

ST JOHN THE BAPTIST

New Inn

Hatherop ST NICHOLAS

Macaroni Fm

Victoria Inn

ST ANDREW

Eastleach Martin

neygar Wood

Quenington ST SWITHUN

Netherton

Hammersmith Bottom

Keble's Bridge

Filkins

ll

Dovecote Former Dwelling of the Knights Hospitallers

Leafield Fm

Fyfield

Broughton Poggs

Way

Donkeywell Buildings

Lea Wood

The Swan

ST PETER **Southrop** Scenic Village

Langford Downs Fm

A361

unhill

Honeycomb Leaze Fm

Farhill Fm

Salt Way

Great Lemhill Fm

River Leach

Jake Sutton Gallery

'Stained Glass' ST MARY THE VIRGIN

Stanford Hall

Little Faringdon

Milton End A417

East End

Nature Reserve

FAIRFORD

A417

Thornhill Fm

Lechlade & Bushleaze Trout Fisheries

Lechlade Mill

Meysey Hampton

Harcott

LECHLADE

The Old Rectory

Horcott Hill

Riverside Park

ST LAWRENCE

Ha'penny Bridge

Lechlade

Marston Hill

Ash Close

ST ANNE

River Coln

St John's Bridge

A361

A417

le Fm

FAIRFORD AIRFIELD

Whelford

Inglesham

ST MARY

Dunfield

Dudgrove Fm

Lynt Bridge Old Parsonage (NT)

Buscot

ST JAMES

Marston Meysey

Kempsford Manor

Kempsford ST MARY

Brazen Church Hill

Thames & Severn Canal

Upper Inglesham

Weston Farm

89

BIBURY

Arlington Row in Summer, Bibury

Geese On Song, River Coln, Bibury

Tombs, St Mary's Churchyard, Bibury   *Wild Purple Garden, Bibury*

BIBURY

William Morris described Bibury as one of the prettiest villages in England, and few would argue with him. It attracts the crowds, and is thus the stop-off point for many coach tours. It is a honey-pot village made up of rose-covered cottages set behind idyllic kitchen gardens, and all, overlook the sleepy River Coln inhabited by swans, trout and duckling. During the C17 Bibury was notorious as a buccaneering centre for gambling and horse racing. (G5)

SPECIAL PLACES OF INTEREST...

Arlington Row (NT). These iconic cottages were originally monastic wool barns. However, in the C17 they were converted into weavers' homes. Now domestic dwellings, they overlook Rack Isle, a four-acre water meadow where cloth was once hung out to dry. (G5)

Arlington Mill. A beautiful, historic C17 watermill beside the River Coln. Formerly a countryside museum, but sadly all the artefacts were sold off, and it is now a domestic property, closed to the public. (F5)

Bibury Trout Farm. This working trout farm lies in a beautiful setting beside the River Coln. You can feed the fish, or try your hand at fly fishing in the Beginner's Fishery (hours vary). There are fresh and prepared trout on sale, as well as plants and shrubs. Gift shop. Light refreshments. Open daily; summer 8-5.30, winter 8-4. (F5) 01285 740215 www.biburytroutfarm.co.uk

Church of St Mary. If you seek refuge from the hurly burly of Bibury's tourists walk along the banks of the River Coln, and you'll soon find the entrance to this pretty church. With evidence of Saxon remains, Norman font, and superb sculptured table tombs. (G5)

Twin Gables, Bibury

New Inn Coln St Aldwyns

Swan Hotel, Bibury

WHERE TO STAY, EAT & DRINK...

Bibury Court Hotel. An impressive Cotswold mansion lying in an idyllic spot beside the River Coln. You are provided with old-style, traditional comfort at an engaging price. The locals are very fond of their lunches in The Conservatory. Open all year. (G5) 01285 740337 www.biburycourt.co.uk

New Inn, Coln St Aldwyn. Charming C16 ivy-clad inn delivers a combination of hotel-pub-restaurant. Efficient service, affordable cuisine, and contemporary-style bedrooms. (H6) 01285 750651 www.new-inn.co.uk

The Swan Hotel. Few hotels have such a fabulous location as this. Overlooking the trout stream that is the River Coln. Photographed by every Bibury visitor. It is an iconic site. Café Swan (brasserie). Fishing rights. 18-luxurious bedrooms. (G5) 01285 740695 www.cotswold-inns-hotels.co.uk

CIRENCESTER

One of the finest and most affluent towns in the Cotswolds lies Cirencester surrounded by a plethora of attractive villages whose populace (often second home owners) tend to shop, and hob-knob in Ciren (as the locals call it). The smart shops, and bars, reflect the riches of its patrons. As the Roman town Corinium, it became the second largest Roman town (after London) in Britain. Its strategic position at the confluence of the major routes (the Fosse Way, Ermin Way and Akeman Street) combined with the vast rolling sheep pastures brought great wealth in the Middle Ages. The history of Cirencester, and the Cotswolds, is ably documented at the impressive Corinium Museum. On the outskirts of the town stands the Royal Agricultural College, famous for producing generations of estate managers and farmers from all classes of society. All the best eating places appear to be on Black Jack Street. Monday and friday are market days. July Carnival. (B8)

SPECIAL PLACES OF INTEREST...

Cirencester Abbey. Only the Abbey grounds remain. A peaceful enclave behind the Parish Church of St John the Baptist. Open daily. (B8)

Cirencester Park. Belongs to the Bathurst family, who have generously opened their grounds for many years, giving you the opportunity to walk in 3,000 acres of landscaped parkland, and along a five-mile avenue of horse chestnuts, and hardwoods that were planted in the early C18. The C18 mansion is home to Lord Apsley, and is closed to the public. If you like hobnobbing with celebrities, you have the opportunity to do so, by watching polo on most Sundays at 3pm, from May to September, see: www.cirencesterpolo.co.uk or 01285 653225. The park opens daily all year from 9am to 5pm. Separate entrance to the cricket and tennis clubs on the Stroud road. (A8) www.cirencesterpark.co.uk

Corinium Museum. An impressive collection of Roman remains clearly displayed to relate the development of the Cotswolds, from earliest times, with special reference to the Roman period. Open daily all year M-Sa 10-5, Su 2-5. Attached to Jack's Coffee Shop. (B8) 01285 655611 www.coriniummuseum.co.uk

New Brewery Arts, Brewery Court. A centre for excellence in contemporary arts and crafts with Exhibition Gallery, coffee house, shop, theatre and resident craft workers and courses. The Barrel Store (Youth Hostel) with 14-rooms to accommodate 43 guests. Open M-Sa 9-5, Su 9.30-4. (B8) 01285 657181 www.newbreweryarts.org.uk

Parish Church of St John the Baptist. A fine mix of the C14 and C15, the largest of the 'Wool' churches, and the easiest to recognize with its three-storied, fan-vaulted porch. The porch, formerly the Town Hall, overshadows the Market Place. C15 'wine glass' pulpit, Ann Boleyn Cup, and many fine brasses. Guided tours. Open M-Sa 9.30-5 Su in winter 2.15-5.30, in summer 12.30-6. (B8) 01285 659317 www.cirenparish.co.uk

St John's Hospital. Founded by Henry II, later absorbed by the Abbey. Next door, Almshouses dated 1826. (B8)

The Organic Farm Shop, Burford Road. Their dictum: 'Eating organic is eating from the Earth, back to nature void of pesticides. All growing freely

New Brewery Arts, Cirencester ss

Parish Church of St John the Baptist

without insecticides,' is their passion and raison d'être. Café. Open Tu-Sa 9-5, Sun 11-4. (C7) 01285 640441 www.theorganicfarmshop.co.uk

Wet Paint Gallery, 14 London Rd. Colourful, abstract and modern landscapes, ceramics and glass. Open M-F 10-5. (C8) 01285 644990 www.contemporary-art-holdings.co.uk

JUST OUTSIDE CIRENCESTER..

Akeman Street. Roman road built to provide communications between military units and their forts. Best seen near Coln St Aldwyn and Quenington. (E7)

Bagendon Earthworks (Dykes). Remains of the Dobunni tribes' headquarters which was the capital of the Cotswolds in the C1 AD. The settlement was abandoned ten years after the Roman Conquest. Iron Age silver coins excavated here. (B6)

Butts Farm (& Farm Shop). Rare breeds, sheep, fowl, pigs and cattle in 30 acres of meadowland. Tractor safari. Picnics. Pets' corner. Open East to Oct half-term Tu-Su & BHs 10.30-5. Farm shop open daily. (D9) 01285 862224 www.thebuttsfarmshop.com

Cerney House Gardens. Just look around, and you will surmise that this garden has been created by persons of immense enthusiasm, passion and experimentation. And, you have a garden of maturity, with old roses and herbaceous borders that sit well beside the walled kitchen-flower garden. You may purchase plants from their expansive plant collections. Teas. Open daily 10-5 Jan to Nov, 10-5. (B5) 01285 831300 www.cerneygardens.com

LIGHT BITES...

If you like your coffee stop, or brunch to have some cultural affinity, then visit the cafe at the **New Brewery Arts,** or opposite, on the other side of the square, Waterstones have their own cafe serving light snacks, from 7.30-5.30. But, more choice can be found on **Black Jack Street** that runs from Park Street beside the **Corinium Museum,** to Gosditch Street, opposite the side of the Parish Church. **Jack's Coffee Shop** serves the best coffee (according to my Octavian spies), and amazing homemade cakes. You can sit, al fresco. Further up the street, **Jesses Bistro,** Black Jack Street. Butchers in the Cotswolds for many generations, so, if they can't get their meat right, what hope is there for the rest of us? The fresh fish trawls in from Newlyn. Open for lunch, M-Sa and dinner, W-Sa. (B8) 01285 641497 www.jessesbistro.co.uk, or, for a more formal affair, the Cote Brasserie (chain) for breakfast, brunch or a substantial lunch. Then turn R into the Market Place, and enter the Corn Hall to **Made By Bob.** Set in the Corn Hall, a popular food emporia open from 7.30 for breakfast, lunch and afternoon teas. It's got Ciren's Ladies of Means in a frenzy of excitement, all rushing in for their champagne cocktails and made-up TV dinners. (B8) 01285 641818 www.foodmadebybob.com

WHERE TO STAY...

Barnsley House. The former home of the garden expert, the late Rosemary Verey. A chic hotel and spa offering discreet and friendly service, great food and state-of-the-art technology. A visit to this extraordinary garden may cost you lunch, but it will be a worthwhile, and memorable experience. Make sure you visit the vegetable garden. Cinema club. (E6) 01285 740000 www.barnsleyhouse.com

Mayfield Park. Set on the north side of Cirencester, this popular site welcomes tents and caravans. (B6) 01285 831301 www.mayfieldpark.co.uk

No.107 Gloucester Street, Cirencester. Tucked away in a narrow courtyard is this delightful B&B with all the comforts of home. Within walking distance of Ciren's pubs and eating-out emporia. (B8) 01285 657861

No.12 Park Street, Cirencester. If style and gracious comfort is to your liking then this Grade II Georgian townhouse offering luxurious B&B may be just what you are looking for. (B8) 01285 640232 www.no12cirencester.co.uk

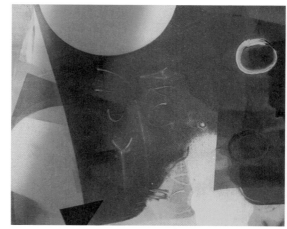

Mosaic, Corinium Museum

Carving of Roman Figures, Corinium Museum, Cirencester

Cerney House Gardens

Laburnam Walk, Barnsley House

EASTLEACH

The twin hamlets of Eastleach Turville and Eastleach Martin face each other across the River Leach. The ancient clapper bridge (Keble's Bridge) connects the two. In spring, hundreds of daffodils grow on both banks, and hidden behind the trees is the Norman Church of St Michael and St Martin. Across the river the tiny church of St Andrews. Rustic village hostelry, the Victoria Inn. (L6)

Keble's Bridge. This was most likely built by the Keble family whose descendant, John Keble, was curate here in 1815. He founded the Oxford Movement, and is know for his volume of religious verse 'The Christian Year.' (L6)

Church of St Michael & St Martin. Founded by Richard Fitzpons, one of William the Conqueror's knights. It has a C14 north transept, decorated windows, and a memorable exterior, beside the river fronted by daffodils in spring. It closed for services in 1982. (L6)

Church of St Andrews. Hidden beneath the trees, this shy, tiny church, has a more interesting interior than its neighbour. Note, the splendid C14 saddleback tower of a Transitional, and Early English, period style. A Norman doorway c.1130 with a carved Tympanum of Christ. (L6)

Macaroni Downs. Quite a sight. These rolling sheep pastures were once the location for Regency derring-do, gambling and horse racing. Now just munched by sheep, cattle and ridden through by mountain bikers. (K6)

Church of St Michael & St Martin, Eastleach

Macaroni Downs Bikers

Seven Tuns, Chedworth ss

FAIRFORD

An attractive market town on the tranquil River Coln, noted for the fine 'Wool' Church with its C15 stained glass windows. Mill. C6 Saxon cemetery. Venue for the annual, Royal International Air Tattoo. (J8)

SPECIAL PLACES OF INTEREST...

Jake Sutton Gallery, 10 High Street. An exhibition of Dance and Ballerinas - bright watercolour scenes, charcoal drawings and prints. Open M-Sa 10-5, or by appointment. (J8) 01285 712500 www.jakesutton.co.uk

Parish Church of St Mary the Virgin. The perfect, late C15 Perpendicular church, that is world-famous for the outstanding 28 stained glass windows, depicting scenes from Genesis to the Last Judgement. Of further interest, the carved misericords and recumbent brasses. Note the stone cat, a memorial to Tiddles who fell off the church roof. Open 9.30-5.30 for visits and guided tours. (J8) 01285 712611

COUNTRY INNS...

Bathurst Arms, North Cerney. Always a favourite with students from the RAC, and families on long summer evenings sitting beside the Churn. (B5)

01285 832150 www. thebathurstarms.co.uk

Seven Tuns, Chedworth. This wonderful, ancient inn has been given a loving make-over by Liz and her sister, Sarah. More comfort and delicious nosh will prepare you for long evenings of vivid conversation, dominoes and bountiful pints of golden ale. Live music and quiz nights. (D3) 01285 720630 www.seventuns.co.uk

The Swan, Southrop. This is a lot more than a stylish inn. As part **of** the Thyme and Southrop Manor Estate, who provide produce from their own kitchen garden and farm, which inspires the chefs to engineer sumptuous meals. There is also luxury B&B, Private Dining and restored barns, and cottages to rent for individuals and house parties, galore. (K7) 01367 850205 www.thyme.co.uk

Village Pub, Barnsley. A warren of little rooms serving ambitious pub food and local beers. Child/dog friendly. Luxurious B&B. Part of the Barnsley House empire, opposite. They have also just taken over the Wagon Wheel in Bibury - a welcome move. (E6) 01285 740421 www. thevillagepub.co.uk

Wild Duck at Ewen. A pub popular with students from the RAC, and Londoners down for the weekend in their Chelsea tractors. If you can put up with the drawling voices, and the posh totty you may enjoy the

comfortable décor and family portraits, the lazy ambience given to long drinking binges and boisterous conversation. But, first book a taxi home, or take your chauffeur. (A10) 01285 770310 www. thewildduckinn.co.uk

WHERE TO STAY...

Brooklands Farm, Ewen. Two miles from the source of the Thames, and close to the National Thames Path. Two comfortable rooms. Home cooked food. Quiet garden to the rear. (A10) 01285 770487

Kempsford Manor, High Street. Beautiful gardens surround this charming C17-18 manor house, that is often a venue for artistic workshops, and village cricket. A place to retreat to, and to be at peace, with yourself, and the world. (J10) 01285 810131 www.kempsfordmanor.com

The Inn at Fossebridge. If Liz Jenkins' enthusiasm and hospitality reaches you, you can be assured of a good time. Here, it's all about old-fashioned manners, comfort food, flagstone floors and log fires. (E3) 01285 720721 www. fossebridgeinn.co.uk

The Old Rectory, Meysey Hampton. Lovely family home. Bask in convivial hospitality surrounded by antiques and aching floorboards. Comfy beds. (G9) 01285 851200 www.meyseyoldrectory.co.uk

Jake Sutton Gallery, Fairford ss

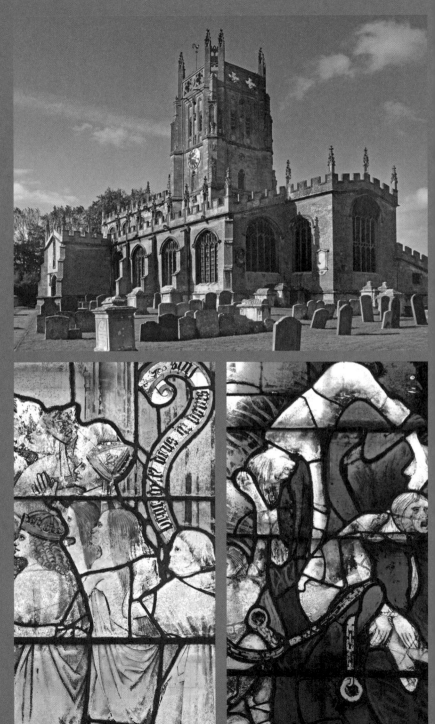

Church of St Peter & St Paul, Northleach

NORTHLEACH

An attractive Cotswold village noted for its exceptional Church and Market Place. Often overlooked, because the A40 now bypasses the village which at first left it out on a limb. However, the village elders have done much to restore the lifeblood of this little community. It is worth a special journey to admire the beautiful church, buildings and museums. (F2)

SPECIAL PLACES OF INTEREST...

World of Mechanical Music, High St. One of the finest attractions in the Cotswolds where you will always be met with a cheery welcome. An enchanting wonderland of mechanical musical instruments, clocks and restored musical boxes. 'Magical Musicals.' Gift shop. Open daily 10-6. (G2) 01451 860181 www.mechanicalmusic.co.uk

Lloyd Baker Countryside Collection. Fascinating medley of agricultural implements: carts and bygone machinery. Free entry via the Cotswold Lion Café - see below. (F1)

Parish Church of St Peter & St Paul. C15. The South Porch has been described as the most lovely in all England: Tall pinnacles and statue filled niches. From afar, the church appears to hover above the town. Brasses of wealthy wool barons. Guided tours: 01451 861172. (F2)

WHERE TO STAY...

Far Peak Camping. A simple, rustic campsite centred conveniently in the centre of the Cotswolds, and all within walking distance of Northleach's amenities. (F2) 01285 720858 www.farpeakcamping.co.uk

Home Farm, Little Barrington. Robin and Sylvia will welcome you warmly to their golden stoned Cotswold home. Robin's family have lived here for 200 years and he will regale you with tales of derring-do. Sylvia's talents lie with interior design, and the culinary arts. Good value B&B. (L2) 01451 844300 www.homefarmcotswolds.com

LIGHT BITES...

Entering from the Cheltenham road, on your left at the traffic-lights resides the Old Prison, and inside the **Cotswold Lion Cafe**, for home-made cakes, soups and wifi. Comfortable and ideal for meeting up with colleagues and friends. Plenty of parking, too. Open daily 9.30-4.30. (F1)

Enter the Market Square and head straight for **The Ox House** housing a wine merchant, wine bar and coffee shop. Brunch and light lunches available, and out back you have the garden room and **Hidden Back Bar** with comfy sofas and log fires, wifi, where you can watch the cricket and rugby, or snooze off their fine wines. Open Tu-Sa 9-11, Su & M 9-9. (G2) 01451 860650 www.northleachwines.com

For the more sober minded, the **Black Cat Cafe**, in the top left corner opens at 8.30 for breakfast, coffee and gluten free bread/cakes. Three cosy rooms with log burners and the morning papers. Cyclists/walkers/young mums/dog/child friendly. Open M-Sa 8.30-4.30. (G2) 01451 861101 www.blackcat-cafe.co.uk

Chedworth Woods & Fields

Mosaic of Spring, Chedworth Roman Villa

World of Mechanical Music, Northleach

Bull in Field, Winson

River Coln at Dawn, Yanworth

River Coln, Coln St Dennis

The Wheatsheaf, Northleach. A friendly C17 coaching inn that invites long hours beside the log fires, and lazy mornings lounging in their comfy beds. Lunch and suppers to be recommended. Luxurious B&B. Book club. Music nights. (G2) 01451 860244 www.cotswoldswheatsheaf.com

SPECIAL PLACES OF INTEREST...OUTSIDE NORTHLEACH...

Chedworth Roman Villa (NT). Discovered in 1864 by a local gamekeeper and later excavated between 1864 and 1866 revealing remains of a Romano-British villa containing mosaics, baths and hypocausts. Family trails. Museum. Open daily mid-Feb to late-Nov, from 10am. (D2) 01242 890256 www.nationaltrust.org.uk

Chedworth Woods. A network of footpaths that crisscross through tangled woodland close to the Roman Villa. (C2)

Churn Valley. A memorable route from Seven Springs to Cirencester follows one of England's most scenic drives. The variety of the trees, and the sunken river valley, are a sight, to behold. Beware, this is a fast road and accidents are frequent. (A2)

Coln Valley. Charming valley with typically quaint Cotswold villages: Calcot, Coln Rogers, Coln St Dennis, Winson and Ablington. (E4)

CHURCHES OF INTEREST...

Ampney Crucis. C14 wall paintings. Saxon, Early Norman, and Perpendicular features. Life-size effigies. Jacobean pews. (D8)

Ampney St Mary. Wall paintings from the C12 to the C15. Norman font with chevron moulding. Isolated in field. Rarely open. (E8)

Baunton. C14 wall painting of St Christopher. Remains of rood screen. Tudor doorway. (B7) **Bagendon.** In fabulous, central position in small hamlet. Stained glass. Norman arcade. (B5) **Chedworth.** Norman origins. C15 'wine glass' pulpit. Gargoyles. 'Wool' church. (D3)

Coln St Dennis. Picturesque. Massive Norman tower. (E3)

Eastleach Martin. Norman. Hipped roof. Beautiful place. Daffodils in spring. (L6) **North Cerney.** Saddle-back tower. Rood loft. C15 stained glass. (B5) **Rendcomb.** Perpendicular. Norman font. (B4) **Southrop.** Norman nave. C12 font. (K7) **Stowell.** Doom painting. Norman. (E2)

LECHLADE

A pleasant market town bejewelled with many fine C18 and C19 buildings. C15 'Wool' Church with fine Priest's Door. A busy boating and fishing centre given that it is the highest navigable point of the River Thames. Marina. (L9)

Lechlade & Bushleaze Trout Fisheries. Stocked with Brown and Rainbow trout (& the odd Pike) for day and half-day, and evening fishing exploits. Tackle shop, loos, tuition and boat hire on hand.01367 253266 www.lechladetrout.co.uk

WHERE TO STAY...

Weston Farm, Buscot Wick. 500-acre organic farm with C17 farmhouse, all tastefully decorated and furnished, inviting comfort and relaxation, both in the house and garden. (M10) 01367 252222

SPECIAL PLACES TO VISIT...

Cotswold Water Park. This covers an area of 40 square miles of countryside and is split into three sections: the Western section, the Keynes Country Park and the Eastern Section (near Fairford). www.waterpark.org. There are 140 lakes, 74 fishing lakes, 10 lakes with SSSI status, 40 different lake owners and 150km of pathways, bridleways and cycleways. 20,000 people live in the park's 14 main settlements. The extraction of the gravel and sand deposits from the 'catchment area' of the Upper Thames left large holes that were in 1967 designated to become a water park. From its humbled beginnings at the South Cerney Sailing Club, the park now attracts more than

The Wheatsheaf ss

half-a- million visitors a year. Children love the sandy beach and sculptures at Keynes, whilst the more active are beckoned to the wakeboarding and slalom skis at WM Ski on Spine Road www.wmski.com. A visit to the Gateway Centre on Spine Road is recommended before you explore the park where you can eat and drink at the Coot's Café daily from 9-5. Just opposite, the retailer, Cotswold Outdoor, for all your walking and camping supplies. Further down the road overlooking Spring Lake, the Lakeside Brasserie for coffees, beers, pizzas, burgers and childrens meals. (D10) www.watermarkclub.co.uk

Lodge Park (NT). A 'little' property with a big (boozy) history. A grandstand (folly) built by John 'Crump' Dutton in 1634 so he could watch deer coursing in comfort, and share his passion for gambling, drinking and entertaining his friends. Open early Mar to 30 Oct, F & W/Es 11-4. (H3) 01451 844130 www.nationaltrust.org.uk

Sherborne Park Estate (NT). Waymarked walks through woods and parkland with fine views. (J2) www.nationaltrust.org.uk

Windrush Valley. A slow, trickling stream in summer with a tendency to flood in winter. The river snakes its way through quiet golden villages, creating the idyllic Cotswold scene. (K2)

Bagendon Church

North Cerney Church

Coln St Dennis Church

Sherborne Brook in Frost, Sherborne

Waterfall, Sherborne Brook

PASTORAL SCENES

Slad Valley

Macoroni Downs, Eastleach

Humblebee, Winchcombe

Summer's Dawn, Sherborne Brook

Footpath into Lower Slaughter

Guiting Power

The Maytime, Asthall

Brewing, scenic villages, blanket making, Blenheim, Birthplace of Sir Winston Churchill.

The West Cotswolds extends from the flat Thames basin in the south up into the more typically hilly undulating countryside around Chipping Norton and the beautiful Windrush Valley dissects the region.

This area has traditionally been a coaching route on the A40 London to Gloucester route. It is awash with hostelries and now has a broad selection of pubs with an excellent reputation for eat-ing and drinking. One of the areas best independent breweries – Hook Norton – is based here too.

Burford was home to one of the area's most famous historic incidents involving the Burford Level-lers who are famed with having started civil rights in this country. During the English Civil War, three Parliamentarian soldiers who felt Cromwell was getting too big for his boots stood up against him and were put to death in Burford churchyard for their troubles. This event is celebrat-ed annually with much gusto and beer.

Many of the villages in the West Cotswolds are feeder villages for Oxford. Great Tew is arguably one of the most beautiful villages in the Cotswolds. Witney is a former blanket making town and was, along with the hilltop village, Chipping Norton, a wool trading market town. And, of course, there is Blenheim, famously the birthplace of Winston Churchill.

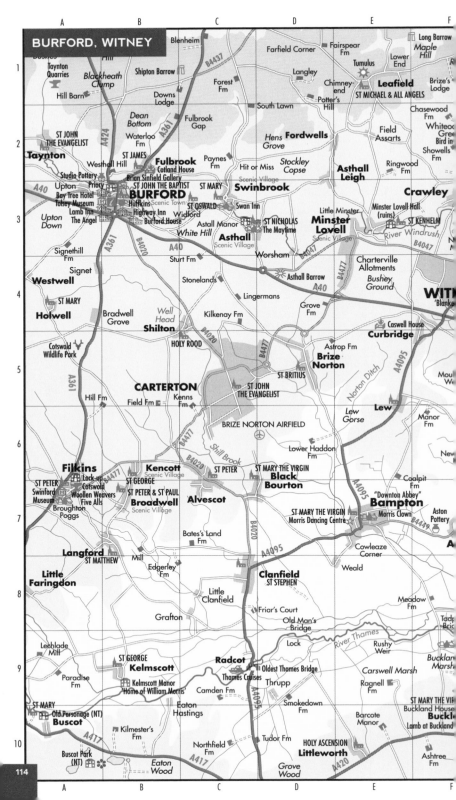

A B C D E F

1
Blenheim
Taynton Quarries
Hill Barn
Blackheath Clump
Shipton Barrow
Downs Lodge
Farfield Corner
Fairspear Fm
Langley
Chimney-end
Potter's Hill
Tumulus
Lower End
Long Barrow
Maple Hill
Leafield
ST MICHAEL & ALL ANGELS
Brize's Lodge
Forest Fm
South Lawn

2
ST JOHN THE EVANGELIST
Taynton
Upton
Bay Tree Hotel
Tolsey Museum
Lamb Inn
The Angel
Dean Bottom
Waterloo Fm
Westhall Hill
ST JAMES
Cotland House
Studio Pottery
Brian Sinfield Gallery
ST JOHN THE BAPTIST
Priory
Huffkins
Fulbrook Gap
Paynes Fm
Fordwells
Hens Grove
Hit or Miss
Stockley Copse
Field Assarts
Asthall Leigh
Chasewood Fm
Whiteoo Gree
Bird in
Showells Fm
Ringwood Fm
Fulbrook
Swinbrook
ST MARY
Crawley

3
Upton Down
Signethill Fm
Westwell
Holwell
ST MARY
BURFORD
Highway Inn
Burford House
Widford
ST OSWALD
White Hill
Asthall
Swan Inn
Astall Manor
The Maytime
ST NICHOLAS
Worsham
Little Minster
Minster Lovell
ST KENHELM
Minster Lovell Hall (ruins)
River Windrush
B4047

4
Signet
Bradwell Grove
Shilton
Sturt Fm
Stonelands
Lingermans
Asthall Barrow
A40
Grove Fm
Charterville Allotments
Bushey Ground
WITI
'Blanke
Kilkenay Fm
Well Head
HOLY ROOD
Caswell House
Curbridge

5
Cotswold Wildlife Park
Hill Fm
CARTERTON
Field Fm
Kenns Fm
ST JOHN THE EVANGELIST
ST BRITIUS
Astrop Fm
Brize Norton
Norton Ditch
Lew Gorse
Lew
Moul We
Manor Fm

6
BRIZE NORTON AIRFIELD
Shill Brook
Lower Haddon Fm
New

7
Filkins
Lock-up
ST PETER
Swinford Museum
Cotswold Woollen Weavers
Broughton Poggs
Kencott
ST GEORGE
Five Alls
ST PETER & ST PAUL
Broadwell
Alvescot
ST PETER
Bates's Land Fm
ST MARY THE VIRGIN
Black Bourton
ST MARY THE VIRGIN
Morris Dancing Centre
Coalpit Fm
"Downton Abbey"
Bampton
Morris Clown
Aston Pottery
A

8
Langford
ST MATTHEW
Little Faringdon
Mill
Edgerley Fm
Little Clanfield
Grafton
Clanfield
ST STEPHEN
Friar's Court
Old Man's Bridge
Weald
Cowleaze Corner
Meadow Fm
Tadp Bri

9
Lechlade Mill
Paradise Fm
ST GEORGE
Kelmscott
Kelmscott Manor
'Home of William Morris'
Radcot
Oldest Thames Bridge
Thames Cruises
Camden Fm
Thrupp
Lock
River Thames
Rushy Weir
Carswell Marsh
Ragnell Fm
Buckla Marsh

10
ST MARY
Old Parsonage (NT)
Buscot
A4417
Buscot Park (NT)
Kilmester's Fm
Eaton Wood
Eaton Hastings
Northfield Fm
Tudor Fm
Grove Wood
Smokedown Fm
HOLY ASCENSION
Littleworth
A420
Barcote Manor
ST MARY THE VIF
Buckland House
Buckle
Lamb at Buckland
Ashtree Fm

A B C D E F

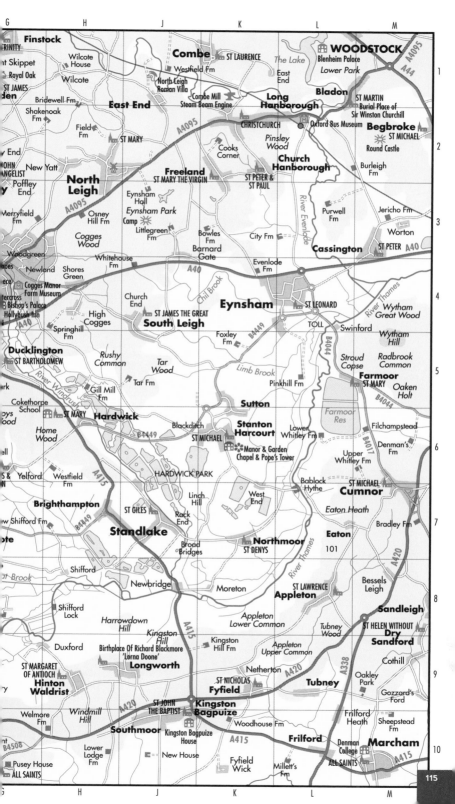

Burford's High Street

Morris Dancing, Burford

BURFORD

The first major Cotswold town you come to if travelling from the East, and what an introduction.   The wide High Street, with its classical gables atop some gracious houses, slopes down to the dreamy, River Windrush. It was once an important coach and wool centre bursting with activity, hostelries and dens of rumbustious entertainment. A history of civil rights and religious tolerance prevailed here with the Burford Levellers. On 17 May 1649, three soldiers were executed in Burford Churchyard on the orders of Oliver Cromwell. These three had sort to undermine the authority of Cromwell whom they considered to be a dictator rather than a liberator. This event is celebrated   every year with song, dance and speeches. Today, there are the splendid inns and pretty cottages hidden down the side streets. The churchyard is a quiet spot with some beautifully decorated table tombs. The town has a wide selection of hotels, inns and tearooms and a couple of delis to make   up lunchtime sandwiches. 'Feast of the Dragon' and Street Fair in June. (B3)

SPECIAL PLACES OF INTEREST...

Cotswold Wildlife Park. A full score of animals, birds and reptiles from all corners of the globe, beautifully laid

River Windrush, Burford

out in 120-acres of gardens and parkland. Adventure playground. Tropical House. Children's farmyard. Facilities for the disabled. Picnic area. Café. Open daily 10-6 (winter to 4). (A5) 01993 823006 www.cotswoldwildlifepark.co.uk

Parish Church of St John the Baptist. One of the great Cotswold churches built in the C15 with proceeds earned by the local wool merchants. Hence, the term 'Wool' church. It has a spacious interior more akin to a small cathedral. The porch and spire c.1450 are outstanding, as are the sculptured table tombs in the churchyard. Inside, don't miss the intricate medieval stained glass and the monuments (painted figures). Open daily 9-5, except during services. (B3)

Burford Priory. This was the former home of Benedictine nuns who have since moved to Broad Marston. It is hidden behind high walls and is Jacobean in style and has a history dating from the C13 when it was a Hospital of St John in 1226. More recently sold as a private residence to a Ms Murdoch. (B3)

Studio Pottery, 4 Bear Court. The work of some of Britain's most respected potters and glassmakers. Open daily 10-5. (B3) 01993 823495 www.saltgallery.com

Tolsey Museum. Burford's social and industrial history; charters, dolls house, objects of many rural trades. Open daily April to October Tu-F & Su 2-5, Sa & BHs 11-5. (B3) 01993 823196 www.tolseymuseumburford.org

Brian Sinfield Gallery, 127 The Hill. Highly respected gallery featuring changing exhibitions of modern and contemporary paintings, sculpture and ceramics. Open Tu-Sa, 10-5. (B3) 01993 824464 www.briansinfield.com

LIGHT BITES...

Quite a choice. Herewith, my favourites, starting at the bottom of the hill with: **Mrs Bumble of Burford, 31 Lower High Street.** A Lancashire lass who knows, and loves her food. It is where I always stop for a baguette, also, a deli to prepare for a walker's picnic. Try her olives, sumptuous cheeses, scotch eggs and pastas..... Open 8.30-5.30. Moving up the High Street, **The Priory, 35 High Street.** Open every day for breakfast, lunch, cream teas and early suppers. Child friendly.B&B. Open 8.30-6. 01993 823249 www.prioryrestaurantburford.co.uk

An alternative for afternoon teas is the Burford House, a home from home, for many wanderers. And, for all cheese lovers continue to ascend the hill until you reach **The Cotswold Cheese Co., 113 High Street.** Sample a cut of cheese, or charcuterie, accompanied by a glass of wine, and freshly roasted coffee. 01993 823882 www.cotswoldcheese.com On the other side of the road, **Maison Blanc** and **Huffkins**.

Bay Tree Hotel, Burford ss

WHERE TO STAY, EAT & DRINK..

Bay Tree Hotel, Sheep Street. This is Burford's most luxurious and smartest hostelry, for that is what they are on this old coaching route, hostelries. It is a traditional and charming inn with oak panelled rooms, stone fireplaces and tapestries. Dinner is quite a formal affair. There is a secluded walled garden for pre-prandials and intimate conversation. (B3) 01993 822791 www.cotswold- inns-hotels.co.uk/baytree

Cotland House B&B, Fulbrook Hill. A substantial Cotswold house in elegant surroundings. A short walk from Burford. Single/double/twin and family rooms. (B2) 01993 822382

Highway Inn, 117 High Street. A choice of 9 cosy bedrooms furnished in a mix of antique and modern styles. The Highway Inn has plenty of character and prides itself on offering an informal and individual experience akin to visiting friends in the country. Simple food made using local and seasonal produce. (B3) 01993 823661 www.thehighwayinn.co.uk

Parish Church of St John the Baptist, Burford

Lamb Inn, Burford ss

Lamb Inn, Sheep St. Your typical olde English hostelry: flagstone floors, low ceilings, nooks and crannies, galore, fine ales (Hookie and 6X) and now with luxurious bedrooms and intimate lounges. Restaurant. Yet, more informal than its sister inn, The Bay Tree, just along the street. (B3) 01993 823155
www.cotswold-inns-hotels.co.uk/lamb

Burford House, 99 High St. Full of character and charm, and you'll never sleep alone in a 4-poster again; there's a teddy bear on every bed! Lunch M-Sa, Dinner Th, F & Sa evenings. No dogs. (B3) 01993 823151
www.burford-house.co.uk

The Angel, 14 Witney St. Relaxed, stylish brasserie in C16 coaching inn provides mouth-watering fare: mediterranean dishes and enormous breakfasts specifically cooked for the adventurous traveller. (B3) 01993 822714
www.theangelatburford.co.uk

Burford Town House

Minster Lovell Hall

SPECIAL PLACES OF INTEREST... MINSTER LOVELL

Arguably, the most beautiful village in the Windrush Valley. There is a fine C15 bridge leading to a street of pretty cottages, and onto the C15 Church, which rests beside the ancient Hall. The Manor House has been associated with the rhyme 'Mistletoe Bough.' (E3)

Minster Lovell Hall (EH). A picturesque C15 ruin beside the River Windrush. Reputed to be the haunted seat of the Lovell family. Open daily. Don't miss the Church, next door. (E3)

WITNEY

The largest shopping centre in West Oxfordshire, and a dormitory town to Oxford that has seen much rapid expansion in the past 25 years. A town of hustle and bustle with a good share of attractive limestone buildings. Note, the C17 Butter Cross with gabled roof, clock turret and sundial, the Town Hall with room overhanging a piazza and across Church Green the unusually handsome spire to the Parish Church, visible from far and wide. There have been signs of Iron Age and Roman settlements but the first records of any activity date from 969 AD. The Bishop of Westminster built a palace in 1044 which was eventually excavated in 1984. In 1277 the town's business centred on the fulling and cloth mills. In the Middle Ages gloves,

blankets and brewing were the staple industries. Earlys of Witney, the blanket makers were in business for 300 years until quite recently. All of this has been ably recorded by the new **Blanket Hall** and **Cogges Manor Farm Museums.** (F4)

SPECIAL PLACES OF INTEREST...

Blanket Hall, 100 High St. When it was built in 1721 every blanket woven in Witney came to Witney Blanket Hall to be tested for quality, and upstairs the weavers sat in court to regulate their affairs. Now,

blanket-making has gone, but the Witney Blanket Hall still proudly stands with its beautiful Great Room, and its famous one-handed clock. A pocket-sized tribute to a proud past. Now, it has once more come to life, as a place where visitors can explore the intricate mysteries of the blanket trade. There's the 1920s blanket warehouse, the soundscape on the grand oak staircase, the re-planted C18 garden by the river... and not forgetting the Blanket Hall Pieshop! Open daily 10-6. (G4) 01367 860660 www.blankethall.co.uk

Bishops Palace. The site of the Bishop's Palace situated near to the Church on Church Green, is   one of 24 luxurious residencies in the diocese and dates from the C12. The archaeological remains   of the great hall and other features are exposed under a modern roof and were discovered in the early 1980s. (G4)

Cogges Manor Farm Museum, Church Lane. Historic buildings, exhibitions, traditional breeds of animals, daily demos and special weekends. Garden, orchard and riverside walk. Café. Open Apr to Oct Tu-F & BH Ms 10.30-5.30, W/Es 12-5.30. (G4) 01993 772602
www.cogges.org.uk

Witney Museum, High Street. Situated in a traditional Cotswold stone building that was once the home of Malachi Bartlett, the proprietor of a well known local building firm. The museum shows the history of Witney and surrounding area featuring local industries such as Witney Blankets, glove making and brewing, together with photographs and artefacts relating to Witney. Open Apr to Oct, Tu-Sa,10-4, Su 2-4. Children free. (G4) 01993 775915.
www.witneyhistory.org

SPECIAL PLACES OF INTEREST...

Aston Pottery. Working pottery, demonstrations, shop and tearoom. Open M-Sa 9-5, Su 11-5. (F7) 01993 852031.
www.astonpottery.co.uk

Buscot Old Parsonage (NT). Early C18 house. Small garden. Open Apr to Oct W 2-6 by written appointment with tenant. (A10) 01793 762209
www.nationaltrust.org.uk

Buscot Park (NT). C18 house with park and superb water garden designed by Harold Peto. Collection of art: Italian, Dutch, Flemish, Spanish and English Schools. Chinese porcelain. Tea room. Open late Mar to Sept W Th & F (including Good F, East W/Es) 2-6, and alternate W/Es in each month 2-6. (A10) 01367 240786
www.buscot-park.com

Caswell House, Brize Norton. An historic 15th century manor house set in 450 acres of Oxfordshire countryside and surrounded by rural views with an ancient orchard, walled gardens and extensive lawns stretching down to the moat. Luxurious and spacious accommodation for up to 20 guests. (E4) 01993 701064
www.caswellhouse.co.uk

Kelmscott Manor. The Elizabethan home of William Morris, the C19 poet, craftsman and socialist. Houses his furnishings which can be identified as examples from the Arts & Crafts Movement. Paintings by his fellow pre-Raphaelite, Dante Gabriel Rossetti. Tearoom. Open Apr to Oct W & Sa 11-5.   Group bookings on Th by arrangement. (B9) 01367 252486
www.sal.org.uk

Kingston Bagpuize House. A beautiful early C18 manor house in parkland setting. The garden contains shrubs, bulbs and herbaceous borders. Teas. Small gift shop. Open all BH W/Es and various Su, Feb to Sept 2-5.30. (J10) 01865 820259
www.kbhevents.uk

North Leigh Roman Villa (EH). This ruin was excavated in 1813 and 60 rooms were revealed surrounding the courtyard with a beautiful mosaic pavement. A charming spot beside the River Evenlode. Open daily in summer.(J1)

Oxford Bus Museum, BR Station Goods Yard. 35 vehicles including the Morris Motors Museum. Open Su, W & BHs 10.30-4.30. (L2) 01993 883617
www.oxfordbusmuseum.org.uk

Cotswold Woollen Weavers, Nr. Lechlade. The story of wool and woollen cloth has woven its way into every fabric of Cotswold life, as has the stone that has built the barns, churches, manor houses and villages. The stone is brilliantly displayed by the masons' sculptures and workmanship. The cloth, and the garments made up in their many guises (scarves, handbags, throws, jackets, skirts, coats, upholstery, as well as rolls of cloth) mirror the delights of this unique establishment. Coffee shop. Picnic area. Open daily M-Sa 10-6, Su 2-6. (A7) 01367 860491
www.naturalbest.co.uk

Kelmscott Manor

Stanton Harcourt Manor House & Gardens. A unique collection of medieval buildings. The house contains fine pictures, silver, furniture and porcelain. Moat and stew ponds. Pope's Tower. Open Apr to Sept 2-6 limited opening, call for details. (K6) 01865 881928

Swinford Museum. Agricultural, craft and domestic bygones. Open May to Sept first Su 2-5, and by appointment. (A7)

CHURCHES OF INTEREST...

Swinbrook. Fettiplace monuments. Mitford family memorials. (C3) Kelmscott. Wall painting. William Morris tomb by Philip Webb. (B9)

INNS WITH ROOMS...

Five Alls (The), Filkins. A comfortable, and charming C18 coaching inn offers log fires, great nosh and luxurious bedrooms, and maybe, the odd celeb in mufty enjoying a Cotswold repast. 01367 860875 www.thefiveallsfilkins.co.uk

Maytime Inn (The), Asthall. Set in an authentic Cotswold stone building situated in a quiet country village. On a winter's day you can duck through the low door into the homely bar and imagine the pub as it was centuries ago. B&B. (C3) 01993 822068 www.themaytime.com

Plough (The), Kelmscott. Recently re-opened (after flooding) by the proprietors of the Five Alls at Filkins, Seb and Lana Snow. Its a pretty Grade 11 listed building of character, good food and 8 luxurious bedrooms. Cottage garden for alfresco dining, and hidden Hideaway Bar in the old stable block. 01367 253543 www.theploughinnkelmscott.com

Swan Inn, Swinbrook. Formerly owned by the late, Dowager Duchess of Devonshire (the former Deborah Mitford, the last of the infamous Mitford sisters). A beautiful dining pub, in a delightful location, with a fair balance between traditional and modern cuisine. Luxurious B&B. (C3) 01993 823339 www. theswanswinbrook.co.uk

COUNTRY INNS...

Lamb at Buckland, Lamb Lane. C18 Cotswold inn patronised by locals provides first class food. B&B. No dogs. Closed M. (F10) 01367 870484 www.thelambbuckland.com

Morris Clown, High Street, Bampton. The headquarters of the Bampton Morris Men is a dark, drinking man's boozer, with a large open fire, and an excellent selection of traditional ales. Operates a no food (only booze) policy. (E7) 01993 850217

Royal Oak, Ramsden. A listed Coaching Inn dating from the C17 that was used as a watering hole for the London to Hereford stagecoach. Traditional, and rustic bar, and restaurant with an excellent reputation for food. (G1) 01993 702576

The Trout, Tadpole Bridge. Remote location beside the Thames footpath manages to be busy at lunchtime. Well worth a visit. Children & dogs welcome. B&B. (F9) 01367 870382 www.trout-inn.co.uk

Dachsund, Five Alls, Filkins ss

Sᴿ
EDMUND FETTIPLACE
BARONET

...ORY OF
...IPLACE
...

IN MEMORY OF
...TTIPLACE
...
...rerfect

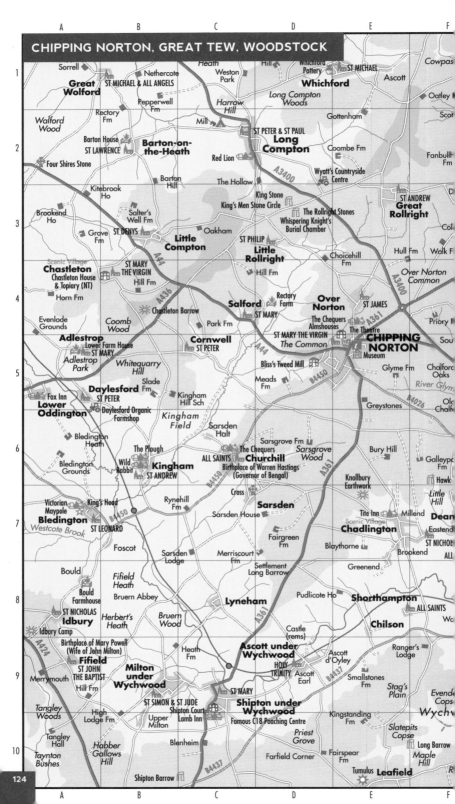

Sorrell
Great Wolford
ST MICHAEL & ALL ANGELS
Nethercote
Pepperwell Fm
Heath
Weston Park
Hill
Whichford Pottery
ST MICHAEL
Cowpas
Whichford
Ascott
Oatley
Scot

Walford Wood
Rectory Fm
Harrow Hill
Long Compton Woods
Gottenham
Barton House
ST LAWRENCE
Barton-on-the-Heath
Mill
ST PETER & ST PAUL
Long Compton
Red Lion
A3400
Coombe Fm
Fanbullh Fm

Four Shires Stone
Barton Hill
The Hollow
Wyatt's Countryside Centre
ST ANDREW

Kitebrook Ho
Salter's Well Fm
Little Compton
Oakham
King Stone
King's Men Stone Circle
The Rollright Stones
Whispering Knight's Burial Chamber
Great Rollright
Col

Brookend Ho
Grove Fm
ST DENYS
ST PHILIP
Choicehill Fm
Hull Fm
Walk F

Horn Fm
Chastleton
Chastleton House & Topiary (NT)
Scenic Village
ST MARY THE VIRGIN
Hill Fm
Little Rollright
Hill Fm
Over Norton Common
A3400

Evenlode Grounds
Coomb Wood
Chastleton Barrow
Park Fm
Salford
ST MARY
Rectory Farm
Over Norton
ST JAMES
A361
Priory

Adlestrop
Lower Farm House
ST MARY
Adlestrop Park
Whitequarry Hill
Cornwell
ST PETER
A44
The Chequers Almshouses
ST MARY THE VIRGIN
The Common
CHIPPING NORTON
The Theatre
Museum
Chalford Oaks
Sou

Fox Inn
Lower Oddington
Daylesford
ST PETER
Daylesford Organic Farmshop
Slade Fm
Kingham Hill Sch
Bliss's Tweed Mill
Meads Fm
Glyme Fm
River Glym
Old Chalfo
B4450
B4026

Bledington Heath
Kingham Field
Sarsden Halt
Greystones

Bledington Grounds
The Plough
Wild Rabbit
Kingham
ST ANDREW
ALL SAINTS
The Chequers
Churchill
Birthplace of Warren Hastings (Governor of Bengal)
Sarsgrove Fm
Sarsgrove Wood
Bury Hill
Galleypo
Hawk

Victorian Maypole
King's Head
B4450
Rynehill Fm
Cross
Sarsden
Knollbury Earthwork
Little Hill
Dean

Bledington
ST LEONARD
Westcote Brook
Sarsden House
Fairgreen Fm
Tite Inn
Chadlington
Millend
Eastend
ST NICHOL
ALL

Foscot
Sarsden Lodge
Merriscourt Fm
Settlement Long Barrow
Blaythorne
Brookend
Greenend

Bould
Fifield Heath
Bruern Abbey
Bruern Wood
Pudlicote Ho
Shorthampton
ALL SAINTS

Bould Farmhouse
ST NICHOLAS
Idbury
Herbert's Heath
Lyneham
Chilson
Wo

Idbury Camp
A424
Birthplace of Mary Powell (Wife of John Milton)
Fifield
ST JOHN THE BAPTIST
Hill Fm
Heath Fm
Castle (rems)
A361
Ascott under Wychwood
Ascott d'Oyley
Ranger's Lodge

Merrymouth
Milton under Wychwood
HOLY TRINITY
Ascott Earl
Smallstones
Stag's Plain
Evende Cops
Wych

Tangley Woods
High Lodge Fm
Upper Milton
ST SIMON & ST JUDE
Shipton Court
Lamb Inn
ST MARY
Shipton under Wychwood
Famous C18 Poaching Centre
Priest Grove
Kingstanding Fm
Slatepits Copse
Long Barrow
Maple Hill

Tangley Hall
Habber Gallows Hill
Blenheim
Farfield Corner
Fairspear Fm
Tumulus
Leafield

Taynton Bushes
Shipton Barrow
B4437
R

124

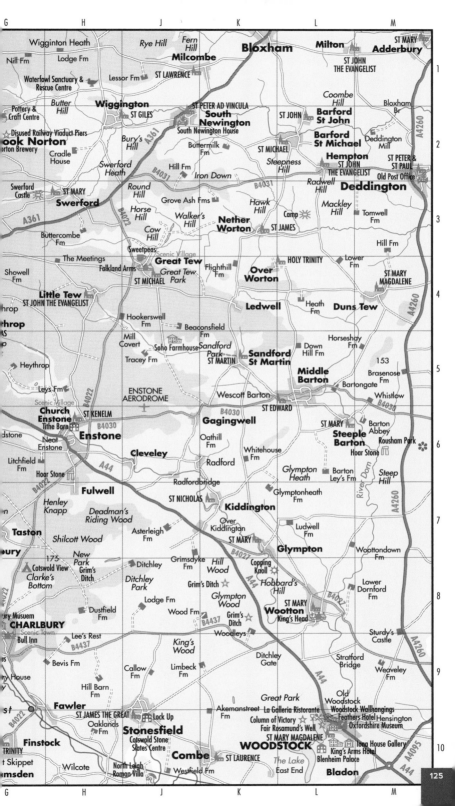

Bliss Tweed Mill, Chipping Norton

CHIPPING NORTON

A well situated hill-top town affording spectacular views over the surrounding countryside. Mentioned in the Domesday Book. The new Market Place was built in 1205 and is today surrounded by elegant houses with Georgian facades. But it was the Wool industry established in the C13 that brought wealth to this corner of Oxfordshire and, like so many before them and after, the wealthy merchants invested their coppers in the C15 'Wool' church in order to guarantee a place in heaven. Its attraction is that it is very much a small market town responding to the demands of the local populace and is little affected by Cotswold tourism. It is home to some celebrities: Jeremy Clarkson, and, until his death, Ronnie Barker, who ran an antique emporium. The 'Chipping Norton Set,' is a close group of powerful politicians and media elite, amongst them is included, The Prime Minister, David Cameron, and his friends, Rebekah and Charlie Brooks, Matthew Freud and Elisabeth

Murdoch (daughter of media mogul, Rupert Murdoch). Fine bookshop with coffee shop. Mop Fair in September. (E5)

SPECIAL PLACES OF INTEREST...

Almshouses. A picturesque row of C17 houses still in use today. The occupants were to be 'Honest women of godly life and conversation.' (E5)

Bliss Tweed Mill. Built by William Bliss in 1872 to house his textile factory. He was instrumental in encouraging the railways to reach Chipping Norton. The mill closed as a factory in 1980 and was converted into domestic apartments. It is still quite a sight from the road and was apparently one of Sir John Betjeman's favourite buildings. (D5)

Chipping Norton Museum, 4 High St. Agricultural equipment, a 30s kitchen and local 'Co-op'. Open Easter to October M-Sa & BH Ms 2-4. (E5) 01608 658518

Rollright Stones. The King's Men is a Bronze Age stone circle 100 feet in diameter, 2,000-1,800 BC and is easily accessible from the road. Just 400 yards east of this circle are The Whispering Knights, remains of a Bronze Age burial chamber. And, isolated in a field, the King's Stone. (D3)

The Theatre, Goddards Lane. Flourishing little theatre puts on dance, music, plays, films, workshops, and is host to touring companies. (E5) 01608 642349
www.chippingnortontheatre.co.uk

WHERE TO STAY...

Bould Farm, Chipping Norton. 400 acre sheep/arable farm with C17 farmhouse in a large garden overlooking beautiful countryside. The owner breeds working sheep dogs. Comfortable bedrooms. 01608 658850
www.bouldfarm.co.uk

Long Compton Camping, Mill Farm. A small, and simple site with only 11 units for pitching a tent. Set close to a good village pub, the Red

Lion and village shop. Ideal for cyclists and hardy campers. (C2) 01608 684663

Rectory Farm, Salford. A 250-year old farm house with its own tranquil 450-acre valley of scenic farmland. The mature 2-acre garden leads down to, two spring-fed trout lakes where fishing is available for guests. (D4) 01608 643209
www.rectoryfarm.info

Cotswold View Campsite, Enstone Road, Charlbury. Spacious pitches set in rolling, wooded farmland. Well-signed trails where you can see a variety of farm animals. Children's playground. Tennis court, skittle alley and well-stocked shop, and off-license. Open late-Mar to Oct. (G8) 01608 810314
www.cotswoldview.co.uk

CHARLBURY

A small town overlooking the Evenlode Valley, towards the Wychwood Forest. Group of stone-roof houses with 30-yard stretch of wisteria. Fine walking and cycling country; the Oxfordshire Way passes through the town, and the Glyme Valley is also a popular walker's destination. Easy rail access to London and Oxford. Charlbury Deli and Cafe, and Bull Hotel. (G8)

GREAT TEW

A sensationally beautiful village lined with ironstone cottages covered in thatch and stone tiles. Many fell into disrepair

Long Compton Camping

Three Views of Great Tew

Oyster Dish, The Plough at Kingham ss

but have now been restored to their former glory. Much of the village was designed by the Scottish architect, John Claudius London. The Falkland Arms is named after Lord Falkland who lived here, and who died fighting for Charles 1 at the Battle of Newbury. (J4)

Cornbury Music Festival (The Original), Great Tew Park. Now establishing itself as a cheaper, and more personal, alternative to Glastonbury. Three days in early July, with a full lineup of stars. (J4)
www.cornburyfestival.com

WHERE TO STAY, EAT & DRINK..

The Falkland Arms. A traditional pub with flagstone floors, oak beams, inglenook fireplace, mugs and bric- a-brac hanging from the ceiling, and real ale in many potions to whet your senses. Garden. B&B, two bedrooms with 4-posters. (J4)
01608 683591
www.falklandarms.org.uk

The Old Post House, New Street, Deddington. Beautiful and luxurious accommodation. Guest's sitting and dining rooms allow you to imagine it all belongs to you. The inner courtyard, walled gardens and swimming pool add a cherry to the top! 01869 338978
www.oldposthouse.co.uk

Soho Farmhouse. A new venture for Soho House (of Babington House fame) who founded clubs for the creative industries, has developed this exclusive member's club in 100 acres of Oxfordshire

countryside with 40 cabins, a 7-bedroom farmhouse, a Main Barn, Mill Room for eating, a Boathouse, in and outdoor pools and the Cowshed spa, plus a lot more for your hedonistic pleasures. It is also very eco and PC. (J5)
01608 691000
www.sohohouse.com

Sweetpeas, 23 The Green. A florists with coffee shop serving a lazy cooked breakfast, home-made cakes, hot chocs, and a pizzeria, on F & Sa nights. (J4)
01608 683600
www.sweetpeasofgreattewox7.co.uk

AND, NEARBY...

Lamb Inn, Shipton-under-Wychwood. Inviting C16 hostelry with a flourish of C21 interior design. Multi-ethnic bedrooms relive the proprietor's past travels. Food is eclectic, too. B&B. Family room. (C9)
01993 830465
www.shiptonlamb.com

Hook Norton Brewery. Visitor Centre displays brewing artefacts from 1849 to today. Two-hour tours M-F. Centre open all year M-F 9-5, Sa & BHs 9.30-4.30. (G2)
01608 737210
www.hooknortonbrewery.co.uk

Hook Norton Pottery & Craft Centre. Workshop and gallery open all year. Local crafts including paintings, basketware, woodcraft and cards. Open M-Sa 9-5. (G2)
01608 737414
www.hooknortonpottery.co.uk

WOODSTOCK

A pretty town of stone built houses, interesting shops and smart hotels, and a practical centre for exploring the eastern Cotswolds and West Oxfordshire. Famous for glove-making in the C16, and for Blenheim Palace, the birthplace of Sir Winston Churchill (1874-1965) who is buried nearby in Bladon churchyard. There are a number of antique shops, art galleries and a fascinating museum plus a melee of delis, inns, restaurants, tearooms and coffee shops. The foodaphile is spoilt for choice, and below are listed a small selection on offer. (L10)

SPECIAL PLACES OF INTEREST...

Blenheim Palace. This is the home of the Dukes of Marlborough and was

Rollright Stones, Chipping Norton

Blenheim Palace, Woodstock

built as Queen Anne's gift to John Churchill, 1st Duke of Marlborough, for his defeat of Louis XIV in 1704 - 'a monument to commemorate a military victory, and to glorify the Queen.' It is considered to be Vanburgh's C18 baroque masterpiece, although much of the detail was by Nicholas Hawksmoor. There are fine paintings, Churchill Exhibition, tapestries, a 10,000 volume library and parkland designed by 'Capability' Brown. Plus, other attractions: the Butterfly House, Marlborough Maze, Adventure Play Area and Herb Garden. Restaurant. Palace open from mid-February to mid-December, daily to 1 November, then W-Su 10.30-5.30 (last admission 4.45pm). Park open daily, all year, for rambling and dog walking, 9-5. (L10) 01993 810530
www.blenheimpalace.com

Combe Mill. A restored C19 beam engine and a breast shot waterwheel. Blacksmith's forge in operation. Open Days are advertised locally.
www.combemill.org

Grim's Ditch. Disconnected series of ditches and banks built by Iron Age tribes (Belgic) to defend their grazing enclosures. Best sections in Blenheim and Ditchley Parks. Grim is one of the names of Woden - the masked one, the god of victory, death and magic power, the high god of the Anglo-Saxons, before their conversion to Christianity in the C7. (K8)

Iona House Gallery. Paintings, etchings, prints, sculpture, ceramics, glass, textiles, silver and wood. Open M-Sa 10-5.30, Su 11.30-5. (L10) 01993 811464
www.ionahousegallery.org

Oxfordshire Museum, Park Street. An exhibition of Oxfordshire, and its people, from earliest times to the present day. Changing exhibitions. Coffee shop. Open daily Tu-Sa 10-5, Su 2-5. (L10) 01993 811456
www.oxfordshire.gov.uk

Woodstock Woolhangings, Town Hall. Story of Woodstock from Norman times, told in thirteen embroidered scenes. Open M, W & F 9-1. (L10) 01993 811216

LIGHT BITES...

Brothertons. Opens at 10.30 for coffee and cakes, lunch and dinner will provide pastas, pizzas and burgers, and daily specials. A family business serving unpretentious, and good-value fare. Closed Tu. 01993 811114
www.brothertonsbrasserie.co.uk

Chef Imperial, High Street. The Chinese arrive here in coach loads from far and wide, the locals will queue patiently outside for a table. It all adds up to a Chinese restaurant in great demand. Need one add more? (L10) 01993 813593

Hampers Food & Wine Company, Oxford Street. A great deli and café provides a wide range of sandwiches, paninis and cakes whilst next door you can sit down, relax and enjoy the crack. Open daily. (L10)

La Galleria Ristorante Italiano, 2 Market Place. Sardinian Italian with an emphasis on simplicity and taste. (L10) 01993 813381
www.la-galleria.co.uk

Tea Rooms. You have a choice of three: **Harriets** on the High Street, the **Blenheim** on Park Street just before you enter the Palace, and **Vickers** on Market Place.

Woodstock Arms, Market Street. This is considered by many locals as the best pub in Woodstock. It serves great value pub-grub, most of the day. (L10) 01993 811251
www.thewoodstockarms.com

WHERE TO STAY, EAT & DRINK..

Feathers Hotel, Market Street. This romantic C17 top-notch hotel has a labyrinth of rooms on all levels; the bedrooms are plush, intimate and hidden up narrow stairwells. The restaurant has been producing superb food for years. Add the log fires and antique furniture, and it makes for a winning combination. (L10) 01993 812291
www.feathers.co.uk

Kings Arms Hotel & Restaurant, 19 Market Street. This has the feel of a trendy wine bar: leather chairs and pine tables and a smart cocktail bar. Upstairs, the bedrooms are trendy with low-slung, sexy beds you can crawl into. (L10) 01993 813636
www.kingshotelwoodstock.co.uk

DINING PUBS...SPOILT FOR CHOICE...A PUB CRAWL BECKONS...

The Chequers at Churchill. A member of The Onion Club assortment of pubs and restaurants who promote local, fine dining in the Cotswolds. All very civilised, and nice and jolly with scrummy food and nectar-like ales. (C6) 01608 659393 www.
thechequerschurchill.com

The Kings Head, Bledington. A former C16 cider house that has a dream-like setting, on a village green beside a meandering brook. A local inn proud to use produce from University Farm in Bledington, and to remain, foremost a pub that serves great food. The bedrooms are pretty special, too. (A7) 01608 658365
www.thekingsheadinn.net

The Plough at Kingham. A long-term favourite of foodie aficionados in West Oxfordshire. You have the laid-back pub area serving local and draught ales, and exceptional bar food. The dining room serves English Classic fare, and you have the 7-luxurious bedrooms. Its all a winning combination, just awaiting your reservation. (B6)01608 658327
www.thekinghamplough.co.uk

The Wild Rabbit, Kingham. A Daylesford (Bamford) creation (or warren, ha-ha) designed for the upwardly mobile Londoner, and or, media-type. It is all glass, and showey food in prep whilst the clientele are busily monitoring their laptops and iPads. The saving grace, the log fire, comfy seating and classy bedrooms. (B6) 01608 658327
www.thewildrabbit.co.uk

Chastleton House

King's Head, Wotton.
Popular eating venue for local foodies and academics. High on personal service and exceptional ingredients. (L8) 01993 811340
www.kings-head.co.uk

SPECIAL PLACES OF INTEREST...

Charlbury Museum. An exquisite little museum with Oxfordshire hay wagon, old photohraphs and domestic bric-a-brac from a bygone age. Open Easter to October Su & BH Ms 2.30-4.30. (G8) 01608 810656
www.charlbury.info

Chastleton House & Topiary (NT). Jacobean Manor associated with the Gunpowder Plot retains its faded glory with a superb collection of tapestries, original furniture and ornamental topiary. Don't miss the church next door. Open April to

October W-Sa 1-5 (-4 in October). (B4) 01494 755560

Daylesford Organic Farmshop. The doyen of farm shops, and an expensive habit for those who can afford it. Takes the Waitrose experience onto another level. On display are the fine foods direct from their organic fields and pastures. Kitchen and bakery. Cafe. Open daily M-Sa 9-6, Su 10-4. (A5) 01608 731700
www.daylesfordorganic.com

Enstone Tithe Barn, Rectory Farm. Dates from 1382 and is built with some magnificent timbers. Used for local functions: craft fairs, harvest festivals. Its future is uncertain, as it has been put on the market along with the farm. Open Days. (H6)

Rousham Park, House & Garden. Castellated house built

c.1635 by Sir John Dormer. Remodelled by William Kent c.1773 to a Gothic style. Royal Garrison in Civil War. Beautiful garden with temples, dovecote and walled garden. No children under 15. No dogs. Garden open all year, 10-4.30. House open May to September for groups only. (M6) 01869 347110
www.rousham.org

Waterfowl Sanctuary & Rescue Centre. A centre for rare breeds, with an emphasis on giving children a "hands-on" experience with the farm animals. Baby barn. Open Tu-Su 10.30-dusk. (H1) 01608 730252

Wyatts Plant Centre. Farm shop with ice cream parlour in organic conversion, plus a garden nursery, animal and play area, and tearooms. Open daily. (D2) 01608 684835
www.wyattsgardencentre.co.uk

The Plough at Kingham ss

The Chequers, Churchill ss

The Wheatsheaf, Northleach ss

Scallops, Seven Tuns, Chedworth ss

The Swan at Southrop ss

The Wild Rabbit, Kingham ss

The Bridge, Lower Slaughter

Galloping country, stonewalls, sheep pastures, hill top towns and villages, honey-pot villages, three Gloucestershire towns, three choirs festival, racing stables.

If the Central Wolds are the centre of the Cotswolds, then Stow-in-the-Wold, sitting atop its hill, is the absolute heart of the region. This is due in part to the original route taken by the all important Fosse Way, a route which passes through Stow.

To the left of the Central Wolds lie three significant and interesting towns: Tewksbury, Chelten-ham and Gloucester. The landscape is very flat here. As you move east, the terrain becomes more undulating and hilly. The Windrush river runs through the Wolds from east to west.

Cheltenham is a Georgian Spa town with interesting architecture and a range of decent places to stay and eat. Tewksbury and Gloucester are older, medieval towns with magnificent churches. Gloucester Cathedral is thought by some to be the birthplace of fan vaulting and Perpendicular architecture.

As well as the towns, there are also many pretty feeder villages to Cheltenham in the area includ-ing the Slaughters, the Swells, the Rissingtons and the twin villages of Stanton and Stanway.

This area is host to a number of festivals and cultural events including the Cheltenham Festivals, the Guiting Festival, and the Three Choirs Music Festival.

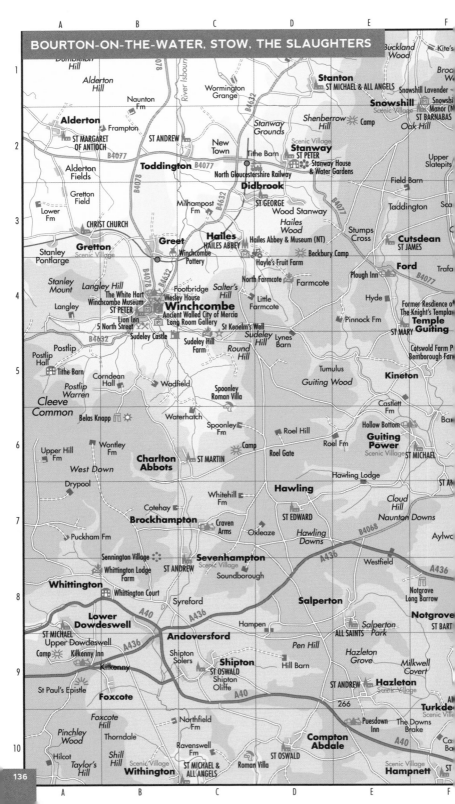

Dumbleton Hill
Alderton Hill
Buckland Wood
Kite's
Broad Wa

Alderton Hill
Wormington Grange
Stanton
ST MICHAEL & ALL ANGELS
Snowshill Lavender
Naunton Fm
Snowshill
Scenic Village
Snowshi
Manor (N
ST BARNABAS

Alderton
Frampton
ST ANDREW
New Town
Stanway Grounds
Shenberrow Hill
Camp
Oak Hill
Upper Slatepits

ST MARGARET OF ANTIOCH
Toddington
B4077
Tithe Barn
Stanway
ST PETER
Stanway House & Water Gardens
Field Barn

Alderton Fields
North Gloucestershire Railway
Didbrook
Taddington
Sca

Gretton Field
Milhampost Fm
ST GEORGE
Wood Stanway
Stumps Cross
Cutsdean
ST JAMES

Lower Fm
CHRIST CHURCH
Hailes
HAILES ABBEY
Hailes Wood
Hailes Abbey & Museum (NT)
Ford
Trafa

Stanley Pontlarge
Gretton
Greet
Winchcombe Pottery
Hayle's Fruit Farm
Beckbury Camp
Plough Inn

Stanley Mount
Langley Hill
Wesley House
Footbridge
Salter's
North Farmcote
Farmcote
Hyde

Langley
The White Hart
Winchcomba Museum
ST PETER
Winchcombe
Little Farmcote
Pinnock Fm
Temple Guiting

5 North Street
Lion Inn
Ancient Walled City of Mercia
Long Room Gallery
St Kenelm's Well
Sudeley Hill
Lynes Barn
ST MARY

Sudeley Castle
Sudeley Hill Farm
Round Hill
Cotswold Farm P
Bemborough Farm

Postlip
Postlip Hall
Tithe Barn
Corndean Hall
Wadfield
Spoonley Roman Villa
Tumulus
Guiting Wood
Kineton

Postlip Warren
Cleeve Common
Belas Knapp
Waterhatch
Spoonley Fm
Roel Hill
Castiett Fm
Hollow Bottom
Ba

Upper Hill Fm
Wontley Fm
West Down
Charlton Abbots
ST MARTIN
Camp
Roel Gate
Roel Fm
Guiting Power
Scenic Village
ST MICHAEL

Drypool
Whitehill Fm
Hawling
Hawling Lodge
ST A

Puckham Fm
Cotehay
Brockhampton
Craven Arms
Oxleaze
ST EDWARD
Cloud Hill
Naunton Downs

Sennington Village
Whittington Lodge Farm
ST ANDREW
Sevenhampton
Scenic Village
Soundborough
Hawling Downs
B4068
Aylwc

Whittington
Whittington Court
Syreford
Salperton
Westfield
A436
Notgrove Long Barrow

Lower Dowdeswell
A40
A436
Hampen
Salperton Park
Notgrove
ST BART

ST MICHAEL
Upper Dowdeswell
Andoversford
ALL SAINTS
Pen Hill
Hazleton Grove
Milkwell Covert

Camp
Kilkenny Inn
Kilkenny
Shipton Solers
Shipton
ST OSWALD
Shipton Oliffe
Hill Barn
ST ANDREW
Hazleton
Scenic Village

St Paul's Epistle
Foxcote
A40
266
Turkde
Scenic Village

Pinchley Wood
Foxcote Hill
Thorndale
Northfield Fm
Ravenswell Fm
Puesdown Inn
The Downs Brake
A40
Ca
Ba

Hilcot
Taylor's Hill
Shill Hill
Scenic Village
Withington
ST MICHAEL & ALL ANGELS
Roman Villa
ST OSWALD
Compton Abdale
Scenic Villa
Hampnett
ST

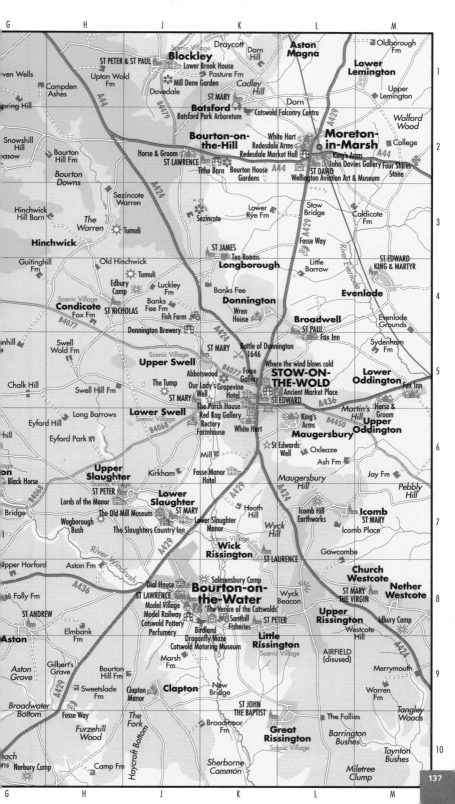

Three Views of Bourton-On-The-Water

BOURTON-ON-THE-WATER

One of the most popular beauty spots in the Cotswolds, but, best visited out of season, or at daybreak. It can be charming on a quiet, frostbitten morning when only the postman is out and about, so be advised to avoid a busy bank holiday when the hordes arrive in coaches and their charabancs. With ice cream in hand the visitors sit beside the river wetting their bare feet in the Windrush, and there's not a stitch of green grass visible through all the paraphernalia. The tourist brochures describe it as 'The Venice of the Cotswolds,' no doubt, because the River Windrush is spanned with low graceful bridges. You must, however, look beyond the crowds and the gift shops and wander the little streets for there are some beautiful houses to admire. Bourton may not thrill the jaded teenager or hard-bitten traveller, but it will delight small children - they loved to run across the little bridges, paddle in the river and feed the ducks, and you have, of course, Birdland, the Model Village, the Motoring Museum and the Model Railway, all devised for family fun and rainy days. The village is built above Salmonsbury Camp, a Roman settlement, and also above a former underground reservoir. It is not an uncommon sight to see a sprightly pensioner move into the village, and within eighteen months, be seen wobbling along the lane, bent double by the   damp. Bourton has its fair share of pubs that cater for the tourist. Perhaps, the most traditional bar is in the Old New Inn. Tearooms are plentiful. July Carnival. Water Game - August BH Sa. (J8)

SPECIAL PLACES OF INTEREST...

Birdland Park & Gardens. Home to over 500 birds on banks of the River Windrush; Penguins, tropical and sub-tropical birds. Feed the penguins, and adopt a bird. Open daily, Apr to Oct 10-6, Nov to Mar 10-4. (J8) 01451 820480 www.birdland.co.uk

Cotswold Farm Park. A unique survival centre for rare historic breeds of British farm animals including the Cotswold Lions (the Golden Fleece), lies elevated, high on the Central Wolds, three miles from Bourton. Pets and tots corner. Farm trail. Lambing, shearing and seasonal exhibitions. Camping. Café. Open daily mid-Feb to Nov 10.30-5. (F5) 01451 850307 www.cotswoldfarmpark.co.uk

Cotswold Motoring Museum. Motorcycles and vintage racing cars in an C18 water mill. Collection of old advertising signs. Open daily mid-Feb to mid-Dec 10-6. (J8) 01451 821255 www.cotswoldmotoringmuseum.co.uk

Cotswold Perfumery. Locally produced fragrances. Exhibition of perfumery. Factory tours. Open M-Sa 9.30-5, Su & BHs 10.30-5. (J8) 01451 820698 www.cotswold-perfumery.co.uk

Cotswold Pottery. Traditional rustic pots, hand-thrown using local materials. Bronze sculptures too. Open daily. (J8) 01451 820173 www.cotswoldpottery.co.uk

Dragonfly Maze, Rissington Road. Search for the Dragonfly within a traditional Yew Hedge Maze with a Rebus Puzzle and look upon the sculptures crafted by Kit Williams. Gift shop. Open daily from 10. (J8) 01451 822251 www.thedragonflymaze.com

Model Railway. Over 400 sq.ft. of exhibits. Continental trains and British Railway trains in HO/OO and N Gauge. Open daily 11-5. (J8) 01451 820686 www.bourtonmodelrailway.co.uk

Model Village, Old New Inn. Bourton in miniature, at the scale of 1/9th of the original. Lovingly tended gardens. Open daily; summer 9-6, winter 10-4. (J8) 01451 820467 www.theoldnewinn.co.uk

Oxfordshire Way. A long distance footpath from Bourton-on-the-Water to Henley-on-Thames, linking the Cotswolds with the Chilterns. Follows the ancient tracks of the county through meadows and woods, along quiet river valleys, and over windy escarpments through many a delightful village. Waymarked. (K8)

Salmonsbury Camp. The Romans' second legion of 5,000 soldiers was encamped here and built Lansdown Bridge to ford the Windrush on the Fosse Way. (K8)

Santhill Fisheries. Mature 26-acre lake stocked with rainbow and brown trout. Open for day, half- day, evening tickets and boat hire. (K8) 01451 810291 www.live4fishing.com/santhill-fisheries

The Lakes. These are flooded gravel pits from the 1960s and 70s. Now used for a carp farm, windsurfing centre and angling lake. There is a great abundance of wildlife: plants, insects and birds. (K8)

Windrush Valley. A slow, trickling stream in summer, with a tendency to flood in winter. The river snakes its way through quiet golden villages to create the idyllic Cotswold scene. (K10)

Cotswold Motoring Museum

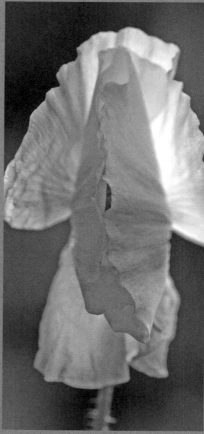

Courtesy of Andrew Dawkes, The Glebe, Bourton-On-The-Water

LIGHT BITES...

Given that I would have tea at my father-in-law's home, the tea rooms on offer do not hold much attraction to me, except for **Bakery On The Water** located just past the bridge, opposite the Cotswold Motoring Museum. An established business for 85-years run by the 4th generation, and now 4-years in Bourton. An artisan bakery, serving a simple breakfast (no fry ups), homemade cakes and bread - all made on the premises. 01451 822748 www.bakeryonthewater.co.uk

Down opposite the Post Office is the **Coffee Hub**, run by enthusiasts who will serve you an espresso, or two. **The Dial House** serves Afternoon Tea, in some style, where you can usher yourself away from the crowds, and if in the mood, a glass of bubbly may entice you to book in for the night?

WHERE TO STAY...

Clapton Manor, Clapton-on-the-Hill. Stunning Grade II listed Tudor house with a beautiful garden created by your host - a garden designer, and historian. (J9) 01451 810202 www.claptonmanor.co.uk

Dial House. A small, intimate hotel with individually designed bedrooms. Informal lunches, candlelit dinners, roaring log fires and romantic rooms are all for your pleasure, and it's nicely tucked away within a large garden. (J8) 01451 822244 www.dialhousehotel.com

Folly Farm Campsite. Set high on the Cotswold Wolds in a drafty and healthy spot. Ideal for tents, and a simple, rustic life. Don't expect 5-star accommodation. (G8) 01451 820285 www.cotswoldcamping.net

MORETON-IN-MARSH

Perhaps the first Cotswold town you'll visit if coming from the north along the ancient Fosse Way. And, what an impressive site it is, too. The wide, main street built by the Abbot of Westminster in 1220 for the sheep and arable sales is today a lively scene on market day, every Tuesday since King Charles I granted the town a Charter in 1637. But, its origins go back to the Romans who built a military camp around 43-50 AD whilst planning the construction of the Fosse Way. It remains the largest town in the North East Wolds and is dominated by the Market Hall built in 1887 by Lord Redesdale, father of the infamous Mitford sisters. Look out for the Curfew Tower, an unusual phenomenon on the corner of Oxford Street, dated 1633, which rung until 1860. A fine centre given to a number of inns, art galleries and independent retailers. Associated with the English Civil War, for the Royalist Cavalry were based here. Just out of town on the Chipping Norton road is the Fire Services' College and HQ of the Institute of Fire Engineers. Moreton (agricultural & horse) show - 1st Saturday in September. (L2

SPECIAL PLACES OF INTEREST...

Batsford Arboretum & Wild Garden. These 56 acres of rare, and beautiful trees, are part of one of the largest private collection of trees in Britain. Visitor Centre, Cafe, garden and gift shop. Dogs welcome. Open daily, all year from 9 (10 on Su & BHs). (K2) 01386 701441

www.batsarb.co.uk

Bourton House Garden. 3 acres of intense planting; topiary, knot garden, potager and a profusion of herbaceous borders and exotic plants. The wonderful C16 tithe barn is host to a gallery of contemporary arts and crafts. Lunches and teas. Open Apr-Oct, Tu-F from 10. (K2) 01386 700754 www.bourtonhouse.com

Cotswold Falconry Centre, Batsford Park. The centre is dedicated to the conservation of eagles, hawks, falcons and owls, with many breeding pairs. Flying displays throughout the day. New parliament of owls. Open daily mid-Feb to mid-Nov, 10.30-5. (K2) 01386 701043 www.cotswold- falconry.co.uk

John Davies Gallery, The Old Dairy Plant. A much-respected Cotswold gallery established in 1977. Six fully catalogued annual exhibitions. Fine period, post impressionist and contemporary paintings. Open daily. (L2) 01608 652255 www.johndaviesgallery.com

Mill Dene Garden, Blockley. A beautiful, mature garden, set around an historic water mill, with rose terrace, grotto and trout stream. Lunches and teas. Open Apr to Sept W-Sa (closed July/early Aug). (J1) 01386 700457 www.milldenegarden.co.uk

Sezincote House & Garden. House designed in the Indian style (and inspiration for the Brighton Pavilion) is beautifully

Bourton House Garden

set in an oriental water garden. House open May to Sept Th F & BH Ms 2.30-5. Garden open Jan to Nov Th F & BH Ms 2-6. (J3) 01386 700754
www.sezincote.co.uk

Wellington Aviation Museum & Gallery. A funky, very personal collection of the late Gerry Tyack's (amateur racing driver) RAF memorabilia, with a corner dedicated to motorsport, plus a choice of 250 aviation prints for sale. Open Su 10-4. (L2) 01608 650323
www.wellingtonaviation.org

Sezincote ss

LIGHT BITES...

For those of you, fortunate enough, to have experienced delicious cakes whilst travelling in Austria and Germany, you are in luck. **Cacao Bean,** just beyond the A44 Oxford road is a pleasure to behold. A coffee, pastry and cake shop. 01608 652060 www.cacaobean. co.uk If you are seeking a more conventional eatery, **Tilleys Tea Room** provides good value fare, and further down the street towards Stow, **Mrs Potts Tea House** specialise in gluten-free dishes. They bake all their cakes, and serve an all-day breakfast from 9am.

WHERE TO STAY, EAT & DRINK...

Horse & Groom, Bourton-on-the-Hill. A modern, and airy ambience permeates this Grade II listed Georgian inn which is peacefully set in a large garden on the hilltop. Bar, en-suite bedrooms, and a blackboard menu changes daily, allowing great variety, even for the most frequent of visitors. 01386 700413
www.horseandgroom.info

Redesdale Arms, High Street. An old coaching inn that mixes the traditional with contemporary designs. (L2) 01608 650308
www.redesdalearms.com

Snowshill Hill Estate B&B. Stay at the heart of a working farm in a comfortable, thoughtfully converted, self-contained dwelling within the extensive grounds of a prestigious and remote estate. 01386 853959
www.snowshill-hill.co.uk

Wren House, Donnington. Wren House accommodation comprises two en-suite bedrooms in the C15 house, recently renovated to a high standard, and the C17 Grade II listed Cotswold stone cottage - an old granary - which has been converted into a surprisingly spacious one bedroom self-catering cottage. (K4) 01451 831787
www.wrenhouse.net

SPECIAL PLACES OF INTEREST... THE SLAUGHTERS

Lower Slaughter is one of the most popular villages in the Cotswolds. Little bridges cross the eye stream which runs beside rows of golden cottages. The much painted C19 red-brick Corn Mill stands on the western edge of the village. Upper Slaughter is a couple of miles upstream and has an old Manor House once lived in by the Slaughter family, an old post office with a beautiful kitchen garden and, along a lane past the church, a ford crosses the stream hidden beneath lush greenery. (J7)

Old Mill Museum, Lower Slaughter. This iconic C19 flour mill has been lovingly restored into a small museum with ice cream parlour, tea room and mill shop. The proprietor is the lead singer in a Jazz band, hence the funky music. Open daily,10-6. (J7) 01451 820052
www.oldmill- lowerslaughter.com

Mill Leat & River Cafe, Old Mill Museum

Lower Slaughter Manor

WHERE TO STAY, EAT & DRINK...

Lower Slaughter Manor. If you seek a hotel with style, and old-fashioned virtues, this perfectly proportioned C17 Cotswold manor house may well be to your liking. There are large, spacious rooms furnished with antiques and classic art. No children U-12. No dogs. (J7) 01451 820456 www.lowerslaughter.co.uk

Lords of the Manor, Upper Slaughter. Classy, well-established country house hotel with C17 origins set in 8-acres of parkland. Child friendly. No dogs. The former home of the Reverend F E B Witts, Rector of this parish who wrote his famous chronicle of the C18, 'The Diary of a Cotswold Parson.' Afternoon Teas. (H7) 01451 820243 www.lordsofthemanor.com

The Slaughters Country Inn, Lower Slaughter. This C17 hotel, once an Eton cramming school, stands in 4-acres of beautiful grounds alongside the river eye. A hostelry, with a pleasing mix of contemporary and historic features, and a reputation for fine food. Afternoon Teas. Fish and Pie Nights. (J7) 01451 822143 www.theslaughtersinn.co.uk

SPECIAL PLACES OF INTEREST... NAUNTON

A pretty village surrounded by rolling sheep pastures, and overlooked by some steep gallops. A noted centre for National Hunt racing stables. The handsome church has some interesting gargoyles, and a stone pulpit. (G6) Naunton Church. Idyllic country setting on edge of village below rolling pastures. Gargoyles. (F6)

SNOWSHILL

(Pronounced Snosill). This charming and unspoilt hilltop village is a short distance by car from Broadway. There's a striking church, a pub and a row of much photographed cottages opposite **Snowshill Manor.** (F1)

Snowshill Lavender. Lavender fields to roam in. Tearoom. Plants. Shop. Open daily late May to Sept 10-5. (F1) 01386 854821 www.snowshill-lavender.co.uk

Snowshill Manor & Garden (NT). A Cotswold manor house containing Charles Paget Wade's extraordinary collection of craftsmanship and design, amounting to some 22,000 items; from toys to musical instruments, Samurai armour, to clocks, and bicycles. Open daily mid-Mar to 30 Oct 11-5.30, house from noon. (F1) 01386 852410 www.nationaltrust.org.uk

STANTON

Charming village with houses of warm honey-coloured stone. Restored by Sir Philip Scott, 1903-37. Centre for equine excellence in the Vine, a popular horse riding centre.

The Mount Inn is a welcome refuge if one's tackling the Cotswold Way, or a fine spot to sink a pint, take in the view, and sample some tasty cuisine. (D1) www.themountinn.co.uk

Stanton Church of St Michael. Impressive Perpendicular tower. Much is C12-15 with wall paintings, Jacobean pulpit, but its fame was associated with the many visits of John Wesley, the Methodist preacher. (D1)

STANWAY

This village is dominated by the outstanding Manor House. In its grounds stands one of the country's finest tithe barns designed with the Golden Proportion in mind, and across the road, a thatched cricket pavilion, set on staddle stones. The beautiful Gatehouse is C17, and was probably built by Timothy Strong of Little Barrington. It bears the arms of the Tracy family. The little church of St Peter has C14 origins and some amusing gargoyles. (D2)

Stanway House & Water Garden. This exquisite Jacobean Manor House and Gatehouse is built from the local stone known as Guiting Yellow which lights up when the sun touches it. All is set within an enchanting and ancient parkland designed by a numerologist, the home of the Earl of Wemyss and March. The restored C18 cascade (fountain) and canal was designed by the highly respected Charles Bridgman, and plays at 2.45-3.15pm and 4-4.30pm. Open June to Aug, Tu & Th 2-5. (D2) 01386 584469 www.stanwayfountain.co.uk

Naunton

STOW-ON-THE-WOLD

With a name like this it is bound to attract visitors, and it has, and does so to this day, for with its exposed position at the intersection of eight roads, (one being the Fosse Way) Stow has been party to some momentous events in history. The Romans used Stow as an encampment and route centre. The Viking merchants traded down the Fosse Way, but it was the Saxon hill farmers who laid the foundations for the "fleece" which created wealth for the wool merchants who used the great Market Place for sheep sales of 20,000, or more. The Kings Arms is named after Charles Stuart who stayed here in 1645 before the Battle of Naseby. In March 1646, the Battle of Stow was the last skirmish, or battle of the English Civil War. Stow has a number of historic hostelries, and is thus, an agreeable place in which to succumb to fine ales and wine, and the comfort of a four-poster bed. Today, the town is a busy and pleasing place to be. It still has free parking and you may wander freely about, and admire the art galleries and many antique shops. 'Where the wind blows cold' so the song goes. (K5)
www.go-stow.co.uk
www.stowonthewold.info

SPECIAL PLACES OF INTEREST...

Abbotswood, Upper Swell. A late C19 park with early C20 formal terraced and woodland gardens. A Manor established by the Cistercians pre-1257. House altered by Sir Edwin Lutyens. Extensive heather and stream gardens. Plantings of spring bulbs. Open for National Gardens Scheme. (K5) 01451 830173
www.ngs.org.uk

Donnington Brewery. Established in 1865 by Thomas Arkell who used the spring water to concoct his delicious potions. The brewery remains independent and supplies 15 tied houses and a number of free trade outlets. (J4) 01451 830603
www.donnington-brewery.com

Fosse Gallery, The Square. Well-established gallery displaying paintings; contemporary and modern, most artists are RA, RAI, ROI members. Open M-Sa 10.30-5. (K5) 01451 831319
www.fossegallery.com

Market Cross. The lantern head represents four meanings: 'A Rood (crucifix/cross),' St Edward, The Wool Trade and The Civil War. (K5)

Parish Church of St Edward (The Confessor). Set behind the Market Place in the centre of town. The building is a mix of the C11 and C15. Originally of Saxon origins, it has an impressive tower of 88 feet that was built in 1447. Modern stained glass is of interest. Seek out the back door within a tree. (K5)

Red Rag Gallery, Church Street. Original paintings from living artists. Sculpture. Scottish art. Open daily. (K5) 01451 832563
www.redraggallery.co.uk

Stow Horse Fair. This is held twice a year, in the spring and autumn. Its origins have been lost in time, but today, it is very much a Romany get-together. They come from far and wide, to trade in ponies, tack and odds and sods. It's quite a sight, but one visit will probably suffice and satisfy your curiosity. On arriving in Stow, one can't help but notice that the police (and RSPCA) presence is considerable, and that most of the shops, tearooms and inns are closed. No doubt the matrons of the town have also locked up their daughters! As you make your way towards the site, gaggles of young girls showing more flesh than common sense (often in freezing conditions), strut their apparel. A rustic type of "Passeggiata." All apparently (according to a 10-year old Romany) to attract members of the opposite sex. I can't imagine that they were successful because the only males I saw were well into their 40s, possibly older, and only intent on doing a deal, often clasping wodges of £50 notes. The elderly female Romanies were fun to talk to, and chivvy with, and were there to meet up with old friends, and to experience the camaraderie of times past. What did impress me was their collection of new motors: black Golf Gtis for the women, and black Land Rovers for the men folk. I was later informed, by what I took to be a reliable source, that they do not pay VAT, corporation or income tax, or are lumbered with hefty mortgages. Well, that beats the system I thought. Perhaps they have something to teach us? (K5)

Peter Martin Gallery, 2 Digbeth Court. An artistic, and creative impression of life in Venice and Paris, through the medium of black-and-white images. Open daily 10-5 07479 610511
www.petermartinstudio.co.uk

Snowshill Lavendar

LIGHT BITES...

Le Patissier Anglais on The Square will be a delectable experience for those with a passion for pastries, home-made mousses, savoy quiches, and coffee. No bread. The Proprietor is a Chocolatier who trained with Albert Roux. So, if you seek a personal service, and to chat with a Maestro…Open M-Sa 9-5, Su 9-1. When he sells out, he closes. 01451 870571 www.lepatissieranglais.co.uk If you seek a fresh, custom-made sandwich you have two choices, either **Cotswold Baguettes** on Church Walk 01451 831362 www.cotswoldbaguettes.co.uk , or bear south-east out of The Square to **Hamptons Fine Foods** on Digbeth Street who also sell cheeses, pies, quiches and cakes. 01451 831733 www.hamptons-hampers.co.uk At the other end of the Square, opposite the Stocks, **The Little Stocks Coffee Shop** run by a Hungarian pastry chef where you can be served soups, savouries and delish cakes. 01451 830666. Next door, a new, small, boutique-style hotel, The Old Stocks Inn www.oldstocksinn.com for a pint of local ale.

WHERE TO STAY, EAT & DRINK...

Grapevine Hotel, Sheep Street. The Conservatory Restaurant serves imaginative food and fine wines. 22 beautifully furnished and decorated bedrooms. Relaxing ambience. (K5) 01451 830344 www.vines.co.uk

Kings Arms, The Square. Fine pub in Market Square set on two levels. Lively and comfortable, matched by well prepared ingredients. Greene King and Hook Norton beers. Children & dogs welcome. B&B. (K5) 01451 830364 www.thekingsarmsstow.co.uk

The Porch House, Digbeth Street. Claims to be the oldest Inn in England, dating from 947 AD. It has a had a complete make-over, and a new name. It is thus, now a luxurious hostelry; cosy and comfy, backed up by fine dining. 13-bedrooms. Adjacent, The Pub and Conservatory for informality. (K5) 01451 830670 www.porch-house.co.uk

The White Hart, The Square. The Inn boasts two cosy bars and an comfortable dining room. The food is recommended by one and all. (K5) 01451 830674. www.whitehartstow.com

WHERE TO STAY, EAT & DRINK...OUTSIDE STOW

Horse & Groom, Upper Oddington. This inn dates back to 1580, and has retained some original features since its early days as a simple hostelry. Set in a beautiful conservation village, this freehouse provides sustenance and comfort. B&B. 01451 830584 www.horseandgroom.uk.com

Rectory Farmhouse, Lower Swell. This fully renovated and comfortable B&B with en-suite bedrooms has had several historical incarnations. Once a monastery whose cellars date back to the C14. Once, a home confiscated from its owner by Henry VIII. And, before its incarnation as a B&B, the Rectory was a working farmhouse. (J6) 01451 832351

William Baron's Fremington Vase, The Long Room, Winchcombe ss

WINCHCOMBE

This small Cotswold town lies cradled in the Isbourne Valley. It was an ancient Saxon burh (small holding) and famous medieval centre visited from far and wide for the market, horse fair and monastery which was destroyed in the C16. You can still walk the narrow streets beside the C16 and C18 cottages, but do look up and admire the many fine gables above the shop fronts. There's a local saying: Were you born in Winchcombe? which is directed at those of us who leave doors open. It can be a wee bit drafty. (B4)

SPECIAL PLACES OF INTEREST...

Belas Knap Long Barrow. In Old English translates 'beacon mound.' A burial chamber, 4,000 years old. Opened in 1863 to reveal 38 skeletons. In superb condition and good viewpoint beside the Cotswold Way. Steep footpath from road. (B6)

Folk & Police Museum. Town Hall. History of the town, police and weapons. TIC. Open East/Apr- Oct M- Sa 10-4. (B4) 01242 609151

Hailes Abbey (EH/NT). Built in 1246 by Richard, Earl of Cornwall, brother of Henry III, having vowed he would set up a religious house if he survived a storm at sea. Museum. The abbey became a popular place of pilgrimage in the Middle Ages until Henry VIII closed it down. It remains an attractive ruin with many surviving artefacts on display in the museum. Open daily Apr to Oct 31 10-dusk. (C3) 01242 602398 www.nationaltrust.org.uk

Hayles Fruit Farm. Wide range of locally produced fruit, cider and home-cured hams. Tea room. Two nature trails. Open daily 9-5. (D3) 01242 602123 www.hayles-fruit-farm.co.uk

Long Room Gallery, Queen Anne House, High St., This is quite a find, and an unusual archival collection of Studio and

WINCHCOMBE GARGOYLES

The word gargoyle is a derivation from the French word gargouille meaning throat or pipe. The carved gargoyles were invented to channel water off, or away, from the roofs of buildings in Egypt and Ancient Greece. Their popularity became almost endemic in Europe during the Middle Ages. Fine examples are to be seen on Notre Dame in Paris, and on Rouen's Cathedral in northern France. In Britain, the Cotswold churches, especially Winchcombe's have some fine, amusing examples, as illustrated.

The reason for these strange and often ugly designs is open to conjecture. Some believe they are caricatures of the clergy, or that they are there to ward off evil spirits. Perhaps, to protect the church's building from the devil. Others believe they are transformed into ghosts and ghoulies at night! They were certainly a popular architectural ornament during dark days of the superstitious, Middle Ages.

Country Slipware from the C19 and C20, and a "must-see" for all ceramic enthusiasts. Open daily. (B4) 01242 602319 www.cotswoldsliving.co.uk

Parish Church of St Peter. One of the great 'Wool' churches. It is of a C15 Perpendicular design but is strangely plain, yet dignified. Not as elaborate as some of the other 'Wool' churches. For example, it has no chancel arch. The gargoyles are the one notable feature, and a circumnavigation of the exterior is advised. The weathercock is the county's finest. (B4)

Postlip Hall & Tithe Barn. A former Jacobean Manor House set in fifteen acres. Postlip Hall has been for the past 40 years a co-housing idyll. Eight families live in separate dwellings, working the organic kitchen garden and grounds, and pursuing their own creative pleasures; be it writing, painting, sculpting or inventing. The original tithe barn is also in continual use except when it is hired out as a venue for weddings, parties and beer festivals. (A5)

Salt Way. This prehistoric track runs east of Winchcombe from Hailes, south towards Hawling along Sudeley Hill. It was used in medieval times to carry salt from Droitwich and coastal salt towns, salt being the essential meat preservative. (D6)

Sudeley Castle. A Tudor house and the original home of the Seymour family. Katherine Parr, widow of Henry VIII lived here and lies buried in the chapel. There is a fine collection of needlework, furniture and tapestries, plus paintings by Van Dyck, Rubens and Turner. All surrounded by award- winning gardens and open parkland. Cafe. The Castle is open daily early Mar to 30 Oct 10-5. (B5) 01242 602308 www.sudeleycastle.co.uk

Winchcombe Pottery. One of the country's most respected potteries, known throughout the ceramic world. A large variety of hand-made domestic ware on sale in the shop. Open daily M-F 8- 5, Sa 10-4 (& Su May to

LIGHT BITES...

There are a number of choices for tea, coffee, pastries, a pre-walk breakfast, and or, brunch and light lunch. Park outside the Church, or in the Square opposite Lloyds Bank.

Taking the RH pavement, you first come to the **White Hart**, and **Wesley House** (described below). Continue along this street, crossing to Hailes Street to **The Lady Jane,** a traditional tea room that welcomes cyclists and walkers with an all-day breakfast. Returning to the **Town Clock/Museum**, and enter North Street. **Cafe 6**, a new venture serving bacon baguettes and Verdi coffee. Next door, the **North Street Bakery** for pasties and pies. A few steps to the food hall, **Food Fanatics, 12 North St.,** a deli and coffee shop serving quiches, cheeses, pates, pastries and cold meats. Open daily. www.food-fanatics.co.uk

WHERE TO STAY, EAT & DRINK...

5 North Street. Has gained a healthy respect from fellow restaurateurs in the Cotswolds. You have a small, and well-run restaurant with low-beamed ceiling in a quaint C17 building providing a relaxed and friendly atmosphere. (B4) 01242 604566 www.5northstreetrestaurant.co.uk

Lion Inn, 33 North Street. A comfortable hostelry serving good-value food within a sympathetically decorated building. You can eat/drink in the bar (and nestle up to the log fire), or dining room; tapas for lunch, Dinner is more dynamic, and sleep in their luxurious bedrooms. 01242 603300 (B4) www.lionwinchcombe.co.uk

Wesley House, High Street. Deserved reputation for excellent food. Locals travel miles to this gastronomic fest, and no wonder. Now, with a chic, new wine bar for the local lovelies. Five bedrooms. (B4) 01242 602366 www.wesleyhouse.co.uk

White Hart, High Street. Variously viewed as an inn or a hotel, the White Hart offers quality in both departments. This C16 inn has eight en-suite bedrooms and a bar, restaurant and wine shop. (B4) 01242 602359 www.wineandsausage.co.uk

WHERE TO STAY... OUTSIDE WINCHCOMBE

North Farmcote. A working family farm producing sheep and cereals situated high on the Cotswold escarpment. Built around 1840 as a dower house for Lord Sudeley's mother, the house is surrounded by a large garden where guests can have afternoon tea. Visit their specialist herb garden (open May to Oct). (C4) 01242 602304 www.northfarmcote.co.uk

Guiting Cottage

Sudeley Hill Farm.
Comfortable C15 listed
farmhouse with panoramic
views onto a working sheep/
arable farm of 800 acres. Three
en-suite bedrooms. (C4)
01242   602344

SPECIAL PLACE OF INTEREST...

Whittington Court. An
impressive, statuesque
Cotswold stone house beside a
pretty church. Home of the
Whittington Press. Open Easter
fortnight, then mid to end Aug,
2-5. (B8) 01242 820724

WHERE TO STAY...

**Whittington Lodge Farm,
Whittington.** Your hostess
takes your comfort and
enjoyment very seriously and
the bedrooms are perfect down
to the smallest details. The
farm has a special emphasis on
conservation and wildlife and
you can take farm wildlife tours
and walks. (B8) 01242 820603
www.whittingtonlodgefarm.com

SPECIAL INNS TO VISIT...

Black Horse, Naunton. A
Donnington Brewery tied-
house, so naturally, there is
an excellent selection of beers
on offer. A little off the beaten
track, so ideal for those wishing
to avoid the crowds. B&B (G6)
01451 850565

Fox Inn, Broadwell. Very
picturesque inn with a large
beer garden situated opposite
the village green thus making
it an ideal pit stop for families.
Real ales from the local
Donnington Brewery, and tasty
pub-grub from the kitchens. Jus
Purrfik, Ma Larkin! (L5)
01451 870909

**Craven Arms,
Brockhampton.** An attractive
C17 inn noted for its fine food
and lovely views, lies   tucked
away on the edge of this hillside
village. Some years ago, it had
but a 'hole in the wall' and
served only ale and lemonade. I
remember watching the stunned
expression on the face of a

young man trying to impress a
young lady who had requested a
g & t, when told, "O no Sir, we
don't av that ere...will lemonade
do?" (C7) 01242 820 410
www.thecravenarms.co.uk

Fox Inn, Oddington. Origins
are C11 with flagstone floors,
open fireplaces and wooden
beams. Wholesome pub grub.
(M5) 01451 870555
www.foxinn.net

Hollow Bottom. Friendly
pub popular with the racing
fraternity. Traditional pub grub
plus more ambitious delights.
(E6) 01451 850392
www.hollowbottom.com

Plough Inn, Ford. The
first pub my 90-year old
Grandmother entered, and
surprisingly, she was markedly
impressed at how civil and well
behaved everyone was. She
was drawn to the advertised,
asparagus. Its all flagstone floors,
beams and old-world charm.
(E4) 01386 584215
www.theploughinnatford.co.uk

GUITING POWER

A hidden, somnolent estate village that surprisingly manages to support two pubs, a village shop
and bakery, a nursery school and an active village hall. The blue-grey cottages belong to the
Cochrane Estate (or Guiting Manor Amenity Trust) that has thankfully saved this village from
greedy developers and second homers. The Church of St Michael & All Angels lies on the edge
of the village and has some Norman features, a beautiful Tympanum and some weather-beaten
tombstones. It was an early Anglo-Saxon settlement called Gyting Broc. A classical and jazz music
festival is held in late July for the past 38 years and attracts many artists of international renown.
www.guitingfestival.org

St Mary's Church, Bibury,

Sapperton Church

Great Tew Church

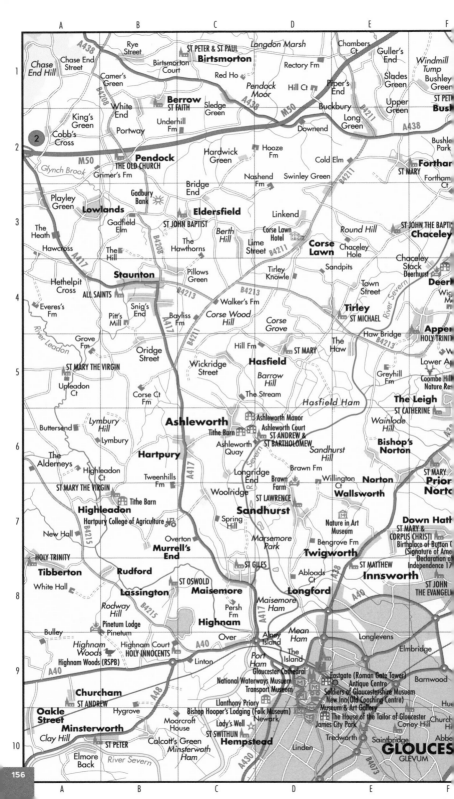

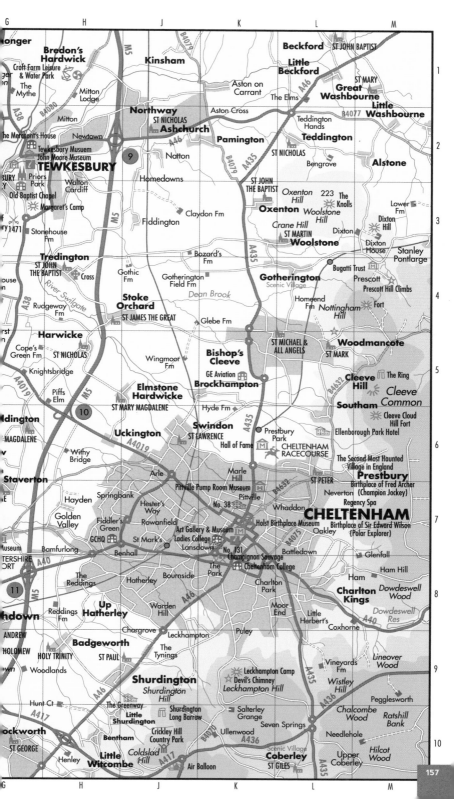

No.11 Suffolk Square, Cheltenham / Lansdown Parade, Cheltenham

CHELTENHAM

A smaller version of Bath, often described as 'the most complete Regency town in England.' Elegant Regency buildings overlook the crescents, squares, tree-lined avenues and spacious parks. Cheltenham remains, in historic terms, a young town of a mere 300-years. It grew as a spa after George III had approved the waters in 1788. Thereafter, distinguished visitors such as George Handel and Samuel Johnson came to be revitalised. The Promenade is one of the most attractive shopping streets in England which becomes progressively more independent and up-market as you trudge with heavy bags and depleted purse west towards Montpelier. Style and fashion epitomise this smart town. Youth and hedonism, a-plenty. Cheltenham has seen a phenomenal explosion of new nightclubs, bars and restaurants patronised by the ever-increasing student population and, come the evening, by an influx of visitors from Birmingham, Bristol and Gloucester and, not least from the surrounding villages and small towns. It is no longer the home of Colonel Blimps and tweedy ladies of means. Cheltenham is proud of its calendar of festivals: Antique, Folk, Jazz, Literature, Music, Science...but it is during the Cheltenham Festival of National Hunt Racing which takes place in March that the town takes on a carnival atmosphere. The Irish arrive in thousands and this brings out the

Cheltenham College, Cheltenham

Cheltonians hospitality. Hotel rooms are like gold dust so many of Cheltenham's citizens open their homes and do a brisk and highly profitable B&B trade for three or four nights. A centre of administration, commerce, education, high-tech industries and secret surveillance. The Countryside Commission and UCAS have their headquarters here. So do a number of large organisations: the Chelsea Building Society, Dowty, Endsleigh Insurance, GE Aviation, Kraft Foods and Zurich Insurance. The University of Gloucestershire has expanded its faculties to countenance the weight of the highly regarded private schools. What stands out for those of us who arrive from the Gloucester side, is the large circular building known as GCHQ, locally known as the Puzzle Palace. This was established after WWII as a secret surveillance centre for the Foreign Office. It is a most congenial town that could

well be described as the centre for the Cotswolds. Its motto Salubritas et Eruditio 'Health and Education.' If you can achieve either of these, then your luck is in. (L7)

SPECIAL PLACES OF INTEREST...

The Wilson - Cheltenham Art Gallery & Museum, Clarence Street. World-renowned Arts & Crafts Movement collection inspired by William Morris. Rare Chinese and English ceramics. The Paper Store, an open archive of local heroes, including the great Edward Wilson, Antarctic Explorer. Social history of Cheltenham. C17 Dutch and C17-20 British paintings.

Wilson Cafe. TIC. Open daily 9.30-5.15. (K7) 01242 237431 www.cheltenhammuseum.org.uk

Bugatti Trust, Prescott Hill. A small exhibition illustrates the work of Ettore Bugatti the genius of industrial design and invention. Study Centre with drawings, photos and some cars. Open M-F 10.30-3.30, and during Hill Climb days. (M4) 01242 673136 www.bugatti.co.uk

Cheltenham College. An independent Public School of architectural renown, distinguished by the superb Chapel and Refectory. The ground for the oldest cricket festival in the world (first staged in 1872) which takes place every summer. (K8) To visit contact 01242 265600 www.cheltenhamcollege.org

Pittville Pump Room

Cleve Hill Walk, Cheltenham

The Paragon Gallery, 4 Rotunda terrace, Montpelier Street. A refreshing, new gallery with a diverse range of stylish, bold, bright and contemporary artworks. The service is friendly and unstuffy, and dog-loving. (K7) 01242 233391 www. paragongallery.co.uk

Cheltenham Ladies College, Bayshill Road. If you see young ladies dressed in green apparel   walking at pace through the streets of Cheltenham (in twos and threes) you can be sure they are educated at this, the most elitist of academies. Its buildings are undistinguished, modern and rarely favourably commented upon. However, the aesthetics of the buildings have no effect on the school's academic achievements, for it usually comes in the Top 3 of all A-Level results. (K7) www.cheltladiescollege.org

Cheltenham Racecourse Hall of Fame. The story of steeple chasing and its immortals, in sight and sound, from Cheltenham's first Gold Cup in 1818 to Desert Orchid's heart-stopping win in 1989. Open M-F and Race Days 9-5. Free. (L6) 01242 513014 www.cheltenham.thejockeyclub. co.uk

Gustav Holst Birthplace Museum, Clarence Road, Pittville. Memorabilia of composer's life. Period furnished rooms. Open all year Tu-Sa 10-4, June to Sept 10-5 & Su 1.30-5. (K7) 01242 524846 www.holstmuseum.org.uk

Pittville Pump Room, East Approach Drive. A masterpiece of C19 Greek Revivalism, adorned with colonnaded facades, portico, pillared and balconied hall. Open daily, except during private functions. (K7) 01242 523852 www.pittvillepumproom.org.uk

Seven Springs. One of the sources of the River Thames. There is a stone plaque here with a Latin inscription which reads, roughly translated: 'Here thou, O Father Thames, hast thy sevenfold beginning.' (L10)

NATURAL PLACES OF INTEREST...

Cleeve Hill. At 1,083 feet this is the highest point in the Cotswolds and thus a superb viewpoint across to the Malvern Hills, Welsh Mountains, and northwards across the Cotswold landscape. A popular dog walking area and, in winter snow, ideal for tobaggan runs.

In 1901 a tramway was built from Cheltenham to Cleeve Cloud but sadly closed in 1930. Cleeve Cloud is the site of an   Iron Age hill fort and just below the scarp is The Ring, a site of religious/pagan rituals, 100 feet in diameter. Castle Rock is popular with novice rock climbers. (M5)

Cleeve Common. A vast expanse of common land where you are free to roam, with dog and friends. It is more like a piece of wild moorland with its extensive horizons, and you may be forgiven for believing you are in the midst of a National Park. There are wild flowers, the Gallops (for exercising race horses) and tracks that lead off in all directions. Park in the golf course, or in the lay-byes on the B4632. (M5)

Coombe Hill Canal Nature Reserve. Two-mile stretch of canal closed in 1876. Habitat of birds, dragonflies, aquatic and bankside plants. Open all year. (F5)

Crickley Hill Country Park. Nature trails, geological and archaeological trails are signposted, as is the Cotswold Way. There are traces of Stone Age and Iron Age settlements. Fine views. Open daily. (J10)

Devil's Chimney. A 50 foot high limestone rock which according to local superstition 'rises from hell.' Its origins resulted from quarrying the surrounding stone. (K9)

Highnam Woods Nature Reserve. 300 acres of broad-leafed woodland, with bluebells in spring. Nightingales call (if you are listening). Open daily. (A9) 01594 562852 www.rspb.org.uk

Leckhampton Hill. A popular dog walking area for Cheltonians that provides superb views towards the Malvern Hills and Wales. The golden stone of 'Regency' Cheltenham was quarried here. Iron Age and Roman camps. (K9)

LIGHT BITES...

Cheltenham provides an amazing choice of bars, coffee shops, hotels, pubs and restaurants. I have selected three areas of the town: **Montpelier, The Promenade and Suffolk Parade**. There were 7 new eateries about to open as I went to press! Where to start? Montpelier - which is the smart, posh, area of town. First up, **The Montpelier Wine Bar**, an old favourite (and the first in town), and perhaps in need of a facelift but it has character, and a pedigree. It opens with a traditional breakfast. Further down Montpelier Street, on the R, the **Gusto Deli and Café**, 12 Montpelier Walk. Great coffee, great breakfasts, a tasty selection of pasta and salads with great views of Montpelier, and Cheltenham life. 01241 239111 www.gusto-deli.com Continue down the street to the corner, and you come to **John Gordons**, 11 Montpelier Arcade. You will be impressed by the bottles on display. 200+ malt whiskeys, 50 gins, 30 rums, an off-license and bar, plus coffee, cakes and tapas with seating outside, too. 01242 245985 www.johngordons. co.uk If you are seeking more formality return to Montpelier Street, and the Montpelier Courtyard.

Upstairs, **Café Deli & Art** where you can buy coffee, and a variety of continental light lunches. Open daily with Evening meals on F & Sa. 01242 237277. Below, the **Montpelier Café**, down the steps. Breakfast and an all-day menu. Child friendly and outside seating. 01241 233534 www.montpeliercafe.co.uk Across the Courtyard in the corner is **Flynns Bar & Brasserie**. This is a well established Cheltenham destination, but more an evening food venue, the lighting is subdued, and romantics hold it dear. 01242 252752 www. flynnsrestaurant.co.uk

Leave **Montpelier**, and with the **Queens Hotel (M Gallery)** on your R descend to the Imperial (Square) Gardens area. **No 131** is worth a look in. Its all about lifestyle and being "Cool" and feeling good about yourself. Ask to see **Crazy Eights**. This boutique restaurant is always booked up way in advance. Breakfast is from 7-11am, brunch 11-4pm and lunch 12-3. There's an outside bar and seating with views over the gardens. 01241 822939 www.no131. com. Across the road you may see folk, in repose, on the grass with glass in hand supplied by the **Imperial Garden Bar**, established in 1903. Open daily from 11am, East until the close of the Literary Festival in October. A popular, al fresco dining experience, where you can meet up with family and friends. Tapas menu. It has a secret garden for intimate assignations. Now, if all this is a bit much, and you just seek a sandwich head towards **The Promenade** to the **Swallow Bakery**, on the corner. There is seating for Brunch, served 8am-3pm to gather your energy and thoughts before tackling the shopping delights of The Promenade where you can buy a fresh coffee from the man with the

Coffee Station. Behind the Promenade, at 16 Regent Street, is **Anderson's Coffee House**, a complete contrast of what has gone before. This quiet and old fashioned, family business provides lunch and teas/coffees to a loyal clientele. Open daily 9.30-4.30.

To reach **Suffolk Parade** you must retrace your steps. Walk to the top of Montpelier Gardens to the roundabout, and turn L down Montpelier Terrace, and take the first R into Suffolk Parade. This area has a full panoply of independent shops and restaurants/bars. A splendid bookshop, The Suffolk Anthology, Lighting and antiques, bike shop and florists. A town within itself. **The Retreat** at 10 Suffolk Parade is an old favourite that has had a loyal following since it opened, years back. Food is served at lunchtime M-Sa 12-3 where you can have ham, egg and chips, to new potatoes and a casserole, to a steak sandwich and rocket salad. A pleasing ambience, with red walls and bare floors gives way to a buzz, come the evening. 01242 235436 wwwtheretreatwinebar. co.uk But, if you seek food of a seasonal variety, try **The Suffolk Kitchen** at No. 8. A passion for fresh, seasonal produce is their raison d'être. Brunch from 9.30-11.30 W/Es, and Tu-Sa lunch 12-2.30, dinner 6-10pm. 01242 237 057 www.thesuffolkkitchen. co.uk. But, if you seek a celebratory lunch, or dinner, and are feeling flush it has to be **Le Champignon Sauvage.**

Devil's Chimney, Leckhampton

38 The Park, Cheltenham

WHERE TO EAT...

Champignon Sauvage, 24-26 Suffolk Road. A two Michelin starred restaurant with a reputation for their original approach to serving fine cuisine. Hence, no cell phones in the Dining Room. Whoopee! **(K7)** 01242 573449
www.lechampignonsauvage.co.uk

Daffodil, 18-20 Suffolk Parade. Converted from a 1920's art deco cinema to a restaurant and mezzanine circle bar and original features, posters advertising films with the original projectors. This is an atmospheric dining experience. Jazz and Martini Mondays. (K7) 01242 700055.
www.thedaffodil.com

www.thebeehivemontpellier.com

Morans Eating House, 123-129 Bath Road. Family owned restaurant, and wine bar, that has been popular and busy since its inception 25 years ago. Squeeze amongst the regulars for a glass of wine or good value, unpretentious fare, from brunch to a bedtime snack. (K8) 01242 581411
www.moranseatinghouse.co.uk

WHERE TO STAY...

Hanover House B&B, 65 St George's Road. An attractive Grade II listed house built in a mix of Italian and Georgian architecture. The B&B is beautifully light and airy inside and the books, flowers and pictures adorning the rooms make you feel at home. Edward Elgar and his wife Alice once lived here. 01242 541297
www.hanoverhouse.org

Georgian House, 77 Montpelier Terrace. Georgian house amidst elegant terrace close to many antique shops. Superb breakfasts. No children U-16. (K7) 01242 515577 www.georgianhouse.net

No. 131 The Promenade. You really can't find a better location than this, in this, Regency town. Smack opposite Imperial Gardens, and a short walk onto the finest shopping street in England. The rooms are all independently decorated, and designed with locally sourced materials. Lavish, and a wee bit over the top, but good fun, too. And, not forgetting the stupendously popular restaurant, Crazy Eights, in the basement. 01242 8229939 www.no131.com

No. 38 Evesham Road. An intimate, Georgian town house overlooking Pittville Park, and a short walk to the Racecourse, and town centre. This, a perfect venue for a house party, catering to 13-rooms can be yours for a small song. 01242 822929 www.no38thepark.com

Hotel du Vin & Bistro, Parabola Road. A little bit of France within a Regency townhouse. The bedrooms are moody, dark and contemporary. The Bistro is inspired by French home-style cooking. The Spa will rejuvenate the senses you thought were missing. 01242 370584 www.hotelduvin.com

The Greenway Hotel & Spa, Shurdington. Elizabethan manor house provides elegance, peace and self-indulgent comfort with easy access to the M5 motorway. (J9) 01242 862352 www.thegreenwayhotelandspa.com

The Greenway ss

Warehouses, Gloucester Docks

GLOUCESTER

The county town of Gloucestershire and its administrative centre is set to the east of the Cotswold Hills, south of the Malvern Hills, and to the west of the Forest of Dean. Originally a port connected to the tidal Bristol Channel and strategic point developed by the Romans into the fort Glevum. This ancient city is today dominated by the magnificent Cathedral. One of the great attractions are the Old Docks where the spectacular C19 warehouses have been restored for commercial and leisure use. It is not unknown to spy tall ships, and ships in the dry dock for renovations. The city is undergoing a great deal of new development on the south side just off the Bristol road. The history of Gloucester is immense and this is well covered in the many museums listed below. (E10)

SPECIAL PLACES OF INTEREST...

City Museum & Art Gallery, Brunswick Road. Roman relics, dinosaurs, aquarium, art exhibitions. Open Tu-Sa 10-4. (D9) 01452 396131
www.venues.gloucester.gov.uk/Freetime/Museums

Eastgate. Roman and Medieval Gate. Towers and medieval stone-lined horse pool (moat). Open May to Sept Sa 10-12, 2.15-5. (D9)

Folk Museum, 99-103 Westgate Street. Medieval timber-framed buildings associated with martyrdom of Bishop Hooper in 1555. Social history, folklore, crafts and industries of city and county. Herb garden. Open Tu-Sa 10-5. (D9) 01452 396868

Glevum, Gloucester. Occupied since Neolithic times. Became of strategic importance to Early Man and the Roman legions. Fort at Kingsholm

Royal Gloucesters' Tableaux, Cathedral Close

beside the River Severn. Lost out to Corinium (Cirencester) in importance in the C3 AD. (D9)

Gloucester Cathedral. The Cathedral Church of St Peter and the Holy and Undivided Trinity. Without exception the most magnificent building in Gloucestershire and one of the finest of all English cathedrals. The building's foundation stone was laid down by Abbot Serlo in 1089 on the site of a religious house founded by Osric, an Anglo-Saxon prince living here in about 678-9 AD. The Nave was completed in 1130. Its architecture is Romanesque, with some early Perpendicular. The reconstruction of the Quire followed the burial in 1327 of Edward II. The East Window behind the altar had at its installation the largest display of medieval stained glass in the world and dates from 1350. The same year, fan vaulting was invented here at Gloucester and its intricate design covers the roof of the cloisters. Some would argue that Gloucester also saw the birth of Perpendicular architecture. In the south transept survives the oldest of all Perpendicular windows. Allow a couple of hours to wander around this spiritual hot house. There are tours of the crypt and tower. You will also be shown the location used for part of Hogwarts in the Harry Potter films.

Evensong is a most magical experience not to be missed, as is the Christmas Carol service. Cafe. Open daily 7.30am to 6pm. (D9) 01452 528095 www.gloucestercathedral.org.uk

Gloucester & Sharpness Canal. Opened in 1827 and built above the River Severn. It's 16 miles long and was originally used by ocean-going ships in transit to Gloucester. (D9)

National Waterways Museum, Llanthony Warehouse. A major national exhibition about the history of the inland waterways. Historic boats and leisure cruises on hand. Café. Open Sa, Su, & BHs 11- 4 and daily during school holidays. (D9) 01452 318200 www.nwm.org.uk

Nature in Art Museum

Nature In Art Museum, Wallsworth Hall. The world's first museum dedicated exclusively to Art inspired by Nature. Life-size sculptures in the garden. Artists at work (Feb-Nov). Coffee shop. Play area. Open all year Tu-Su & BHs (E7) 01452 731422 www.nature-in-art.org.uk

Soldiers of Gloucestershire Museum, The Docks. 300 years' service portrayed by sound effects and life-size models, weapons and uniforms. Open Mar to Oct, daily 10-5, Nov to Feb Tu-Sa, 10-5. (D9)

01452 522682 www.soldiersofglos.com

WHERE TO STAY...

Pinetum Lodge, Churcham. This historic Victorian hunting lodge sits well off the beaten track, situated in 13 acres of woodland garden (otherwise known as a Pinetum) planted by Thomas Gambier Parry in 1844, The owners encourage you to shrug off the city on your arrival, and to surround yourself with nature. 01452 750554 www.thepinetum.co.uk

TEWKESBURY

One of England's finest medieval towns set at the confluence of the rivers Avon and Severn. Just look up at the gables of the many ancient buildings and admire (or venture into) one of the 30 narrow alleyways that make up this historic place so magnificently brought to life in John Moore's Brensham Trilogy. In the Middle Ages Tewkesbury was a flourishing centre of commerce: flour milling, mustard, brewing, malting, shipping. Today, it has its flourmills and is a centre for boating and tourism. It is still a busy market town of half-timbered buildings, overhanging upper storeys and carved doorways. Following the recent floods the town has a new energy and purpose. Note the new Tourist Information Centre and Out of the Hat Museum which symbolises the ambitions of the Town's elders. (G2)

SPECIAL PLACES OF INTEREST...

Old Baptist Chapel. Reputed to be the first Baptist Chapel in southern England. Restored in 1976. Open daily 9-dusk. (G3)

John Moore Countryside Museum, 41 Church Street. Dedicated to children and all aspects of nature conservation displayed in a C15 timber framed house. Open Apr to Oct Tu-Sa & BHs, 10-1 & 2-5. (G2) 01684 297174

Tewkesbury Abbey. Founded in 1087 by the nobleman Robert Fitzhamon. However, the present building was started in 1102 to house Benedictine monks. The Norman abbey was consecrated in 1121. The Nave and roof finished in the C14 in the Decorated style. Much is Early English and Perpendicular, although it is larger than many cathedrals and has according to Pevsner 'the finest Romanesque Tower in England.' The Abbey opens its doors to three major music festivals: Musica Deo Sacra, the Three Choirs Festival and the Cheltenham Music Festival. You can park opposite and take a tour. Info on: 01684 850959. Shop and refectory. Open daily 7.30am to 5pm. (G2)
www.tewkesburyabbey.org.uk

Merchant's House, 45 Church Street. Restored medieval merchant's house. Open Apr to Oct Tu-Sa & BHs 10-1 & 2-5 (G2) 01684 297174

Tewkesbury Museum, Barton Street. Local folk history and heritage centre. Open Mar to Aug Tu- Fri 1-4.30, Sa 11-4, Sept to Oct Tu-F 12-3, Sa 11-3, Nov to Mar, Sa & for special events. (G2) 01684 292901
www.tewkesburymuseum.org

WHERE TO STAY...

Brawn Farm, Sandhurst. Historic farmhouse set in a beautiful landscaped garden with far-reaching views. Three en-suite guest bedrooms. 01452 731010
www.brawnfarmbandb.co.uk

Deerhurst B&B. Deerhurst Priory is a solid working farm adjoining the ancient Saxon Priory Church of St Mary. Pets welcome. 01684 293358
www.deerhurstbandb.co.uk

SPECIAL PLACES OF INTEREST BESIDE THE RIVER SEVERN...

Ashleworth Court. C15 limestone manor with a notable stone newel staircase. Closed to the public. All is overlooked by the tithe barn, next door which can be visited. (D6) 01452 700241

Ashleworth Manor. C15 timber framed and E-shaped. Open by written appointment for parties of eight or more. (C6) 01452 700350

Ashleworth Tithe Barn (NT). This C15 barn has an impressive stone-tile roof and two projecting porch bays. The roof timbers are held together by Queenposts. Open daily, all year 9-6. (C6) 01452 814213
www.nationaltrust.org.uk

Deerhurst (St Mary). C9 Saxon with superb font. (F4)

Deerhurst (Odda's Chapel). One of the few surviving Saxon chapels left in England. Earl Odda dedicated this rare chapel to the Holy Trinity on the 12th April 1056, in memory of his brother. Open daily. (F4)

LIGHT BITES...

For a Light Bite, I would recommend **1471 Delicatessen**, next door to **Out of the Hat Museum.** They know their coffee, hot chocolates, and can make up super sandwiches from their chutneys, cheeses and salads. 01608 2991471
www.AD1471.co.uk

Ashleworth Tithe Barn

Bredon Tithe Barn

Stanway

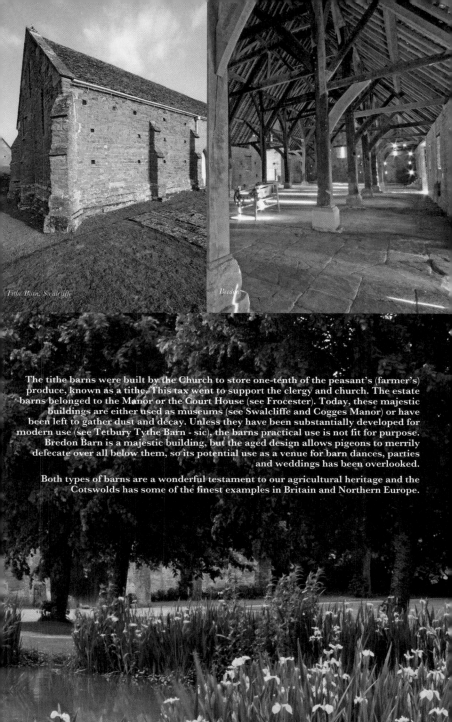

Tithe Barn, Swalcliffe

Bredon

The tithe barns were built by the Church to store one-tenth of the peasant's (farmer's) produce, known as a tithe. This tax went to support the clergy and church. The estate barns belonged to the Manor or the Court House (see Frocester). Today, these majestic buildings are either used as museums (see Swalcliffe and Cogges Manor) or have been left to gather dust and decay. Unless they have been substantially developed for modern use (see Tetbury Tythe Barn - sic), the barns practical use is not fit for purpose. Bredon Barn is a majestic building, but the aged design allows pigeons to merrily defecate over all below them, so its potential use as a venue for barn dances, parties and weddings has been overlooked.

Both types of barns are a wonderful testament to our agricultural heritage and the Cotswolds has some of the finest examples in Britain and Northern Europe.

SAXTON'S MAP 1576

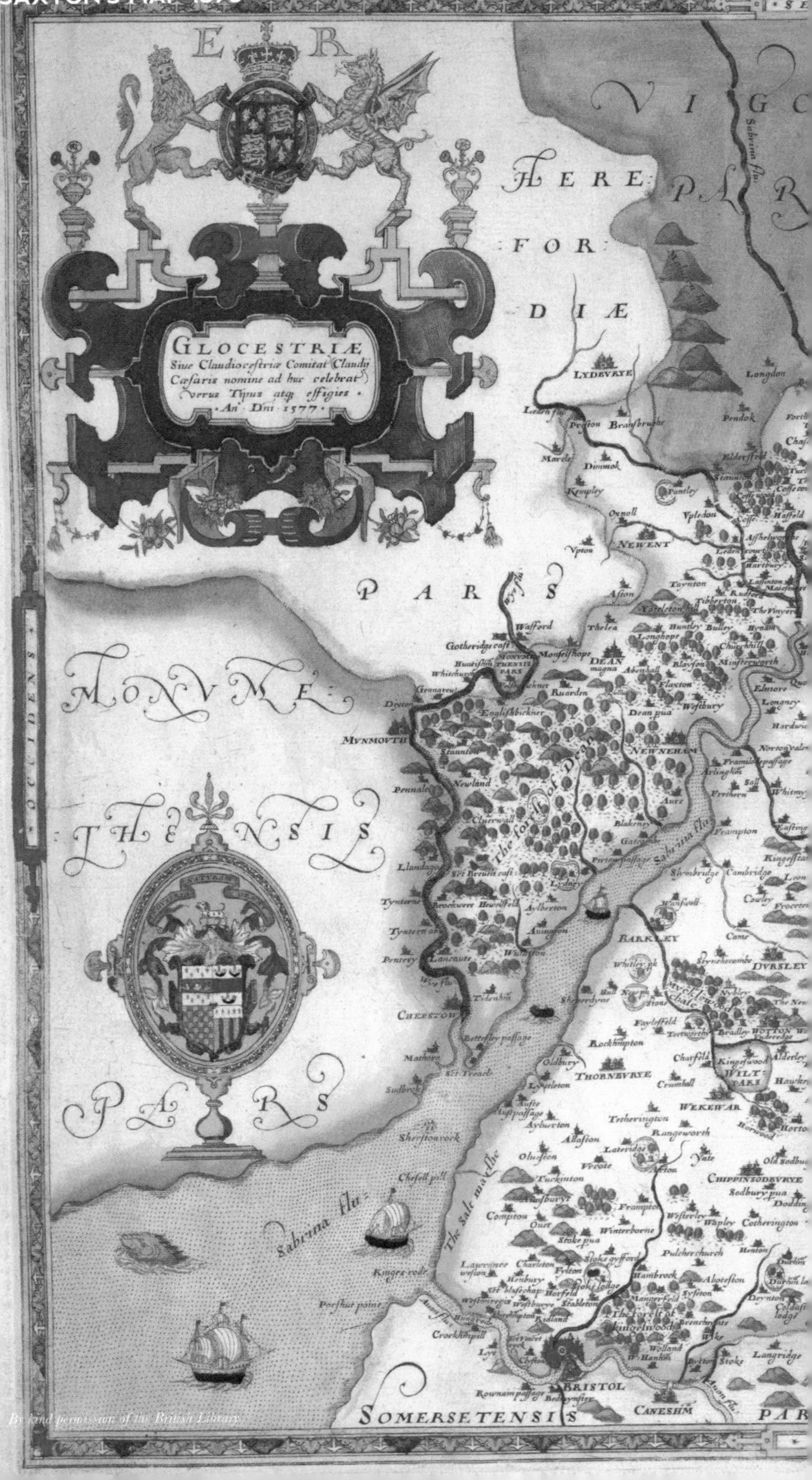

Seymour House, Chipping Campden

Theatre, festivals, Elgar and Shakespeare, Bredon Hill, poets laments, Cotswold jewels, Blossom Trail...

The Northern Cotswolds incorporates Stratford-on-Avon, the birthplace of England's greatest po-et, William Shakespeare, and site of many Shakespearian locations of interest. The area was also the birthplace of England's finest composer – Edward Elgar, who hailed from Lower Broadheath, on the outskirts of Worcester. Perhaps there was, and still is, something in the water!

This area also contains a pair of villages of note which are the jewels in the Cotswold crown: Chipping Campden and Broadway. Chipping Campden is an outstanding example of medieval architecture whilst behind the high walls and hedges of Broadway stand the very epitome of Cotswold domestic architecture

Just off the North Cotswold escarpment, the Evesham Vale, a verdant and productive fruit and vegetable farming area with many farm produce stores beside the road. And, in late May you can follow the annual Blossom Trail, a bonanza of colour and new growth.

Bredon Hill is in the centre of the region and is a very beautiful spot. So beautiful, that poets and writers have been moved to describe it in verse and prose. A E Houseman and John Moore wrote poems and novels about this area. The Gloucestershire composer Ralph Vaughan Williams' 'Lark Ascending' could have been inspired from a field atop this hill, for from the peak are stunning views across to the Cotswolds, the Malverns and the distant, Welsh hills.

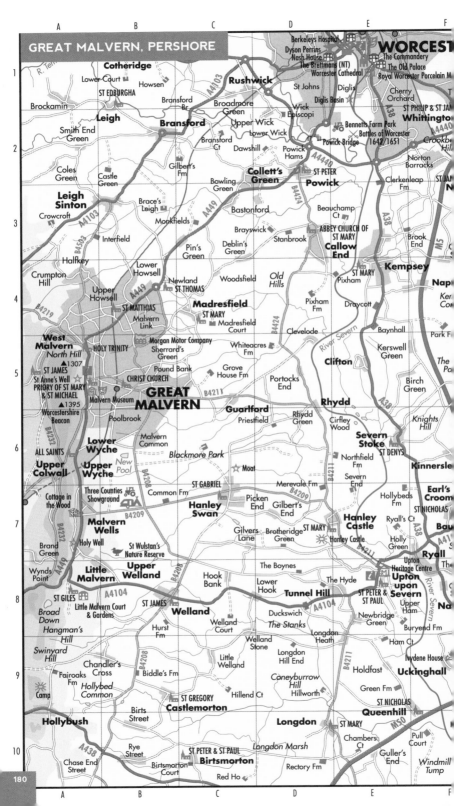

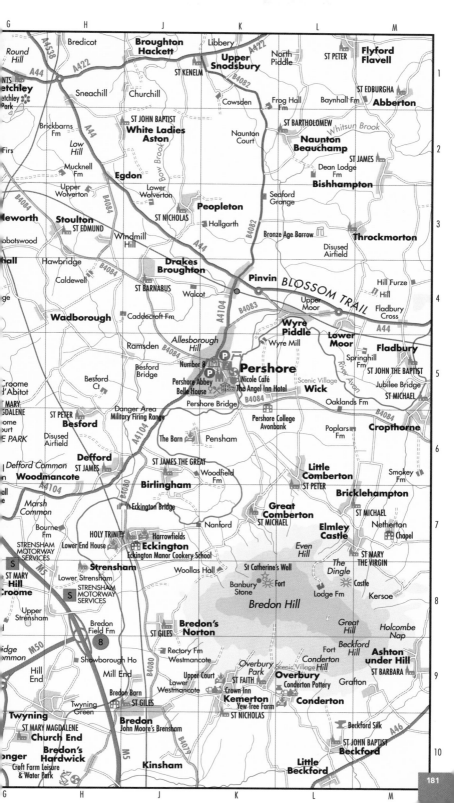

GREAT MALVERN

Pull the word Malvern out of a hat and what does its name conjure up? Edward Elgar, education, festivals, open-top sports cars, spring water, stained glass, walking holidays...quite a diverse spectrum of interests. There has been a settlement here since Iron Age man built forts at the British Camp on Herefordshire Beacon and on the southern tip at Midsummer Hill. Work began on the Priory in the C11 and continued well into the C16. But, it was not until a Dr Wall promoted 'Taking The Waters' that Malvern developed as a spa town in 1756. The town's true popularity took shape when the Baths and Pump Room opened in the 1820s. It even attracted the desperate Charles Darwin to bring his beloved ten-year old daughter Annie here for a cure. She had developed scarlet fever and possibly tuberculosis. She died and was buried in the Priory's churchyard. Her death had a profound and lasting effect on Darwin's attitude and philosophy.

Worth a quiet moment of reflection, in this bicentennial year of his birth. It remains a popular walking centre and once up on the hill there are fine views across to Wales, the Severn Vale and the Cotswolds. The healthy rigour of the town encouraged the Victorians to open schools for both sexes. Even George Bernard Shaw visited and help co-found the Theatre. The busy calendar of events is made up of various arts festivals: Elgar, Fringe, Music, Three Counties.

Edward Elgar, Great Malvern

The show goes on. Be prepared for some steep climbs - take comfy footwear. There are a number of coffee shops and delis on the main street below the Elgar statue. C15 Priory Church with famous medieval stained glass and tiles. (B5)

SPECIAL PLACES OF INTEREST...

Croome Park (NT). 'Capability' Brown's first significant landscape project. A restoration plan has begun - dredging and replanting the Lake Garden. Open Mar, Sept & Oct W-Su, daily Apr to Aug, Xmas & Jan W/Es, 11-5. (G6) 01905 371006 www.nationaltrust.org.uk

Little Malvern Court & Gardens. Former Benedictine monastery. Home of the Russell and Berington families since the Dissolution. Priors Hall with needlework, family and European furniture and paintings. 10 acre garden; spring bulbs, rose garden and views. Open mid-Apr to mid-July W & Th only 2.15-5. (A8) 01684 892988 www.littlemalverncourt.co.uk

Malvern Hills. A superb viewpoint. 6 paths and more criss-cross these hills. The highest point is Worcestershire Beacon at 1,394 feet. (A5)

Malvern Hill's Ancient Settlements. A natural location for Early Man; Herefordshire Beacon is the site of the Iron Age, British Camp. At the southern end is the monument and fort, Midsummer Hill. Superb views. (A5)

Morgan Car ss

Pershore Abbey

Morgan Motor Company.
You can take a factory tour
from the new Visitor Centre
in Spring Lane from late Apr
through to Dec. It will cost you
£10. Tours from 9-12 & 1-2.30
M-Th and 9-12 F. (B4) Pre-book
on 01684 800040
www.morgan-motor.co.uk

Spetchley Park. 25 acres of
rare and unusual trees, shrubs
and plants. Red and fallow deer
in park. Open late-Mar to Sept
W-Su & BH Ms 11-6, Oct W/
Es 11-4. (G1) 01905 345106
www.spetchleygardens.co.uk

**The Priory of St Mary &
St Michael.** The Abbot of
Westminster Abbey decreed
that work begin in 1085 on a
church to cater for 30 monks.
Extensions to this Norman
church were added between
1440 and 1500. The Tower was
built by the self-same masons
at work on nearby Gloucester
Cathedral. There are two quite
outstanding subjects to savour
here. The first is the great East
window that in its day was the
largest piece of stained glass
in England. The second is the
collection of bells that some
consider to be the Priory's finest
possessions. These were built
in Gloucester. The oldest built
between 1350 and 1380 weighs
some 8 cwt. The others were
made in 1611, 1706 and 1707.
Also to look at, the Victorian

glass in the North Aisle, modern
glass in the Millennium window
and another magnificent
window in the North Transept
given by Henry VII portraying
scenes from Mary's life. A good
deal of restoration was carried
out by the ubiquitous Sir Gilbert
Scott, in 1860. (A5)

WHERE TO STAY...

**Cottage in The Wood,
Holywell Rd.** Superb hillside
location with panoramic views
across the Severn Vale towards
the Cotswold Hills. Walks from
hotel onto the Malvern Hills.
Child friendly. (A7)
01684 588860
www.cottageinthewood.co.uk

Ivydene House, Uckinghall.
A special B&B for garden lovers,
so before settling in to your
sumptuous bedroom with all the
luxuries to hand, you must take
a stroll in their beautiful garden
that has plenty of nooks and
crannies, ideal for a quiet read.
07879 463291
www.ivydenehouse.net

PERSHORE

A market town well known
for its plums and elegant
Georgian buildings. The
Abbey was founded c.689, and
established in the late C10 by
the Benedictine monks who
later built the six-arched bridge
across the River Avon. (K5)

SPECIAL PLACES OF INTEREST...

Number 8, High Street. This is
Pershore's new community centre
for the arts, cinema and theatre. It
holds live events, creative courses
for adults and children. Coffee
shop. Open daily. (K5) Box office
01386 555488
www.number8.org

Pershore Abbey. Established in
the late C10 by Benedictines. C14
tower and the superb vaulting
of the Prestbytery, remain.
Beautiful Early English Choir,
but sadly much was destroyed by
Henry VIII. Visitor Centre open
summer weekends. Look out for
the intricate wooden sculpture in
the grounds. Open daily 8-5.30.
(K5) 01386 552071
www.pershoreabbey.org.uk

**Eckington Manor Cookery
School, Manor Road,**
Eckington. This is a cookery
school with state of the art
facilities, and a team of passionate
tutors who use fresh, locally
sourced seasonal ingredients, and
much more. The accommodation
is run separately from the school,
and is in one of the oldest houses
in Worcestershire. A period
house full of character that
has been renovated, with the
emphasis on quality and style.
Perfectly located for walking on
the nearby, Bredon or Malvern
Hills. (J7) 01386 751600
www.eckingtonmanor.co.uk

Riverside Walk, Upton-Upon-Severn

WHERE TO EAT, DRINK & SLEEP...

Belle House Restaurant, Bar & Traiteur, Bridge Street. There are a number of good reasons to visit Belle House: the exterior and interior architecture, the adjacent Traiteur-Deli, the aroma of newly ground coffee, and the mouth-watering restaurant run with great enthusiasm. Ideal for morning coffee, lunch or dinner. (K5) 01386 555055
www.belle-house.co.uk

Nicole Café, 4 High Street. Breakfast is served from 8.30am. All day sandwiches, baguettes, paninis and jacket potatoes. A friendly, little town café open daily. (K5) 01386 555005

The Angel Inn Hotel, High Street. Refurbished inn marries period detail with contemporary décor in   a stylish format. Special weekend breaks with coffee, lunch and dinner for two. (K5) 01386 552046
www.theangelinnpershore.co.uk

OUTSIDE PERSHORE...

Harrowfields, Cotheridge Lane, Eckington. This picturesque black- and-white timbered country cottage nestles peacefully in the Cotswold landscape. Fine attention to detail and guests needs.
01386 751053
www.harrowfields.co.uk

The Barn B&B, Pensham. A large and spacious barn ideally suited for a large family or group. No dogs or children U-12. (J6) 01386 555270
www.pensham-barn.co.uk

UPTON-UPON-SEVERN

An attractive town beside the River Severn that has been an important river crossing and route centre for centuries, thus, the profusion of medieval buildings and hostelries. The 2007 floods left a devastating mark on the town, so much so, that many inns were closed for 12 months. The rush to generate cash has encouraged cheaper beer, binge drinking and unsavoury behaviour at night. Not the venue for a quiet pint or romantic evening. Better to visit during the day, and enjoy the riverside walk and views, a visit to the International Map Shop, to plan further adventures. (E8)

Upton Heritage Centre. History of the town, and the River Severn's activities. Civil War connections. Open daily Apr-Sept M-Sa except Th, 10-5, Oct-Mar M, F & Sa 10-4. (E8) 01684 594200

SPECIAL PLACES OF INTEREST...BREDON HILL & VILLAGES

A circumnavigation of Bredon Hill is a fine introduction to the beautiful villages of Kemerton, Overbury, Conderton, Ashton-under-Hill and Elmley Castle. A lovely mixture of Cotswold stone,

Tof MIlway's Conderton Pottery

Beckford Silk. Hand printers of silk, with silk store, digital print room, hand print rooms, dye kitchen and tenter room. Open M-Sa 9-5 (Coffee shop for light meals, 10-4). (L10) 01386 881507 www.beckfordsilk.co.uk

and black-and-white timbered buildings with many fine Inns, and peaceful churchyards. Various footpaths lead up to the summit from Elmley and Kemerton. Superb views from this isolated limestone hill at 961 ft. (K8)

Bredon Barn (NT). A beautifully constructed large medieval threshing barn extending to 132 feet. Expertly restored after fire. Open mid-Mar to end Oct W Th & W/Es 10-6. (H9) 01452 814213 www.nationaltrust.org.uk

Bredon Hill Fort. Iron Age fort with two ramparts. Scene of great battle at time of Christ, possibly against the Belgic invaders. The hacked remains of 50 men were found near entrance. Superb views over to Wales, Vale of Evesham, the rivers Severn and Avon, and to the Cotswolds. (K8)

Conderton Pottery. Distinctive stoneware pots by specialist saltglazed country potter, Toff Milway. Open M-Sa 9-5. (L9) 01386 725387. www.toffmilway.co.uk

Croft Farm Leisure & Water Park. Bredons Hardwick. Lake and river fishing, camping, windsurfing tuition, and supervised health centre (Gym & Tonic). Cafe. Open daily Mar-Dec. (H10) 01684 772321 www.croftfarmleisure.co.uk

Eckington Bridge. Built between the C16 and C17s. A car park beside the river with a map board detailing a circular walk. (H7)

WHERE TO EAT, DRINK & BE MERRY...

Yew Tree Inn, Conderton. One of the most popular local pubs around Bredon Hill. Conveniently situated for pre- or post-walk, refreshments. Basic pub grub. (L9) 01386 725364 www.yewtreepub.com

Upper Court, Kemerton. Self-catering within a very grand house. Minimum stay for 2 nights. 01386 725351 www.uppercourt.co.uk

Lion Statue, Upton-Upon-Severn

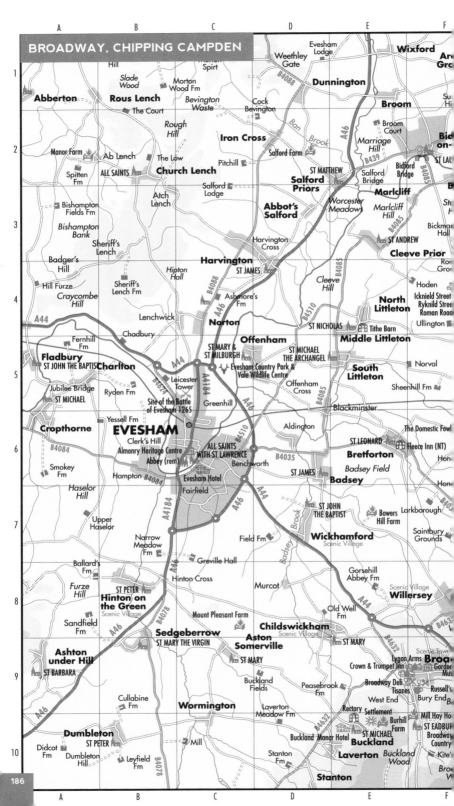

A B C D E F

1

Hill
Slade Wood
Morton Wood Fm
French Spirt
Weethley Gate
Evesham Lodge
Dunnington
B4088
Wixford
Are Gro

Abberton
Rous Lench
The Court
Bevington Waste
Cock Bevington
Broom
Broom Court
Su Hi

2

Manor Farm
Spitten Fm
Ab Lench
ALL SAINTS
Rough Hill
The Low
Church Lench
Pitchill
Iron Cross
Ban
Brook
Salford Farm
ST MATTHEW
Salford Priors
Marriage Hill
B4088
B439
Salford Bridge
Bidford Bridge
Bidon-
ST LAL
Bid on-

3

Bishampton Fields Fm
Bishampton Bank
Badger's Hill
Hill Furze
Craycombe Hill
Sheriff's Lench
Sheriff's Lench Fm
Atch Lench
Hipton Hall
Salford Lodge
Abbot's Salford
Harvington Cross
Worcester Meadows
Marlcliff
Marlcliff Hill
B4085
ST ANDREW
Cleeve Prior
Ro Gro
Bickman Hall
Ste

4

A44
Lenchwick
Chadbury
Harvington
ST JAMES
B4088
Ashmore's Fm
A46
Norton
Cleeve Hill
B4085
B510
ST NICHOLAS
Tithe Barn
North Littleton
Middle Littleton
Hoden
Icknield Street
Ryknild Stree
Roman Roai
Ullington
Norval

5

Fernhill Fm
Fladbury
ST JOHN THE BAPTIS
Charlton
Jubilee Bridge
ST MICHAEL
Ryden Fm
Leicester Tower
Site of the Battle of Evesham 1265
B4077
A4184
ST MARY & ST MILBURGH
Evesham Country Park & Vale Wildlife Centre
Greenhill
A46
Offenham
ST MICHAEL THE ARCHANGEL
Offenham Cross
B4085
South Littleton
Sheenhill Fm
The Domestic Fowl

6

Cropthorne
B4084
Smokey Fm
Yessell Fm
EVESHAM
Clerk's Hill
Almonry Heritage Centre
Abbey (rem)
Hampton
B4084
ALL SAINTS WITH ST LAWRENCE
Benchworth
Aldington
ST JAMES
B4035
Badsey Field
ST LEONARD
Bretforton
Badsey
Fleece Inn (NT)
Hon
Hon

7

Haselor Hill
Upper Haselor
Evesham Hotel
Fairfield
A4184
Narrow Meadow Fm
A46
A44
Field Fm
Badsey
Brook
ST JOHN THE BAPTIST
Wickhamford
Scenic Village
Bowers Hill Farm
Larkborough
Saintbury Grounds
B40

8

Ballard's Fm
Furze Hill
Sandfield Fm
A46
ST PETER
Hinton on the Green
Scenic Village
B4078
Greville Hall
Hinton Cross
Murcot
Mount Pleasant Farm
Childswickham
Scenic Village
Old Well Fm
Gorsehill Abbey Fm
A44
Scenic Village
Willersey

9

A46
Ashton under Hill
ST BARBARA
A46
Sedgeberrow
ST MARY THE VIRGIN
Aston Somerville
ST MARY
ST MARY
Buckland Fields
Peasebrook Fm
ST MARY
Rectory
Settlement
West End
B4632
Lygon Arms
Crown & Trumpet Inn
Broadway Deli
Tisanes
Broa
Gordo
Mus
Russell's
Bury End

10

Didcot Fm
Dumbleton
ST PETER
Dumbleton Hill
Cullabine Fm
Leyfield Fm
B4078
Mill
Wormington
B4078
Laverton Meadow Fm
Buckland Manor Hotel
Stanton Fm
ST MICHAEL
Buckland
Laverton
Buckland Wood
Burhill Farm
Mill Hay Ho
ST EADBUF
Broadway
Country
Kite's
Bro
V

Stanton

A B C D E F

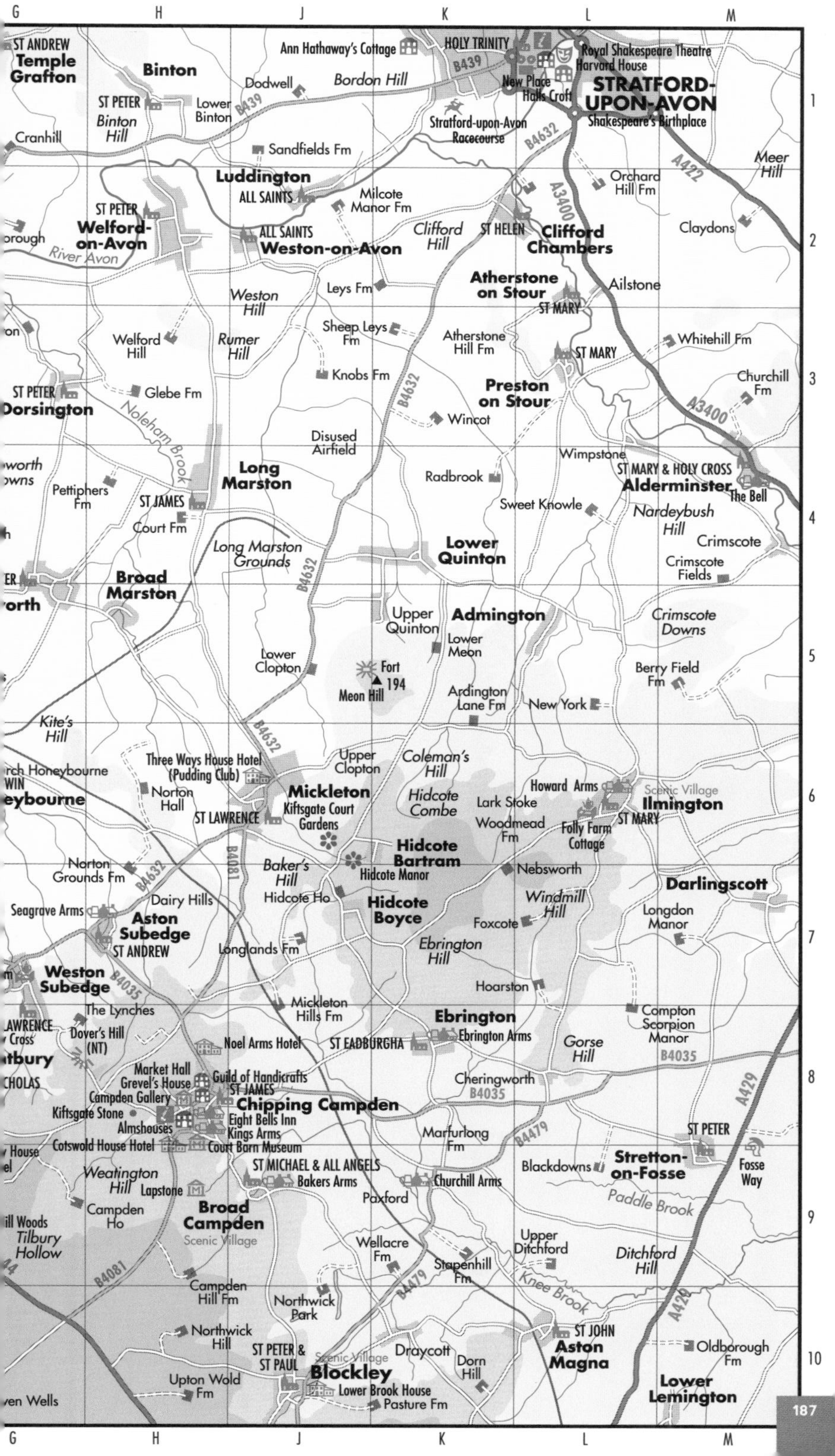
G
H
J
K
L
M
ST ANDREW
Temple Grafton
Binton
Ann Hathaway's Cottage
HOLY TRINITY
Royal Shakespeare Theatre
Harvard House
B439
New Place
Halls Croft
STRATFORD-UPON-AVON
Shakespeare's Birthplace
Dodwell
Bordon Hill
ST PETER
Lower Binton
Binton Hill
Cranhill
Sandfields Fm
Stratford-upon-Avon Racecourse
B4632
A422
Meer Hill
Luddington
ALL SAINTS
Milcote Manor Fm
Orchard Hill Fm
A3400
Welford-on-Avon
River Avon
ALL SAINTS
Weston-on-Avon
Clifford Hill
ST HELEN
Clifford Chambers
Claydons
Leys Fm
Atherstone on Stour
ST MARY
Ailstone
Weston Hill
Sheep Leys Fm
Welford Hill
Rumer Hill
Atherstone Hill Fm
ST MARY
Whitehill Fm
Knobs Fm
Preston on Stour
Churchill Fm
ST PETER
Dorsington
Glebe Fm
Noleham Brook
Wincot
Disused Airfield
Wimpstone
ST MARY & HOLY CROSS
Long Marston
Radbrook
Alderminster
The Bell
Pettiphers Fm
ST JAMES
Sweet Knowle
Nardeybush Hill
Court Fm
Long Marston Grounds
Lower Quinton
Crimscote
Crimscote Fields
Broad Marston
Upper Quinton
Admington
Crimscote Downs
Lower Meon
Lower Clopton
Fort
194
Meon Hill
Berry Field Fm
Ardington Lane Fm
New York
Kite's Hill
B4632
Upper Clopton
Coleman's Hill
Three Ways House Hotel (Pudding Club)
Mickleton
Howard Arms
Scenic Village
Norton Hall
Hidcote Combe
Lark Stoke
Ilmington
ST LAWRENCE
Kiftsgate Court Gardens
Woodmead Fm
Folly Farm Cottage
ST MARY
B4081
Hidcote Bartram
Norton Grounds Fm
Baker's Hill
Hidcote Manor
Nebsworth
Darlingscott
Dairy Hills
Hidcote Ho
Hidcote Boyce
Windmill Hill
Seagrave Arms
Aston Subedge
Longdon Manor
Foxcote
ST ANDREW
Longlands Fm
Ebrington Hill
Weston Subedge
B4035
Hoarston
The Lynches
Mickleton Hills Fm
Ebrington
Compton Scorpion Manor
Dover's Hill (NT)
Ebrington Arms
Gorse Hill
Noel Arms Hotel
ST EADBURGHA
B4035
Market Hall
Grevel's House
Guild of Handicrafts
Cheringworth
ST JAMES
B4035
A429
Campden Gallery
Chipping Campden
Kiftsgate Stone
Eight Bells Inn
Almshouses
Kings Arms
Marfurlong Fm
B4479
ST PETER
Cotswold House Hotel
Court Barn Museum
ST MICHAEL & ALL ANGELS
Blackdowns
Stretton-on-Fosse
Fosse Way
Weatington Hill
Bakers Arms
Churchill Arms
Lapstone
Paxford
Paddle Brook
Broad Campden
Campden Ho
Scenic Village
Tilbury Hollow
Wellacre Fm
Upper Ditchford
Stapenhill Fm
Ditchford Hill
B4081
Campden Hill Fm
B4479
Knee Brook
Northwick Park
A429
Northwick Hill
ST JOHN
ST PETER & ST PAUL
Scenic Village
Draycott
Aston Magna
Oldborough Fm
Dorn Hill
Blockley
Upton Wold Fm
Lower Brook House
Lower Lemington
Pasture Fm
1
2
3
4
5
6
7
8
9
10
G
H
J
K
L
M

Row of Cottages, Broadway

High Street, Broadway

St Eadburgh's Churchyard, Broadway

BROADWAY

'The Painted Lady of the Cotswolds' is a term often used to describe this beautiful village. The honey-coloured stone captivates the visitor today, as it did in the C19, when William Morris and his pre-Raphaelite friends settled here. A slow walk up the High Street will unfold some large, and impressive houses, former homes to Edward Elgar, JM Barrie (Peter Pan), Ralph Vaughan Williams, Sir Gerald Navarro MP and Laura Ashley. These great houses with bow windows, dormers and finely graduated stone roofs are usually hidden behind statuesque gates. There are a number of fine hotels, restaurants, tearooms, art galleries and a splendid bookshop. (F9)

SPECIAL PLACES OF INTEREST...

Ashmolean Museum, 65 High Street. Exhibits on display over 3-floors include decorative art from the C17-C21; paintings by Gainsborough and Millais, Armorial ceramics, and Sheldon tapestries. Much was donated to the University of Oxford in 1683, by Elias Ashmore. Open Tu-Su 10-5 (F9) 01386 859047 www.ashmolean.org

Broadway Tower Country Park. A unique Cotswold attraction: an C18 folly tower with historical and geographical

exhibitions. Country retreat of the pre-Raphaelite, William Morris. Breeders of red deer with adventure playground, nature walks and Morris & Brown Cafe with quality giftshop. Superb views from the top of the Tower - a clear day gives a view of 12 counties. Nuclear Bunker. Open daily all year, the Cafe from 9-5, Tower 10-5, NB 10-4.45 at W/Es & BHs. (F10) 01386 852390 www.broadwaytower.co.uk

Buckland Church, St Michaels. An exquisite church preserved with an almost undisturbed history from the C13 to the C17. Beautiful roof: painted and wood panelled. C14 tower with gargoyles. C15 stained glass in East window restored by William Morris. Not to be missed, the Wainscotting: medieval wooden benches along the far wall as you enter. The Hazel Bowl made in 1607 of Dutch maple with a silver rim. The Buckland Pall, C15 embroidered vestments from the V&A, London. Sadly, the medieval frescoes were removed by the restorer FS Waller in 1885. (E10)

Buckland Rectory. The oldest, and most complete rectory in the county. Notable Great Hall with timbered roof. Open occasionally for village events. (E10)

Fish Hill Woods. Attractive woodland providing superb views. (G9)

Gordon Russell Museum, 15 Russell Square. A collection spanning 60 years that is dedicated to one of the C20s finest furniture designers. With original design drawings and furniture embracing the 'Arts & Crafts' movement. Open Tu-Su 11-5 & BH Ms. (F9) 01386 854695 www.gordonrussellmuseum.org

Richard Hagen Gallery, Stable Lodge. One of the Cotswold's finest galleries, and after 40-years in the business Richard specialises in contemporary artists; Stephen Mangan, Jean B Martin, Linda Styles, Linda Smith, Emma S Davis. Many awash with bright colours. Open daily, except W & Su, 10-1, 2-5. (F9) 01386 853624 www.richardhagen.com

St Eadburgh's Church. A rare architectural gem of almost perfect proportions with a mix of C12-C18 additions. Superb brass work, topiary in churchyard, interesting tombstones and a welcome retreat from the hustle and bustle of Broadway. (F10)

Trinity House, 20 High Street. Modern British Paintings are their speciality; Dame Laura Knight, Donald McIntyre, Edward Seago, amongst others. All from £2,000. Open daily. (F9) 01386 859329 www.trinityhousepainting.com

Broadway Tower Walk, Broadway

Buckland Manor ss

Oak Suite, Foxhill Manor ss

Mill Hay ss

LIGHT BITES...

On entering **Broadway** from the south along the **Cotswold Way**, and you will spy the **Crown & Trumpet Inn**. A necessary pit stop after a hard slog across the hills. You may be persuaded to stay for the monthly jazz and blues nights. (F9) 01386 853202. Then onwards to **The Green**, opposite the **Broadway Hotel** on the RH pavement there is **Tisanes, 21 The Green**. A friendly tea room set in a C17 Cotswold stone building full of charm. Homemade cakes. (F9) 01386 853296 Further up the High Street on your R, **Broadway Deli at No.16**. You can't miss it, with fruits and veg outside, and once inside you will salivate at the mouth-watering cakes, pastries and pies. Open for breakfast at 8-11.30, lunch 12-4.30. (F9) 01386 www.broadwaydeli.co.uk Further up the Street, **Market Pie**, for an alternate choice. If you seek a yearning for the grape, then turn down **Kennel Lane** for a glass, or two, of Champagne, Chardonnay, Pinot Noir at the **Broadway Wine Co**. Open M-Sa 10-5 where you can sit outside and smoke a cheroot. Further up the **High Street**, beyond **Landmark** is the **Hunters Restaurant and Tearoom** for a more conventional repast. If you like Pizza, then cross the road to **Prego**. But, if you demand a grand location for afternoon tea, try the **Lygon Arms**, 2- 5pm, where you can soak up some history, and wonder what happened to all their earlier, fine furniture?

WHERE TO STAY...

Barn House, High Street. Fabulous gardens surround large barn conversion. Chintz and pine bedrooms. Indoor pool. (F9) 01386 854858

Buckland Manor Hotel. The benchmark for the Country House Hotel: quiet, understated luxury, set within a 10-acre garden of sweeping lawns amidst stunning countryside. A lovely, modest-minded contrast to the ephemeral boutique hotel; oak-panelled walls, oil paintings, porcelain, antiques and traditional fireplaces with roaring log fires, and discreet staff on hand. There's a formal dress code for dinner - the exquisite cuisine deserves your respect. Displays of flowers in abundance. Open all year. (E10) 01386 852626 www.bucklandmanor.co.uk

Burhill Farm, Buckland. Peaceful setting. Two en-suite bedrooms. 01386 858171 www.burhillfarm.co.uk

Dormy House Hotel & Spa, Willersey Hill. C17 farmhouse converted into a comfortable hotel with a multitude of leisure facilities. Adjacent, an 18-hole golf course. Popular dining room and barn owl bar. (G9) 01386 852711 www.dormyhouse.co.uk

Foxhill Manor. The old, (traditional architecture) meets the new, (bespoke baths, and beds) in a titanic clash that will seduce all those seeking a hedonistic break. Your very own private Cotswold retreat. Only 8-luxurious rooms. Butler service. 01386 852711 www.foxhillmanor.com And, down a swirling drive you come to **The Fish**, an exclusive, up-market style of centre-parc. www.thefishhotel.co.uk. All part of the Farncombe Estate, previously known as Group 4 who used to run HM Prisons.

Luggers Hall, Springfield Lane. Built by the Victorian Royal Academy artist Alfred Parsons, this listed building is set in two acres of landscaped gardens. Peaceful and tranquil setting, yet less than two minutes walk from Broadway Village centre. B&B. (F9) 01386 852040 www.luggershall.com

Lygon Arms. This former coaching inn of renown, has recently been re-branded into a luxurious Spa, and Country House Hotel. The centrepiece is the Great Hall with imposing barrel-vaulted ceiling, C17 Minstrel's Gallery, suits of armour and oak panels, and off the hall are cosy lounges with log fires and deep armchairs. Many additional, contemporary rooms, but when you book ask for a 'traditional' bedroom. (F9) 01386 852255 www.lygonarmshotel.co.uk

Mill Hay House. Imposing Queen Anne house provides luxurious B&B on the outskirts of Broadway. No children U-12. No dogs. (F9) 01386 852498 www.millhay.co.uk

Mount Pleasant Farm, Childswickham. 900 acre mixed family farm in a quiet rural area with stunning views from all of the en-suite bedrooms. Traditional farmhouse English breakfast. B&B and holiday cottages. 01386 853424 mountpleasantfarmbroadway.co.uk

Russell's, 20 High Street. This has gained quite a reputation, as a great place to eat in the North Cotswolds. So, feast on their food, then settle into one of their contemporary, comfy bedrooms with all the latest mod cons, and indulge yourselves. (F9) 01386 853555 www.russellsofbroadway.co.uk Fish and chip shop, behind.

Seated Figure by Joan Gillespie, Richard Hagen Gallery, Broadway ss

CHIPPING CAMPDEN

If you choose to visit just one Cotswold village, make sure it's this one. There is no better introduction. The harmony of Cotswold stone mirrors the town's prosperity in the Middle Ages. The Gabled Market Hall was built in 1627 by the wealthy landowner Sir Baptist Hicks, whose mansion was burnt down in the Civil War, and the remains are the two lodges beside the Church. The Church of St James is a tall and statuesque 'Wool' church. William Grevel, one of the wealthiest wool merchants, is remembered in the church on a brass transcription which reads: 'the flower of the wool merchants of all England.' Opposite his house (Grevel's House) on the High Street, the Woolstaplers Hall, the meeting place for the fleece (staple) merchants. The Dovers Cotswold Olympick Games & Scuttlebrook Wake is held in June. (H8)

SPECIAL PLACES OF INTEREST...

Almshouses. You will pass these on your left as you make your way toward the parish church. Built about the same time as the Market Hall (in 1627) by the town's wealthy benefactor, Sir Baptist Hicks. (H8)

Campden Gallery, High Street. One of the most respected of Cotswold galleries has constant changing exhibitions of paintings, sculpture and prints. Open daily. (H8) 01386 841555 www.campdengallery.co.uk

Court Barn Museum. A celebration of the town's association with the Arts & Crafts Movement. An exhibition of silver, jewellery ceramics,

Almshouses, Chipping Campden

sculpture, industrial design and more, all beautifully set up by the Guild of Handicraft Trust. Open Apr to Sept Tu-Sa 10.30-5.30, Su 11.30-5.30, Oct to Mar Tu-Sa 11-4, Su 11.30-4. (H8) 01386 841951 www.courtbarn.org.uk

Cotswold Way. A long distance footpath covering 97 miles from Chipping Campden to Bath. It follows the edge of the escarpment, meanders through picturesque villages, past pre-historic sites and provides spectacular views. It is signposted. For short excursions set out from Cleeve Hill, Winchcombe, Broadway, Painswick, Coaley Peak or Brackenbury Ditches. (H8) www.cotswold-way.co.uk

Dover's Hill. A natural amphitheatre on a spur of the Cotswolds with magnificent views over the Vale of Evesham. The 'Olympick Games & Scuttlebrook Wake' have been held here since 1612, and take place on the Friday and Saturday, following the Spring Bank Holiday. (G8)

Grevel's House. Built by the wealthy wool merchant, William Grevel: 'The flower of the Wool Merchants of England.' The house has intricately decorated windows, gargoyles and a sundial. (H8)

Guild of Handicraft and The Gallery @ The Guild - The Old Silk Mill. Founded in 1888 as part of the 'Arts & Crafts' movement. The Harts gold and silversmith workshops (open Tu-Su) remain in situ and the Gallery @ The Guild is a co-operative of artists and craftspeople. Open daily, all year. Coffee shop. (H8) 01386 841100 www.thegalleryattheguild.co.uk

Hidcote Manor Garden (NT). One of the finest gardens of the C20 designed by Major Lawrence Johnston in the 'Arts & Crafts' style. It is made up of garden rooms with rare trees, shrubs, herbaceous borders and 'old' roses. The all-weather court has recently been restored. Barn café, plant sale and restaurant. Open mid-Mar to Oct M Tu W & W/Es, 10-6. (J6) For other (more complex) times phone 01386 438333
www.nationaltrust.org.uk

Kiftsgate Court Garden. Rare shrubs, plants, and an exceptional collection of roses in a magnificent situation. Water Garden. Plants for sale. Tearoom. Open Days. Open Apr-Sept Su, M & W 2-6, May to July Sa-W 12-6. (J6) 01386 438777
www.kiftsgate.co.uk

Lapstone, Westington Hill. A different shopping experience for the design conscious. Shop, café, hairdresser and beauty salon, in a contemporary barn conversion, set in the middle of a Cotswold field. (H9) 01386 841611.
www.lapstone.net

Market Hall. This iconic image of Chipping Campden was funded by Sir Baptist Hicks (merchant banker) in 1627, for the sale of cheese and butter. It is Jacobean, with pointed gables. (H8)

Meon Hill. Iron-age hillfort. The locals keep well away from this spot for fear of the spookery of witchcraft. (J5)

Parish Church of St James. A fine old 'Wool' church, of Norman origin, restored in the C15, with a tall and elegant tower, and a large Perpendicular nave. The 'Brilliant' gold stone is startling in late summer afternoons. C15 Cope, and a unique pair of C15 Altar Hangings. Brasses of Woolstaplers. C15 Falcon Lecturn. Open daily. (H8)

WHERE TO STAY EAT, DRINK & BE MERRY...

Bakers Arms, Broad Campden. Good old-fashioned, traditional Cotswold pub with no jarring modernities serving fine ales. (J9) 01386 840515
www.bakersarmscampden.co.uk

Cotswold House Hotel & Spa, The Square. Bespoke luxury, blissful comfort and informality, on hand for your every need. Two restaurants; Juliana's (formal) and Hicks' Brasserie, innovative and deliciously sublime. Two bars. Spa with 6-treatment rooms, hydrotherapy pool and aromatic steam room. (H8) 01386 840330
www.cotswoldhouse.com

Eight Bells Inn. Church Street. C14 inn, full of rustic charm, contrasts well with the modern cuisine and bright bedrooms. Fresh fare. B&B. (H8) 01386 840371
www.eightbellsinn.co.uk

Kings Arms, The Square. Handsome Cotswold hotel and brasserie with spacious interior. Drop in for their delicious breakfast, as I did pre-walk. Chic bedrooms. French-ambience to decor. B&B. (H8) 01386 840256
www.kingscampden.co.uk

Noel Arms Hotel, High Street. A C16 coaching inn that has been transformed into a luxurious contemporary hotel:

Parish Church of St James, Chipping Campden

it's all log fires, four-posters and fine ales. Event Nights; curry, mexican, beer…to keep you wanting more. (H8)
01386 840317
www.noelarmshotel.com

Volunteer. Named The Volunteer in the mid 1800's because local men used to visit to 'sign on' for   the volunteer armies: the Volunteer is now a popular local pub not least because of the excellent curries available from the kitchen. B&B. (H8) 01386 840688
www.thevolunteerinn.net

WHERE TO STAY EAT, DRINK & BE MERRY… NEAR CHIPPING CAMPDEN…

Bowers Hill Farm. Large Victorian farmhouse on a remote mixed working farm. What your hosts don't know about the local history of the area, isn't worth knowing. Sit in their 40' conservatory, and soak in the atmosphere. Double and twin rooms. (E7) 01386 834585
www.bowershillfarm.com

Churchill Arms, Paxford. Nick Deverell-Smith has transformed, brought new life and expertise, into this ancient C17 hostelry. Great british food, and a full panoply of pub characteristics; log fires, flagstone floors and local ales plus cosy, boutique bedrooms on hand. (K9) 01386 593159
www.churchillarms.co

Ebrington Arms, Ebrington. An C17 traditional inn full of charm, character and popular as a community pub with both locals, and visitors to the area. Luxurious, old-pine bedrooms. English breakfasts. Dogs welcome. Garden. Closed M except BH Ms. (K8)
01386 593223
www.theebringtonarms.co.uk

Folly Farm Cottage, Back Street. No stone is unturned, in order to make your visit a happy, and comfortable one. Set in golden stone village. No dogs. (H8) 01386 682425
www.follyfarm.co.uk

Howard Arms, Ilmington. Fine selection of local beers. Pubby atmosphere serving interesting food. Dining Room. B&B. (L6) 01608 682226
www.howardarms.com

Manor Farm, Weston Subedge. Beautifully restored, and renovated traditional oak-beamed farmhouse built in 1624, and set within an 800-acre working farm with pedigree Charolais cattle, and sheep. Bedrooms with power-showers. Also self-catering cottage. (G7) 01386 840390
www.manorfarmbnb.demon.co.uk

Seagrave Arms, Weston Subedge. An other hostelry with style, comfort and great-value food that will tempt you back, time and again. On hand 8-luxurious bedrooms to indulge oneself. Added to which, they have Wild Food Breaks, Bloody Mary Sundays, Monday Pie Nights, and more.
01386 840192
www.seagravearms.com

Three Ways House Hotel, Mickleton. Home of the Pudding Club since 1985. Walking tours arranged (to burn off the calories!). Special themed 'Pudding Club' bedrooms. (J6)
01386 438429
www.puddingclub.com

Chipping Campden

William Grevel's House, Chipping Campden

EVESHAM

An attractive market town with tree-planted walks and lawns beside the River Avon. Centre for the Vale of Evesham's fruit growing industries. Abbey remains. Simon de Montfort, who fell at the Battle of Evesham in 1265, is buried in the churchyard. (B6)

Almony Heritage Centre. Displays of the Romano-British, Anglo-Saxon, medieval and monastic remains, in an exquisite C14 timber-framed building. TIC. Open daily 10-5 M-Sa except W, Su 2-5 (Mar-Oct). (C6) 01386 446944 www.almonryevesham.org

The Valley, Evesham Country Park & Vale Wildlife Hospital. Wildlife rescue centre supporting animal welfare. Set in country park that has shopping outlet stores, fishing, light railway, walks, carrot cake café and garden centre. Open daily from 10.30. (C5) 01386 882288 www.vwr.org.uk www.thevalleyshopping.co.uk

Domestic Fowl Trust. A collection of rare and minority breeds; hens (for sale), turkeys, ducks, geese and farm animals in grass paddocks. Visitor Centre. Playground. Teas.

Open daily except Tu 10.30-4 (3 at W/Es). (F6) 01386 833083 www.domesticfowltrust.co.uk

Middle Littleton Tithe Barn (NT). This C13 barn is considered one of the finest in the country with ten bays and 130 feet long. Open daily Apr to Oct 2-5. (E4) 01905 371006 www.nationaltrust.org.uk

WHERE TO STAY, EAT, DRINK & BE MERRY...

Evesham Hotel, Cooper's Lane. The child-friendly (of all ages) hotel, and a wee-bit old-fashioned that endears itself to many, for the service is supplied with great humour, and dedicated professionalism. Local produce from the Vale to succour your appetites. If your companions disappear to the loo for hours, fear not, for it is unlikely to be their digestion. More so, the WCs are a hilarious museum of comic bric-a-brac, and the ultimate, in lavatory humour. (C6) 01386 765566 www.eveshamhotel.com

Fleece Inn, Bretforton. A half-timbered medieval farmhouse that became an inn in 1848. Fine collection of pewter. Morris dancing, and folk music are regular events.

Almony Museum, Evesham

Pretty garden. Fine ales and menus using local produce. B&B. (E6) 01386 831173 www.thefleeceinn.co.uk

Manor Farm House B&B, Ab Lench. A luxurious but homely B&B tucked away in a beautiful garden and packed with original features as well as treasures from far flung places. (B2) 01386 462226 www.wolseylodges.com

Salford Farm House, Salford Priors. A quintessentially English B&B. The owner has a fruit farm and farm shop nearby, and guests dine well on its produce, as well as that of other local farmers. (E2) 01386 870000 www.salfordfarmhouse.co.uk

Evesham Abbey

Holy Trinity Church, Stratford Upon Avon

Narrow Boats, Stratford Upon Avon

Holy Trinity Church, Stratford Upon Avon

STRATFORD UPON AVON

The birthplace of William Shakespeare, home to the Royal Shakespeare Company and one of the great tourist destinations in England. The town was established as a Romano-British settlement beside the river crossing on the busy Exeter to Lincoln route. In 1086 during the Domesday survey Stratford was a manor house belonging to Wulstan, Bishop of Worcester. In 1196 Richard I granted permission for a weekly market thereby establishing Stratford's early days as a market town. This instigated the annual Mop Fair on October 12 where local labourers sought employment. The tradesman's society, the Guild of the Holy Cross, was later formed to promote the crafts and local industries. During Shakespeare's time Stratford was home to 1,500 persons and was a bustling centre for the marketing of corn, malt and livestock, as well as being a centre for local government, and proud to foster one of the country's finest grammar schools. The town's buildings were predominantly Elizabethan and Jacobean. Today, there are C15 half-timbered buildings on Church Street, and C16 to C17 timber-framed houses in Chapel Street, the High Street and Wood Street plus a number of C18 period buildings of re-frontings with brick and stucco. It is not strictly a Cotswold town, but is included as it lies on the edge of the map, and is worthy of a day's visit from Broadway, or Chipping Campden. (L1)

SPECIAL PLACES TO VISIT...

Brass Rubbing Centre, Avon Bank Gardens. Learn how to make brass rubbings using some of the best national and local brasses. All materials and instruction included in the price. Open daily summer 10-6, winter 11-4. (L1) 01789 297671 www.stratfordbrassrubbing.co.uk

Butterfly Farm & Jungle Safari, Tramway Walk. Europe's largest butterfly farm where you can wander through a jungle of exotic plants, fish filled pools, and waterfalls amid hundreds of tropical butterflies. (L1) 01789 299288 www.butterflyfarm.co.uk

Clopton Bridge. Built in late C15 by Sir Hugh Clopton who became the Lord Mayor of London, and who died circa 1496. (L1)

Falstaff's Experience, 40 Sheep Street. A waxworks museum recreates Stratford's darkest hours. Ghost tours from 6pm. Open daily 10.30-5.30. 01879 298070 (L1) www.falstaffsexperience.co.uk

Gower Memorial (Shakespeare Statue). This was presented to the town in 1888 by Lord Gower. The statue is made up of figures depicting Hamlet, Lady Macbeth, Falstaff and Prince Hal, which in turn, symbolizes philosophy, tragedy, comedy and history. (L1)

Guild Buildings. Guild Chapel, Guildhall, Grammar School and Almshouses, Chapel Street. (L1)

Holy Trinity Church, Southern Lane. The burial place of William Shakespeare, and his family, and a magnificent building, too. Note the Clopton Chapel, C15 vestry screen, C15 misericords, C15 font, The Bible c. 1611, the stained glass windows and the Chapel of Thomas a Becket. Open daily. (L1) 01789 266316 www.shakespeareschurch.org

Mason's Court, Rother Street. A beautifully preserved C15 domestic building of red brick and timber-framing. Views of exterior only. (L1)

Mason Croft, Church Street. C18 property of the Shakespeare Institute of Birmingham University. The home, until 1921, of Marie Corelli, the Victorian novelist. Open for academic studies. (L1) 01789 293127

Open Top Bus tours. Travel to 14 stops including all the Shakespeare landmarks. Tickets are valid for 24 hours and passengers can hop on and off. Main departure point outside the TIC. (L1) 01789 412680

Royal Shakespeare Theatre, Waterside. The home of the Royal Shakespeare Company, was built in 1932 to Elizabeth Smith's design, following the fire of 1926, and then fully renovated in 2010, known as the Transformation Project, into a 1,040 +seat thrust stage, Rooftop Restaurant & Bar, Riverside Cafe and Observation Tower. Officially opened on 4th March, 2011 by HM Queen Elizabeth 11. Its dedicated to the works of the poet and playwright, William Shakespeare. (L1) 01789 403493 Box Office. www.rsc.org.uk

Shakespearience, The Waterside. A hi-tech show full of special effects and the latest developments in show technology takes you through the life and legacy of WS. Open daily (except Christmas). Shows on the hour from 10. (L1) 01789 290111 www.shakespearience.co.uk

Town Hall, Sheep Street. Originally built in the reign of Charles I and throughout its chequered history has seen calamitous events including being extensively damaged from a gunpowder explosion in 1643. (L1)

LIGHT BITES...

Sheep Street has the best restaurants in town: **Lambs, The Vintner** (also teas and coffees) and **The Opposition.** Just around the corner, **The Shakespeare Hotel** where you can have morning coffee and afternoon teas in the hotel or next door at **Othello's Bar Brasserie**, or perhaps stay the night. Down by the Waterside is **Carluccio's**, an ideal spot for coffee and sandwiches, and people watching. Most, or all, eating places cater for pre-theatre suppers. (L1)

Mary Arden's House, Wilmcote, Stratford Upon Avon

Shakespeare's Birthplace, Stratford Upon Avon

The Garrick Inn, Stratford Upon Avon

IVDICIO PYLIVM GENIO SOCRATEM ARTE MARONEM,
TERRA TEGIT, POPVLVS MÆRET, OLYMPVS HABET

STAY PASSENGER, WHY GOEST THOV BY SO FAST,
READ IF THOV CANST, WHOM ENVIOVS DEATH HATH PLAST
WITH IN THIS MONVMENT SHAKSPEARE: WITH WHOME,
QVICK NATVRE DIDE WHOSE NAME, DOTH DECK Y TOMBE,
FAR MORE, THEN COST: SIEH ALL, Y HE HATH WRITT,
LEAVES LIVING ART, BVT PAGE, TO SERVE HIS WITT.
OBIIT ANO DO 1616
ÆTATIS 53 DIE 23 AP.

WILLIAM SHAKESPEARE

"The Swan of Avon" as Ben Jonson described his friend, was born in Henley Street on 23rd April, 1564. His father, John Shakespeare was the son of a yeoman farmer from nearby Snitterfield who traded as a glover and wool-dealer and who later was to become the town's mayor. His mother, Mary Arden married John Shakespeare in 1557 and was the daughter of a prosperous gentleman- farmer from an old Warwickshire family. Although we know little of William's early life we know that he attended the local Grammar School where he took a close interest in the touring actors who performed in the Guildhall below the Grammar School. In 1582 he married Ann Hathaway, a farmer's daughter from Shottery and six years older than he. Shottery is still today linked to Stratford by a footpath that the courting William must have trod.

One wonders at the success of their marriage for he soon fled to London in 1587 after having been caught poaching Sir Thomas Lucy's deer in Charlecote Park. The more likely reason was to pursue his ambitions in the theatre. In London he joined the Leicester Players, and later, the King's Company which was patronised by the Elizabethan court and men of the Inns of Court. Despite his success in London he retained a close association with Stratford. In 1597 he bought New Place, the finest house in Stratford and took up permanent residence in 1611. He died in 1616 on his 52nd birthday following a merry meeting with his fellow poets Ben Jonson and Michael Drayton. He is buried in Holy Trinity Church beside members of his family. The statue which overlooks his grave was placed there seven years after his death.

QUOTES FROM HIS PLAYS:

"If music be the food of love, play on." **Twelfth Night**

"The course of true love never did run smooth." **A Midsummer Night's Dream**

"She's beautiful, and therefore to be wooed; She is woman, and therefore to be won." **Henry VI Part 1**

"She is spherical, like a globe. I could find countries in her." **The Comedy of Errors**

"Thou Mother took into her bed some stern, untutored churl...whose fruit thou art." **Henry VI, Part 11.**

"More of your conversation would infect my brain." **Coriolanus**

"It is a tale told by an idiot, full of sound and fury, signifying nothing." **Macbeth**

"Better a witty fool, than a foolish wit." **Twelfth Night**

"Nothing in his life Became him like the leaving it." **King Lear**

"Death lies on her, like an untimely frost Upon the sweetest flower of all the field." **Romeo and Juliet**

"Love is blind, and lovers cannot see, The pretty follies that themselves commit." **The Merchant of Venice**

PROPERTIES OF THE SHAKESPEARE BIRTHPLACE TRUST

This Trust was established in 1847, and is probably the oldest conservation society in Britain. Its purpose, to promote the appreciation, and study, of William Shakespeare's plays and prose, to an international audience, and to protect, and care, for the buildings associated with the poet for future generations. You can purchase a ticket that covers all of their properties. 01789 204016 www.shakespeare.org.uk

Anne Hathaway's Cottage, Shottery. This is the picturesque home of Anne before her marriage to WS in 1582. A large 12- room farm house surrounded by a colourful and charming garden of perennial shrubs, box hedges and apple orchard. This cottage belonged to descendants of the Hathaway family until 1892. Open daily 9-4. (K1)

Hall's Croft, Old Town. A fine Tudor house beautifully furnished with a walled garden. It was the home of WS's daughter Susanna and her husband Dr John Hall who in his day was considered an advanced medical practicioner. Open daily 10-5. (L1)

Mary Arden's Farm, Wilmcote. Mary Arden was WS's mother and she lived in this beautiful C16 farmhouse with Jacobean furniture and bygones from a former time. There is a farm museum exhibiting carts, carriages and a 650-hole dovecote. Open daily Mar-Nov. (North of map)

New Place & Nash's House, Chapel Street. Sir Hugh Clopton built New Place in 1483. In 1597 it was bought by WS and was one of the finest and most prestigious houses in Stratford. WS retired here in 1610, and it was where he died on 23rd April 1616 whilst celebrating his 52nd birthday. In 1702 it was almost completely rebuilt but was demolished by the Reverend Francis Gastrell in 1759 following a dispute with the corporation about his rates. The foundations of New Place remain in the garden adjoining Nash's House, formerly the home of Thomas Nash, husband of Elizabeth Hall, who was WS's granddaughter. It remains half-timbered with an ancient interior and is a museum of local history. The Great Garden of New Place has the original orchard and kitchen garden with a mulberry tree raised from a cutting of WS's tree. Adjoining, the Knot Garden, a replica of an enclosed Elizabethan garden with old English flowers and herbs. Open daily. (L1)

Shakespeare's Birthplace, Henley Street. William Shakespeare was born here on 23rd April, 1564. The house was originally divided into two buildings and used as a home and a workshop for his father, a wool-dealer and glove maker. It is half-timbered with strong oak framing, leaded windows and wide sills. The building was restored in the C18 by the Actor- Manager David Garrick. There is a comprehensive collection of Shakespeariana and the garden displays flowers named in his plays and poems: daisies, violets, pansies, lady smocks and mary buds. Open daily. (L1)

Harvard House & Pewter Museum, High Street. Harvard House was built in 1596 by a wealthy townsman, Alderman Thomas Rogers, who had twice served as High Bailiff. His initials are carved on the front of the house (with a bull's head to denote his trade as a butcher) together with those of his wife Alice and his eldest son, William, and the date 1596. The elaborately carved facade, by far the richest example in the town, is testimony to Rogers's wealth and standing. From the mid C17, there was a succession of owners until the Shakespeare Birthplace Trust assumed responsibility for the building and, in 1996, it became the Museum of British Pewter. Open daily. (L1)

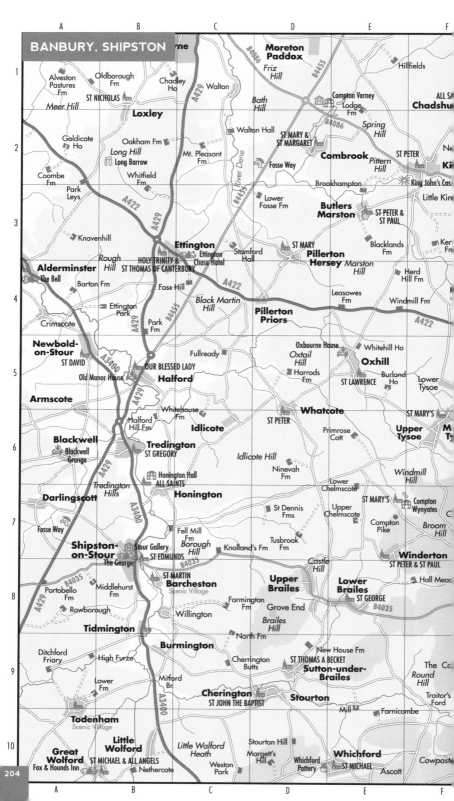

A   B   C   D   E   F

Moreton Paddox

Hillfields

Alveston Pastures Fm
Oldborough Fm
Chadley Ho
Walton
Friz Hill
ST NICHOLAS
Meer Hill
Loxley
Bath Hill
Compton Verney Lodge Fm
Spring Hill
ALL SA
Chadshu

Goldicote Ho
Oakham Fm
Long Hill
Long Barrow
Mt. Pleasant Fm
Walton Hall
ST MARY & ST MARGARET
Combrook Pittern Hill
ST PETER
Ki
Ne

Coombe Fm
Park Leys
Whitfield Fm
Fosse Way
Brookhampton
King John's Cas
Little Kin

Knavenhill
Ettington
Ettington Chase Hotel
Stamford Hall
Lower Fosse Fm
ST MARY
Pillerton Hersey
Butlers Marston
ST PETER & ST PAUL
Blacklands Fm
Ker Fn

Alderminster
The Bell
HOLY TRINITY & ST THOMAS OF CANTERBURY
Rough Hill
Foss Hill
Marston Hill
Herd Hill Fm

Barton Fm
Ettington Park
Black Martin Hill
Pillerton Priors
Leasowes Fm
Windmill Fm

Crimscote
Park Fm
A422

Newbold-on-Stour
ST DAVID
Old Manor House
Fullready
Oxbourne House
Oxtail Hill
Whitehill Ho
Oxhill
Burland Ho
Lower Tysoe

Halford
Harrods Fm
ST LAWRENCE

Armscote

Whitehouse Fm
Idlicote
ST PETER
Whatcote
ST MARY'S
Upper Tysoe
M
Ty

Halford Hill Fm
Blackwell
Blackwell Grange
Tredington
ST GREGORY
Idlicote Hill
Ninevah Fm
Primrose Cott
Windmill Hill

Honington Hall
ALL SAINTS
Honington
Lower Chelmscote
ST MARY'S
Compton Wynyates
C

Darlingscott
Tredington Hills
St Dennis Fms
Upper Chelmscote
Compton Pike
Broom Hill

Fosse Way
Fell Mill Fm
Borough Hill
Knolland's Fm
Tusbrook Fm
Castle Hill
Winderton
ST PETER & ST PAUL

Shipston-on-Stour
Stour Gallery
ST EDMUNDS
The George

Barcheston
Scenic Village
ST MARTIN

Portobello Fm
Middlehurst Fm
Upper Brailes
Lower Brailes
ST GEORGE
Hall Mead

Rawborough
Farmington Fm
Grove End
B4035

Willington
Brailes Hill

Tidmington

Ditchford Friary
High Furze
Burmington
North Fm
New House Fm
The Co
Round Hill

Lower Fm
Mitford Br.
Cherrington Butts
ST THOMAS A BECKET
Sutton-under-Brailes
Traitor's Ford

Cherington
ST JOHN THE BAPTIST
Stourton
Mill
Farnicombe

Todenham
Scenic Village

Little Wolford
Little Walford Heath
Stourton Hill
Margett's Hill

Great Wolford
Fox & Hounds Inn
ST MICHAEL & ALL ANGELS
Nethercote
Weston Park
Whichford Pottery
Whichford
ST MICHAEL
Ascott
Cowpast

A   B   C   D   E   F

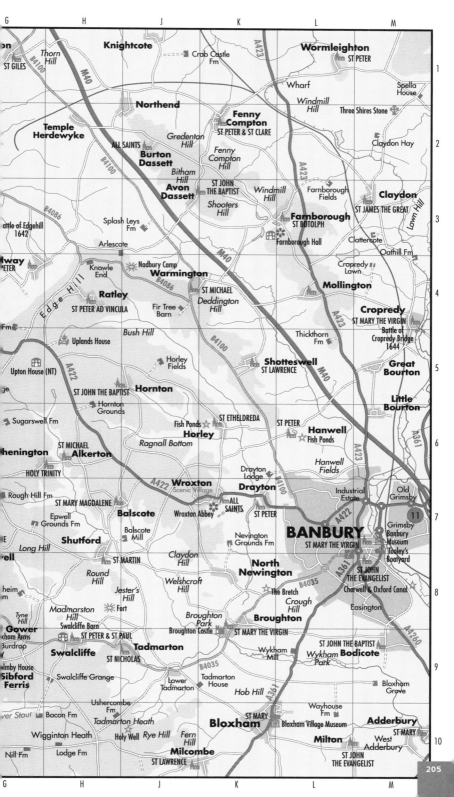

BANBURY

A prosperous commercial and retail centre situated on the northern edge of the Cotswold escarpment. The extension of the M40 in 1991 has provided access to Birmingham, London and Oxford and thus given Banbury infinite opportunities. Since 2005 a massive influx of Polish immigrants has boosted the local economy and the congregation in the Catholic churches. Kraft Foods has the largest coffee processing plant in the world here. Famous for Banbury cakes (similar to Eccles cakes), and the celebrated 'Banbury Cross.' Man has lived here since an Iron Age settlement of 200 BC, a Roman villa at Wykeham Park around 250 AD and a Saxon stronghold in the C5. The Danes developed trade routes and the Salt Way came through Banbury. A focus of Civil War hostilities in the C17 - the first battle took place at Edgehill in 1642. Shortly after Banbury became a centre of Puritanism. From about 1700-1800 cloth making took a hold on the local economy producing shag, then plush. With the expansion of the Oxford Canal in 1790 Banbury again prospered. The Cattle Market was once the largest in Europe but sadly closed in 1998. You can follow a Town Trail around all the historic buildings. (M10)

Ride a cock horse to Banbury Cross,

To see a Fyne lady ride on a white horse.

With rings on her fingers and bells on her toes, She shall have music wherever she goes.

SPECIAL PLACES TO VISIT...

Banbury Museum. The new canal side location features interactive art and historic exhibitions with some fabulous displays of clothes, bicycles, a timeline of events and changing exhibitions. Café Quay. Open daily 9.30-5, Su and BHs 10.30-4.30. (M7) 01295 753752 www.banburymuseum.org

Broughton Castle. Moated medieval manor house, substantially enlarged in the C16. Magnificent plaster ceilings, fine panelling and

Oxford Canal, Banbury

fireplaces. Interesting Civil War connections. In the family of the Lords Saye and Sele for over 600 years. Multi-coloured borders. The location for much of the film, Shakespeare in Love. Open East & BH Ms, then W & Su May to mid-Sept, also Th in July & Aug 2-5. (K9) 01295 276070 www.broughtoncastle.com

Oxford Canal. Built by James Brindley in 1769 to connect the industrial Midlands with London via the River Thames. Financial problems delayed the construction but it was eventually to reach Oxford in 1789. Today, it runs for 77 miles from Hawkesbury Junction, south of Coventry to Oxford. You can enjoy a multitude of leisure activities, from solitary walks to boating, canoeing, cycling, fishing and, the wildlife. (M7) www.waterscape.com

Tooley's Boatyard & Tours, Spiceball Park Road. This is the oldest working dry dock boatyard on the inland waterways of Britain. Established in 1790 to build and repair the wooden horse-drawn narrow boats. 200-year old forge, chandlery and gift shop. Self drive hire and private boat trips. (M7) 01295 272917 www.tooleysboatyard.co.uk

LIGHT BITES...

S H Jones Wine Merchants, 27 High Street. Enjoy a coffee or snack in one of Banbury's oldest buildings, or sample a soupçon of fine wine. Open daily. (M7) 01295 251179 www.shjoneswines.com

Ye Olde Reindeer Inn, Behind Parson Street. Visit this inn for its Civil War associations, and superb C17 panelling, and gate. (M7) 01295 270972 www.ye-olde-reindeer-inn. co.uk

Whately Hall Hotel, Horse Fair. A pragmatic destination for morning coffee, business meetings and lunch. The building is impressive from the exterior, and once inside look to the superb Jacobean staircase. It is an old fashioned hostelry with a long history of ghosts, Regal visits and town functions. Sadly, let down by the modern additions. (M7) 01295 253261 www.mercure.com

SHIPSTON-ON-STOUR

A working town with some attractive Georgian inns and houses amidst some rich pastoral farmland. In the C16, a prosperous weaving centre holding one of the great sheep markets. (B7)

SPECIAL PLACES TO VISIT...

Stour Gallery, 10 High Street. A popular and long running gallery displaying contemporary paintings, studios ceramics and sculpture, all set on three floors. Open M-Sa except Th, 10-5.30 (B7) 01608 664411 www.thestourgallery.co.uk

WHERE TO EAT, DRINK & BE MERRY...

The George, High Street. A handsome building that has been given a contemporary makeover. The downstairs has a pleasing ambience. Upstairs, the 16 bedrooms have been designed with a food theme: chocolate, strawberry, meringue, fig, lobster. You can chose a savoury, a fruit or a dessert. Chocolate is apparently the most digestible. (B7) 01608 661453 www.georgehotelshipston.com

Mrs Baldwin in Eastern Dress, Joshua Reynolds, Compton Verney ss

The Horseshoe Inn, 6 Church Street. This is where the locals go for a pint and some conversation. It is pretty basic. Curry nights and unpretentious pub grub, for those in need of the simple life. (B7) 01608 662190 www.horseshoeshipston.com

The Old Wine House

SPECIAL PLACES OF INTEREST...

Adderbury Church. Early C13 cruciform. C14 West tower with massive carvings. Superb chancel and vestry. (M10)

Bloxham Church. C14 spire. Carvings. C15 wall paintings. East window by William Morris and Edward Burne-Jones. (K10)

Battle of Edgehill site. The battle of Edgehill on Sunday 23rd October, 1642 was the first major battle of the English Civil War. It was fought in the open fields around the villages of Radway and Kineton in Warwickshire between the army of the Earl of Essex, the parliamentarian Lord General, and the King's army. The outcome was deemed indecisive. (G3)

Compton Verney. Art Gallery in C18 Robert Adam mansion set in parkland by 'Capability' Brown. Naples School, British portraits, folk art. Open mid-Mar to mid-Dec Tu-Su & BHs 11-5. (D1) 01926 645500 www.comptonverney.org.uk

Compton Wynyates. A Tudor dream house built 1460 with multi-coloured bricks; pale rose, crimson, blood red, shades of orange and bluish brown. Twisted chimneys. Panelled rooms. Plaster ceilings. Perhaps, the most romantic of all England's country houses. Sadly, no longer open. May be glimpsed through the trees from the nearby road. (F7)

Farnborough Hall (NT). A beautiful honey-coloured stone house sits in parkland crated in the 1740s. Noted for the exquisite C18 plasterwork. Parkland walks and lake views. Open Apr to Sept, W & Sa 2-5.30. (L3) 01295 690002 www.nationaltrust.org.uk

Honington Hall. Small house c.1680 with fine plasterwork. Open W in June, July & Aug (also BH Ms) 2.30-5, and by appointment. (B6) 01608 661434

Swalcliffe Barn. Early C15 tithe barn with fascinating displays of Oxfordshire's agricultural and trade vehicles. Exhibition of 2,500 years of the area. Open East Su to Oct Su & BH Ms 2-5. (H9) 01295 788278

Upton House & Gardens (NT). This house exhibits the lifestyle of a 1930s millionaire. It also has an outstanding display of English and Continental Old Masters paintings plus a wealth of herbaceous borders, terraces and tranquil water gardens. Open most days. See website for details. (G5) 01295 670266 www.nationaltrust.org.uk

Whichford Pottery. Hand-made English terracotta flowerpots of immense size. Thirty craftsmen and women. Shop. Open daily. (E10) 01608 684416 www.whichfordpottery.com

WHERE TO EAT, DRINK & BE MERRY...

The Bell, Alderminster. Former C18 coaching inn now run by the Alscot Estate. It is spacious, comfortable, and serves good, solid food. Perhaps, more restaurant, than inn. (A4) 01789 450414 www.thebellald.co.uk

Wykham Arms, Sibford Gower. Thatched inn set in pretty North Oxford village. The proprietors, Damian and Debbie, are chefs so expect pub food of the highest order. Open for coffee and pastries, lunch and dinner. Sundays are special. (G9) 01295 788808 www.wykhamarms.co.uk

WHERE TO STAY...

Blackwell Grange. C17 Working farm with charming cottage garden. Beams, inglenook fireplaces and flagstones conjure up a relaxing hideaway. Suppers (of local produce). Stabling for horses. Two self-catering cottages. 01608 682357 www.blackwellgrange.co.uk

Ettington Chase Hotel. Flamboyant Victorian Gothic hotel with rococo plasterwork, many leisure activities has recently undergone a massive renovation. Very much aimed at the corporate and wedding markets. Open all year. (C3) 01789 740000 www.ettingtonchasehotel.co.uk

Holmby House, Sibford Ferris. An elegant wisteria-clad Victorian house set in fragrant gardens complete with heated outdoor pool and tennis and croquet equipment for the restless. The en- suite bedrooms are spacious and light. Dinner available if pre-booked. 01295 780104 www.holmbyhouse.com

Old Manor House, Halford. English country house style B&B at its finest. From lounging black Labradors to chintz and marmalade, and family antiques. Anyone for tennis? (B5) 01789 740264 www.oldmanor-halford.co.uk

Oxbourne House, Oxhill. Only 15 minutes from Stratford set on the edge of the village of Oxhill, Oxbourne House is a tranquil oasis. Choose from the comfortable en-suite bedrooms or the self- contained Annexe with bedroom, sitting/dining room, kitchen and shower room. 01295 688202 www.oxbournehouse.com

Uplands House, Upton. The owners of this Country House B&B are former Olympic fencers with interesting stories, aplenty, as well as detailed, rapier-like knowledge to help you plan your break. A comfortable, and welcoming home-from-home. 01295 678663 www.cotswolds-uplands.co.uk

Swalcliffe Tithe Barn

Bather by Joan Gillespie, The Richard Hagen Gallery, Broadway 55

Sarah Dee - Artist in Studio, Brian Sinfield Gallery, Burford.

CALENDAR OF EVENTS

JANUARY

• Gloucester Cajun & Zydeco Festival

• Royal Shakespeare season ends

FEBRUARY

• Snowdrops at Colesbourne Park

• Snowdrops at Rococo Gardens, Painswick

MARCH

• Cheltenham National Hunt Festival

• Chipping Norton Music Festival cnmf.org.uk

• Evesham Spring Regatta

• Lambing, Cotswold Farm Park cotswoldfarmpark.co.uk

• Royal Shakespeare Theatre season begins

• West Country Game Fair, Royal Bath & West Showground

APRIL

• Adderbury Day of (Morris) Dance adderbury.org

• Broadway Spring point-to-point

• Cheltenham International Jazz Festival cheltenhamfestivals.co.uk

• Cirencester Beer Festival

• Evesham Vintage Easter Gathering shalespearerally.com

• Great Blenheim Palace Easter Egg Challenge

• GWR Toddington Spring Diesel Gala

• Nailsworth Festival nailsworthfestival.org.uk

• Highnam Court Spring Fair

• Shakespeare Birthday celebrations, Stratford

• Stratford-Upon-Avon Literary Festival stratfordliteraryfestival.co.uk

MAY

• Badminton Horse Trials badminton-horse.co.uk

• Banbury Beer Festival northoxfordshirecamra.org.uk

• Bath International Music Festival bathmusicfest.org.uk

• Burford Levellers Day levellers.org.uk

• Chipping Campden Music Festival campdenmusicfestival.co.uk

• Coopers Hill Cheese Rolling cheese-rolling.co.uk

• Dover's Olympick Games, Chipping Campden olimpickgames.co.uk

• Gloucester Tall Ships Festival gloucester.gov.uk/tallships

• Kemble Great Vintage Flying Weekend

• Malvern Arts Festival

• Malvern Spring Gardening Show threecounties.co.uk

• Pershore Carnival

• Prescott Hill Classic Car Eventcleevevale.org.uk

• Randwick Cheese Rolling

• South Cerney Street Fair BHM

• Stow Horse Fair

• Tetbury Woolsack Races BHM tetburywoolsack.co.uk

• Tewkesbury Festival of Food & Drink (&Merriment)

• Tortworth Vintage Rally shakespearerally.com

• Upton Folk Festival uptonfolk.org

• Wychwood Music Festival, Cheltenham Racecourse wychwoodfestival.com

JUNE

• Banbury Show banbury.gov.uk

• Bledington Music Festival bledingtonmusicfestival.co.uk

• Bloxham Steam Rally banburysteam.co.uk

• Cheltenham Science Festival cheltenhamfestivals.com/science

• Deddington Festival deddingtonfestival.org.uk

• Gloucester Medieval Fayre

• Kemble Air Day

• Longborough Festival Opera lfo.org.uk

• Pershore Festival of Arts

• Severn Project severnproject.com

• Sudeley Castle Rose Week

• Three Counties Agricultural Show, Malvern

JULY

• Banbury Hobby Horse Festival banbury.org.uk

• Cornbury Music Festival, Charlbury cornburyfestival.com

• Cotswold Show, Cirencester Park

• Fairford Air Tattoo

• Fairport Convention, Cropredy fairportconvention.com

• Gloucester Festival

• Gloucester Rhythm & Blues Festival

• Hook Norton Fetsival of Fine Ales hookybeerfest.co.uk

• Music Deo Sacra, Tewkesbury Abbey

• Music At The Crossroads, Hook Norton hookymusic.co.uk

AUGUST

• Bourton Water Games BH M

• Evesham Flower Show

• Prescott Vintage Hill Climb

• Three Choirs Festival

• Winchcombe Flower Show

SEPTEMBER

• Banbury Cavalcade of Sport

• Battle of Britain Weekend, Kemble Airfield

• Cheltenham Carnival

• Chipping Norton Mop Fair

• Moreton-in-Marsh Show

• Painswick Church clipping & 'Puppy-dog pie' is eaten - 19th

OCTOBER

• Banbury Canal Day

• Cheltenham Literary Festival

• Shipston Medieval Fun Fair

• Stratford Mop Fair

• Tewkesbury Mop Fairt

NOVEMBER

• Bonfire Show, Cheltenham Racecourse

Banbury
Castle Quay Shopping Centre
OX16 0AA
banbury.tic@cherwell-dc.gov.uk
01295 753752

Bath
Abbey Chambers
Abbey Church Yard
BA1 1LY
tourism@bathtourism.co.uk
0844 8475256

Bourton-on-the-Water
Victoria Street
GL54 2BU
info@visitbourton.com
01451 820211

Bradford-on-Avon
The Greenhouse
50 St. Margaret's Street
BA15 1DE
tic@bradfordonavon.co.uk
01225 865797

Broadway
Unit 14 Russell Square
High Street
WR12 7AP
01386 852937

Burford
33A High Street
OX18 4QA
burford.vic@westoxon.gov.uk
01993 823558

Cheltenham
The Wilson
Clarence Street
GL50 3JT
info@cheltenhamtrust.org.uk
01242 237431

Chippenham
Yelde Hall
Market Place
SN15 3HL
tourism@chippenham.gov.uk
01249 665970

Chipping Campden
The Old Police Station
High Street
GL55 6HB
info@campdenonline.org
01386 841206

Cirencester
Corinium Museum
Park Street
GL7 2BX
cirencestervic@slm-ltd.co.uk
01285 654180

Corsham
Arnold House
31 High Street
SN13 0EZ
enquiries@corshamheritage.org.uk
01249 714660

Evesham
The Almonry
Abbey Gate
WR11 4BG
01386 446944

Gloucester
28 Southgate Street
GL1 2DP
tourism@gloucester.gov.uk
01452 396572

Malvern
21 Church Street
WR14 2AA
info@visitthemalverns.org
01684 892289

Moreton-in-Marsh
Moreton Area Centre
High Street
GL56 0AZ
moreton@cotswold.gov.uk
01608 650881

Nailsworth
Old Market
GL6 0DU
01453 839222

Painswick
Grave Digger's Hut
St Mary's Churchyard
GL6 6QA
painswicktourist@gmail.com
01452 812278

Pershore
Town Hall
34 High Street
WR10 1DS
tourism@pershore-tc.gov.uk
01386 556591

Stow-On-The-Wold
St Edwards Hall
The Square
GL54 1AG
stowvic@gloucestershire.gov.uk
01451 870998

Stroud
Subscription Rooms
George Street
GL5 1AE
tic@stroud.gov.uk
01453 760960

Tetbury
33 Church Street
GL8 8JG
tourism@tetbury.org
01666 503552
Seasonal opening

Tewkesbury
Out of the Hat Tewkesbury
Heritage and Visitor Centre
100 Church Street
GL20 5AB
tewkesburytic@tewkesbury.gov.uk
01684 855040 W

Upton Upon Severn
4 High Street
WR8 0HB
upton.tic@malvernhills.gov.uk
01684 594200

Winchcombe
Town Hall
High Street
GL54 5LJ
winchcombetic@tewkesbury.gov.uk
01242 602925
Seasonal opening

Witney
3 Welch Way
OX28 6JH
tourism@westoxon.gov.uk
01993 775802

Woodstock
Oxfordshire Museum
Park Street
OX20 1SN
woodstock.vic@westoxon.gov.uk
01993 813276

Wotton-Under-Edge
The Heritage Centre
The Chipping
GL12 7AD
wuehistsoc@gmail.com
01453 521541

ACKNOWLEDGMENTS

I would like to thank my darling wife, Caroline, for her constant support and encouragement. Thank you, too, to my mother, Margaret, for her hospitality, often at a moments notice, and for her constant support over the years, to Phil Butcher for his design skills and enthusiasm for this project, to my daughters, Izy for her proof reading, and Flora for coming in at the end of the design process to finish off the book given Phil's sudden illness, to Richard Martin for allowing me to print extracts from his essay on the Golden Fleece. And, finally, to Richard Vaughn-Davies, and his entourage of foodies for their feedback. Not to be forgotten, all the kind persons at the many attractions, places to stay and eat, for showing me around their establishments, and for putting up with my endless questions.

And, thank you, to Sebastian Faulks for permitting me to quote your praiseworthy comments on the cover of this book.

Loan of Images:

Goldeneye would like to thank the following for allowing us to photograph their property, or for providing us with an image to illustrate their property. It is now not uncommon for a tourist attraction (e.g. Blenheim Palace) or a charitable organisation (The National Trust) to charge a fee for photographing their property. Goldeneye makes it a policy not to pay a fee given that: a) We are promoting these properties (free of charge), and b) The cumulative expense would make this book an unfeasible production. We would hope that this policy may change, and that a more mutually beneficial outcome may arise. A good number of illustrations used in this book were shot with permission before these organisations had a policy change at head office. Goldeneye would therefore prefer to illustrate a lesser-known property, rather than the expected. Therefore, if you wonder why we have not illustrated the obvious key attraction in a town (a rare occurrence) that is the reason. So, again, thank you:

Abbotswood, Andrew Dawkes Custodian of The Glebe, Barnsley House, Bath Priory Hotel, Beaufort Polo Club, Bennetts Fine Wines, Bibury Trout Farm, Blenheim Palace, Bliss Tweed Mill, Bradford Old Mill, Buckland Manor Hotel, Burford Parish Church, Calcot Manor & Spa, Campden Gallery, Celia Wet Paint Gallery, Cerney House Gardens, Chipping Campden, Parish Church, Colin Carruthers Red Rag Gallery, Compton Verney Trust, Corsham Court, Cotswold Inns, Cotswold Motoring Museum, Cotswold Woollen Weavers, Cowley Manor, Dalton Cotswold Falconry Centre, Daylesford Organic Farm, Dyson, Earl of Wemyss & March Stanway, Fairford Parish Church, Frocester Estate Barn, Gallery Pangolin, Gerald Harris Old Mill Museum, Gloucester Cathedral, Great Tew Estate, Guiting Power Parish Church, Henson, Cotswold Farm Park, Holy Trinity Church, Jack Russell Gallery, Jake Sutton, Jane Bury, Jeremy George of The Glebe, World of Mechanical Music, Kelmscott Manor Trust, Kiftgate Court Gardens, Lords of the Manor Hotel, Lords Saye & Sele Broughton Castle, Lower Slaughter Manor, Mike Finch Winchcombe Pottery, Mill Farm Long Compton, Morgan Motor Company, Bourton House Garden, National Trust Ltd, Nature In Art Museum, New Inn Coln St Aldwyn, No 1 Royal Crescent, No 12 Park Street Cirencester, Owlpen Manor, Oxford Canal Trust, Oxfordshire Museums Trust, Painswick Rococo Garden, Pershore Abbey, Royal Crescent Hotel, Edward Peake of Sezincote, Shakespeare Birthplace Trust, Sudeley Castle, Tewkesbury Abbey, The Old Passage, The Rectory Crudwell, The Wheatsheaf, Westonbirt Arboretum, Wild Garlic, Wildfowl & Wetlands Trust, William Grevel's House, Winchcombe Parish Church.

And, for the 2nd Edition: Ruth Overton at Lucknam Park, Johnny Chambers at Kiftsgate Court, Kardien Gerbrands of Stroud Farmer's Market, Abigail of Museum in the Park,

Milky House, Elena of Frampton Court, Rousham Park Gardens, Amelia Bird of The Wild Rabbit, Nina Lloyd-Jones of Badminton HT, Caroline Lowsley-Williams of Chavenage, Kate Cleaver of the Lucky Onion, Tom of The Sign Of the Angel Lacock, The Long Room Winchcombe, Tof Milway Conderton Pottery, Beckford Silk, Foxhill Manor, Mill Hay, Holy Trinity Church, The Swan at Southrop, Richard Hagen Gallery Brian Sinfield Gallery.

Bounce Wake, Burton Hill

INDEX

INDEX

Winchcombe Pottery

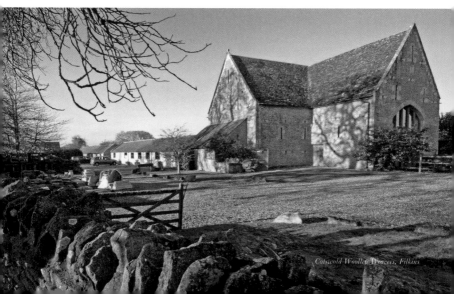

Cotswold Woollen Weavers, Filkins

Cerney House Gardens

Cirencester Park

MAP SYMBOLS EXPLAINED

♏ Abbey/Cathedral	☕ Pub/Inn	⊕ Leisure/Sports Centre
✕ Battle Site	🚋 Railway Interest	⛵ Lifeboat
Bed & Breakfast Accomodation	✕ Restaurant	Ⓟ Parking
☕ Café	Self Catering Accommodation	♒ Picnic Site
Castle	Standing Stone/Barrow	Tents & Caravans
Church/Chapel of Interest	Theatre/Concert Hall	△ Sailing
Cinema	⅃ Tourist Information	🏄 Surfing
Craft Interest	☼ Tumulus/Tumuli	⅃ Tourist Information
Cross	Viewpoint	Windsurfing
Cycleway	Windmill/Wind Farm	▲ Youth Hostel
Fun Park/Leisure Park	⊕ Airfield	Agricultural Interest
Hill Fort/Ancient Settlement	Aquarium	♧ Arboretum
Historic Building	Boat Trips	Bird Reserve
Hotel	Camping Site (Tents)	Garden of Interest
Industrial Interest	Caravan Site	♨ Vineyard
Karting	Ferry (Pedestrians)	Walks/Nature Trails
Lighthouse	Ferry (Vehicles)	Wildlife Park
Mining Interest/Engine Houses	Fishing Trips	Zoo
☆ Miscellaneous/Natural Attraction	⁹⁄₁₈ 9/18 Hole Golf Course	Ⓟ National Trust Car Park
Museum/Art Gallery	Harbour	
Pottery	Inshore Rescue Boat	

- 381m.
- 305m.
- 229m.
- 152m
- 76m.

———— A Road

———— B Road

———— Minor Road

------------ Other Road or Track
(not necessarily with public
or vehicular access)

———•———— Railway

·············· Cycleway

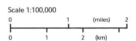

Open Space owned
by the National Trust

Built-up Area

Scale 1:100,000

0   1   (miles)   2

0   1   2   (km)

The Circus, Bath

William Fricker, photographed by his son Harry, checking out an off-road route.

William Fricker was born in Somerset and educated at Stonyhurst College, Lancashire, and in various places of learning in Austria and Germany. He has worked in publishing for over forty years.

William first worked for William Collins (now Harper Collins) in London, where he became a Creative Director in their paperback division before taking a sabbatical, to make a 4,000 mile trek across Europe (France-The Alps-Italy, to Greece) along the old mule tracks, footpaths and pilgrim's routes. Inspired by Patrick Leigh Fermor's A Time of Gifts, and Laurie Lee's As I Walked Out One Midsummer Morning. On reaching Greece, his original plan was to then head south and walk up the Nile, but he believes his better judgement prevailed, and returned on a bicycle via North Africa, Spain and France. For the past thirty years he has built up Goldeneye compiling the research, editorial and photography, for more than two hundred UK travel guides and books; on cycling, touring and walking. More recently, he plans to revise his Guidebook series, and expand his books of photography titled: "The Landscape of Britain". Last year he moved with his wife Caroline, and their children, to Penryn, Cornwall.